THE CHEAP BASTARD'S GUIDE TO
NEW YORK CITY

"A penny-pincher's nirvana—it's as if we wrote it!"
—*Arthur Frommer's Budget Travel Magazine*

"A book that reinforces one of the classic family values that New Yorkers hold dear—never pay retail."
—Brian Lehrer, WNYC New York Public Radio

"But does it work? You bet. . . . Grader hilariously dissects the city to come up with his innovative money savers."
—John Deiner, *The Washington Post*

"There are a lot of ideas worth considering. . . . Plenty of attractions for the casual visitor."
—Richard P. Carpenter, *The Boston Globe*

"The [money] you spend on this book will be recouped in no time."
—*Brooklyn Parent* magazine

"Brings on attitude and humor in its revelations of how to obtain assorted freebies."
—*Publishers Weekly*

"The last word on living well and cheaply in the Big Apple—and, no, it is not an oxymoron."
—June Sawyers, *The Chicago Tribune*

"If you are planning a trip to the Big Apple, this book is a must. . . . You will enjoy the wit and humor Grader has inserted into this delightful guide."
Gillette News-Record (Gillette, Wyoming)

HELP US KEEP THIS GUIDE UP TO DATE

We would love to hear from you concerning your experiences with this guide and how you feel it could be improved and kept up to date. Please send your comments and suggestions to:

editorial@globepequot.com

Thanks for your input, and happy travels!

CHEAP BASTARD'S® SERIES

THE CHEAP BASTARD'S® GUIDE TO

New York City

Secrets of Living the Good Life—For Less!

Fifth Edition

Rob **Grader**

gpp®
travel

Guilford, Connecticut
An imprint of Globe Pequot Press

All the information in this guidebook is subject to change. We recommend that you call ahead to obtain current information before traveling.

To buy books in quantity for corporate use
or incentives, call **(800) 962–0973**
or e-mail **premiums@GlobePequot.com.**

Text design by Sheryl P. Kober
Lyrics on page 26 from "Grand Central Station, March 18, 1977" by Steve Forbert, reprinted by kind permission of Welk Music (ASCAP, adm. Lichelle Music Co.).

ISSN 1549-5116
ISBN 978-0-7627-6458-7

Printed in the United States of America
10 9 8 7 6 5 4 3 2 1

For Dad, the one, the true, the Original Cheap Bastard,
and for Mom, though not always cheap,
one true original in her own right.

CONTENTS

Introduction: The Land of the Free xiii

SECTION 1: Entertainment in New York

Theater: Free Speech 2

Volunteer Ushering 3

Cheap Seats 17

Just Plain Free Theater 20

Free Will(iam): Free Theater in the Parks 25

Music: Of Free I Sing 26

Rock, Pop, Folk & Alternative 27

Jazz & Blues 30

Classical Music 33

Outdoor Summer Concerts 36

Film: Cheap Shots 44

Free Flicks 45

Better than the Book 53

Television Tapings: Public Access 55

Comedy: Cheap Jokes 61

Dance: Free Expression 64

Watching It 65

Doing It 68

So You Want to Be a Dancer: Work-Study Dance Classes 69

Magic: Cheap Tricks 72

SECTION 2: Living in New York

Food: On the House 76

Happy Hours 77

Free Samples: A Sampling 84

Eat Late, Eat Cheap! 90

Wine Tastings: Cheap Drunk 93

  East Side 94

  West Side 97

  Downtown East 101

  Downtown West 101

Hair, Beauty & Massage: Free-Style 103

  Product Testing Centers 104

  Hair Salons 105

  Beauty Schools 111

  Massage 113

  Makeup 115

Real Estate: This Land Is Your Land 116

  Low-Rent, No-Fee Apartments 117

Children & Teens: Olli Olli Oxen Free 121

  After-School Programs 123

  Arts & Crafts 124

  Films 128

  Sports & Games 132

  Health Insurance 135

  Museums 136

  Stores for the Fun of It 137

  Storytelling 139

Education: Cents-Less Smarts 143

  Arts 144

  Food & Wine 148

  Mind 150

  Body 155

  Spirit 157

Health & Medical: Live Free or Die 160

  To Your Health: Free Clinics 161

  Whatever Ails You: Clinical Studies 162

  HHC to the Rescue 164

    Depression/Mental Health Studies & Clinical Trials 167

    STD Clinics 167

Fitness, Fun & Games: Cheap Thrills 170

    Park It Here! Parks Offering a Variety of Activities 171

    Recreation Centers 174

    Skating, Biking & Running 175

    Boating 179

    Everybody In! Public Pools 180

    Beaches 183

Libraries: Free Access 186

    Research Centers 187

    Private Libraries 190

Newspapers: The Free Press 192

Furniture & Household Goods: One Man's Trash 198

    Favorite Finds 200

    Curbside Shopping Tips 200

Shopping: A Tale of Two Streets 204

    32nd Street: Bargain Paradise 205

    17th Street: First in Secondhand. 206

Pets: Canine, Feline, Bottom Line 208

    Low-Cost Pet Care & Adoptions 210

    Pet Postings 211

SECTION 3: Exploring New York

Walking Tours: The Freedom Trail 214

Travel: Free-Wheelin' 224

    Getting Around New York 225

    Getting Out of New York 226

    The Train to the Plane 229

Gardens & Gardening: Dirt Cheap 232

    Public Gardens 233

    Gardening Education 235

    Community Gardens. 236

Art Galleries: Show Me the Monet 237

    Chelsea 238

    SoHo 241

    Williamsburg, Brooklyn 243

    Other Galleries & Shows Around New York 245

Museums: Free to See 249

    Always Free 250

    Sometimes Free. 256

    Museums with Suggested Donations 262

Zoos: Born Free 264

Appendices

    Appendix A: Romance: Sweet Nothings. 266

    Appendix B: Parades: Gratis Gatherings. 271

    Appendix C: Public Library Branch Locations 277

    Appendix D: New York City Recreation Centers 284

    Index 291

ABOUT THE AUTHOR

Born and bred in New York City, **Rob Grader** is a writer, actor, and massage therapist and has lived in four out of the five boroughs (he'll make it to Staten Island one of these days). Rob's other writing credits include *The Cuddle Sutra* (Sourcebooks, 2007), scripts for the National Public Radio series *Jazz From Lincoln Center,* as well as articles for local newspapers and magazines. He has also created and produced the A&E reality show *House of Dreams*. As an actor, Rob has appeared at many regional theaters across the country; on the television shows *Law & Order, Law & Order: SVU, The Job, All My Children,* and *Who's the Boss?;* in the HBO film *American Splendor;* and in a number of national commercials. He's a graduate of the American Repertory Theater's Institute for Advanced Theater Training at Harvard University. As a massage therapist, he has rubbed many sore and aching backs around New York. Rob currently lives, works, and does his darndest not to spend any money in Manhattan. Check out his website, www.thecheapbastard.com.

ACKNOWLEDGMENTS

No one becomes a Cheap Bastard on his own, and here are the names to prove it. There are many people I need to acknowledge who've helped me along the way. From the very beginning, I had training from the best, the ultimate Cheap Bastard himself, my dad, Jack Grader. Thanks also to Mom, Bernice Grader, and everyone in my family for their support, encouragement, and suggestions while I was putting this opus together. In particular, thanks to Scott Grader (with two *t*'s, right?) for all the free legal counseling, to Trish Lande Grader for all the free publishing know-how, and to all the rest of the Graders: Jessica, Michelle, Emily, Sally, Jonas, Jeff, Lisa, Stu, and Ellen. Special thanks to Shari Springer Berman and Bob Pulcini for all the free writing advice and consultations. I am also indebted to Steve Harper for the free proofreading services (and the constantly free ear!), to Harry Mizrahi of American Spectrum Realty for the free use of the office equipment and for giving me plenty of free time while I was working for him, to Hans Kriefall and his mom for the free Latin lesson, and to Chiori Miagowa, Suzi Takahashi, Nilaja Sun, Ignacio Lopez, Ken Bolden, Danny Weiss, Patricia Kelley, Bill Quigley, Bill Driscoll, Mark Farnan, Sue Barret, Helen Mandlin, and Karen Raksis (the best things in life are free!) for all giving so freely of their spirits. My gratitude also goes out to Mark S. Roy and Brian DeFiore of DeFiore and Company, and to Laura Strom, Shelley Wolf, Maureen Graney, Jennifer Quint, Mike Urban, and everyone at Globe Pequot Press for their invaluable assistance. There is also a nasty little secret about New Yorkers I must expose: Contrary to popular belief, they truly are the friendliest, smartest, most generous, and helpful people in the world. Innumerable friends, acquaintances, associates, and strangers helped me out in countless ways throughout the development of this book. I'm sorry I cannot name you all, but please know you are appreciated. Thanks to all—you're a wonderful bunch of Bastards!

INTRODUCTION:

THE **LAND** OF **THE** FREE

A few years back while I was visiting England, I found myself low on cash—but still wanting to see the sights. Not to be deterred by this minor detail, I proceeded to figure out ways to sneak into some of the Brits' most expensive and heavily guarded tourist attractions. My proudest feat was making my way into the impenetrable Tower of London. Take that, William the Conqueror! I was having such a good time getting around the system that I thought this would make a great first in a series of books—*Getting Around London: How to Sneak into Anywhere*. Upon further consideration (and after speaking with my brother the lawyer), it seemed there might be an array of legal problems with this kind of book. But somehow the idea wouldn't go away.

Then back home in New York, I watched the Pulitzer Prize–winning play *Wit* one evening for free (and legally!). After the show, I stopped by a favorite haunt of mine to get a little snack (free, thank you) and made it home to my spacious Upper West Side apartment (for which I paid $560 a month in rent and found without paying any broker's fee). As I sat relaxing in my leather easy chair (free, too!) and thinking about my yoga class the next morning (you guessed it, free), it dawned on me—I am one cheap bastard. I also understood that I have a mission in life to figure out how I can get or do practically anything I want without paying one red cent, and usually on the up and up. And I felt compelled to share this—my life's work—with the world. So I humbly offer to you *The Cheap Bastard's Guide to New York City*.

The *CB Guide* is not only a collection of specific destinations, listings, and tips on how to get almost anything imaginable for free or ridiculously cheap (more on my definition of these later), it's also a celebration of life on the cheap. The myth is that New York is a great place to live or visit if you have the money to enjoy it. The truth is, no place offers more for free than New York, but only if you know how to find it. And once you find it, oh the joy! Anyone can pay their way into a Broadway show, but when you get in for free, somehow the lights are brighter, the songs are sweeter, the drama so much more heartbreaking. There is no thrill in buying a dinner, but the taste of a free Buffalo wing is spiced with adventure, the crunch of a crisp free Granny Smith apple is the sound of triumph, and the kick of getting a free cup of coffee puts just that extra spring in your step.

A big part of the value of getting something for nothing is the story that goes with it—the history, the event. What can you tell me about any piece of furniture in your house that you bought? *I went to the store. I liked it. I bought it.* But everything in my house comes with a heritage. Every time I sit in my leather easy chair, I'm reminded of how I came to own this piece of furniture that by all rights I could never afford to buy. I was walking along a few blocks away from my apartment, my arms loaded down with books I was donating to my local library, when I saw a chair sitting on the curb waiting to be picked up by the next sanitation truck. While at first glance it looked like it might truly be ready for the trash heap, with its torn-up seat cushion, I knew right away I wanted it. Still, I couldn't stop to grab it then. I hurried to the library, dropped off my books, and rushed back to the chair. Of course, someone else was checking out the merchandise by the time I got back. I thought I had lost it. Who would pass up such a great find? I waited on the corner sending evil thoughts his way . . . and miraculously, he walked away. *Great, it's mine!* When I was in the middle of inspecting my chair, seeing if the cushion really was beyond repair, another guy walked up to offer his advice. "Eh, you don't want that—it's falling apart," he said. I thanked him for his words of wisdom and continued to poke and prod at the chair. He then walked away, and I noticed him heading back to his double-parked van just down the block. *Nice try, buddy,* I thought. I knew I had to grab it now or kiss it good-bye. I heaved it over my head, managed to lug it the few blocks home—and the rest is history. All I had to do was fashion a new cover for the cushion, which cost me no more than $30. The chair has now served me well for many years.

Each and every listing in this book offers you an opportunity for something more valuable than money: a memory, an experience, a story (and of course, the chance to save a boatload of cash ain't such a bad thing, either).

The listings in this book can be split into two categories: "Free" and "Ridiculously Cheap," with the vast majority of the listings being free. So let's define what I mean by these terms.

Simply stated, *free* is getting something without having to pay any money for it. So, here are some of the things you will *not* find in this book: "Buy One, Get One Free"; "First Month Free"; "Mention the Cheap Bastard and get in for half price"; or any other scheme that is ultimately about getting cash out of your wallet. What kind of free listings *will* you find in this book? Two basic kinds: free-free and free-with-a-catch. *Free-free* is just that: no-strings-attached, give-it-to-me-but-I'm-not-giving-you-anything free. For example, you can get a free personalized guided tour of any neighborhood in the five boroughs from Big Apple Greeters, plus they will even give you a free one-day unlimited MetroCard, no strings attached. *Free-with-a-catch* generally means you'll need to exchange some time or effort to get that something for free. For example, you can see almost any Off Broadway and some Broadway shows for free by being a volunteer usher. Show up an hour early, help seat the paying folks, and watch the show for nothing. I have tried to clearly lay out any catch you may need to know about by including the category *The Catch* (ingenious, eh?) wherever necessary.

"Ridiculously cheap" listings are those things that, yes, you will have to lay out some money to get. Still, the cost is so minimal that when you're asked to pay, you do it quickly for fear they'll realize their mistake. For example, does $75 a year for a gym membership sound pretty ridiculous to you?

Let me also mention what makes someone a Cheap Bastard. I see *Cheap Bastard* as a proud term referring to someone who enjoys the thrill of the hunt, not someone whose end-all and be-all is not spending money. This isn't someone who will deny himself or anyone else anything simply because it will cost some money. Most importantly, this isn't someone who is looking to cheat another person; nor is it to be confused with *stingy*. A Cheap Bastard is not out to beat another person out of a few cents; he is out to beat the system.

This book is intended for visitors and natives alike. Whether you're a backpacker from Australia who has just shown up in the city at the end of your round-the-world jaunt with less cash than you planned; a born-and-bred New Yorker who needs to stretch that paycheck a little farther; someone who's just moved to the city and working his first (low-paying) job out of college; a college student who needs to figure out how to make that student loan last all year; or even one of those folks for whom money is no worry, but, hey, you just like getting something for nothing (and who doesn't?)—this book is for you.

Finally, all the information in this guide is accurate as of press time, but things change quickly in New York, so I have included as much contact information as possible for each listing. Always call, check the website, or stop by to make sure all the information in this book is still accurate.

I've had a ball putting this book together, and I hope it helps you get the most out of the greatest city in the world.

Live well, live free,

Rob Grader
The Cheap Bastard
New York City
www.thecheapbastard.com

SECTION 1:

Entertainment in New York

THEATER:
FREE SPEECH

"Of all men, physicians and playwrights alone possess the rare privilege of charging money for the pain they inflict on us."

—SANTIAGO RAMÓN Y CAJAL

From the bright lights of Broadway to the cutting-edge antics of the downtown performance world, New York is the undisputed capital of the theater world. Any day of the week, literally hundreds of performances are going on in every corner of the city. And while the top ticket prices for a Broadway show have surpassed $400, you can spend endless evenings in the theaters of New York without spending a cent. By taking on the role of a volunteer usher, you can make your way into some Broadway shows and almost any Off Broadway show absolutely free. You can also keep yourself very busy attending any of the many just-plain-free performances at theaters throughout the city. These run the gamut from full productions to staged readings of new plays and musicals.

VOLUNTEER **USHERING**

Every time you walk into a theater to see a show, some kind person takes your ticket and shows you to your seat. Often you find that these folks are just thrilled to be doing this job. Ever wonder why? Well, this isn't their regular job; they're just there to see the show, like you. The only difference is, they haven't paid a cent to get in. Yes, they're volunteer ushers, and you'll find them at almost all Off Broadway and some Broadway theaters. Considering the ticket prices of these shows (from $25 to more than $400), volunteer ushers get "paid" very well for basically one hour's work, so why wouldn't they be pretty darn happy? And it's easy to join their ranks.

Each theater has its own protocol, but essentially all that's involved is making a reservation a week or two in advance, then showing up an hour before the curtain rises. The house manager will give you a quick rundown on the seating plan (warning: you do need to be able to count to twelve to understand this; sometimes you even need to count backward); then you help seat the paying folks. During the performance, enjoy the show. Ushers get to watch from seats that remain empty as the show is about to start. There are almost always good seats—many times the best seats in the house—for you to fill, even if the show is officially sold out. On the very rare occasion that there are absolutely no seats available, they will set up chairs for you, or in extremely rare cases, ask you to sit in the aisles. Occasionally you need to stay a couple of minutes after the show to help pick up stray playbills. It's as simple as that.

Why do theaters do this? Economics. It's cheaper to let you in for nothing than it is to hire a full-time ushering staff. You can even bring a friend. Most theaters need at least two ushers per show (some as many as ten) and are happy to let you reserve more than one slot. Some theaters that officially only use one usher per show will even let you bring a companion to usher with you if you ask nicely. Talk about your cheap dates!

BROADWAY

Manhattan Theatre Club at the Biltmore Theatre

261 W. 47th St. (between Broadway and Eighth Avenue)
(212) 394-3000, ext. 5463 (usher hotline)
volunteer@mtc-nyc.org
www.manhattantheatreclub.com
Ushers per performance: 5

Dedicated to producing and developing new plays and musicals, Manhattan Theatre Club has built a sterling reputation that began as a small Off-Off Broadway showcase more than thirty years ago and has now claimed some prime Broadway real estate for itself. Over the years they have presented new works by such acclaimed playwrights as Sam Shepard, Terrance McNally, A. R. Gurney, Harold Pinter, John Patrick Shanley, and countless others. The production often attracts big-name Hollywood and Broadway talent. Each year they present a full season of new plays. They usually begin taking phone or e-mail reservations two weeks before performances begin, but call their hotline earlier to find out the specific day they will start accepting reservations. The slots for the entire run usually fill up that day.

The Roundabout Theatre Company
The American Airlines Theater
227 W. 42nd St. (between Broadway and Eighth Avenue)
(212) 719-9393, ext. 523 (usher hotline)
www.roundabouttheatre.org
Ushers per performance: 6

After years of hopping from theater to theater, one of New York's most renowned theater companies has found a permanent home on Broadway. And since they remain a not-for-profit theater, this is one of the few opportunities to volunteer-usher on Broadway. They also maintain productions at Studio 54 and the Off Broadway performances at the Laura Pells Theatre, the Harold and Miriam Steinberg Centre for Theatre, and the Roundabout Underground Black Box Theatre (see below for information on these theaters). Their productions often attract star performers and are almost always of a high caliber (particularly the musicals). To book a slot at the American Airlines Theater, sign up with the security guard in the lobby of the theater Mon through Fri between 10 a.m. and 5 p.m. (but just from 10 a.m. to noon on Wed). They generally make dates available about two weeks before previews begin and fill the dates for the entire run on a first-come, first-served basis. These slots go fast, so sign up early. Call their hotline (listed above) to find out when they are accepting ushers. They are very serious about the black-and-white dress code for ushers.

Studio 54
254 W. 54th St. (between Broadway and Eighth Avenue)
(212) 719-9393, ext. 523 (usher hotline)
www.roundabouttheatre.org
Ushers per performance: 10

The Roundabout Theatre Company has taken ownership of the legendary disco and turned it into its own permanent home for musicals and high-profile plays. After playing host to the longtime Broadway hit *Cabaret,* the Roundabout will now continue to fill this theater with its own brand of high-quality, often star-studded revivals and original musicals for both limited and extended runs. To nab yourself an ushering slot, stop by the theater

Mon through Fri from 10 a.m. to 5 p.m. (but just 10 a.m. to noon on Wed.) Be sure to call the usher hotline before you head down there to find out when they accepting ushers.

OFF BROADWAY

Atlantic Theater Company
76 Ninth Ave. (between West 15th and West 16th Streets)
(212) 691-5919
atlanticushers@atlantictheater.org
www.atlantictheater.org
Ushers per performance: 2

Followers of the David Mamet school of acting founded this theater company, and it is known for producing his works and others of the same ilk. Productions all have limited runs, and ushering slots fill quickly. They start taking ushering reservations three weeks prior to the start of performances and are usually "sold out" by the time the reviews come out. The dress code is all black.

Blue Man Group
Astor Place Theatre
434 Lafayette St. (between East 4th and 8th Streets)
(212) 254-4370, ext. 220
www.blueman.com
Ushers per night: 4

You've seen the long-running Off Broadway Blue Man Group on the Intel commercials, Jay Leno, David Letterman, and every other talk show imaginable, and if you still haven't seen enough of them, come on down to the theater where the whole thing started and see them for free (they don't need any more money). They will also ask you to stay about fifteen minutes after the show is over to clean up. Warning: It's a messy show. To make an ushering reservation, call about a week in advance, Mon through Fri from 9 a.m. to 9 p.m.

The Cherry Lane Theatre
38 Commerce St. (between Bedford and Hudson Streets)
(212) 989-2020, ext. 23
www.cherrylanetheatre.com
Ushers per performance: 3

Since 1924 this theater has been home to many of the early works of such playwrights as Edward Albee, Beckett, Ionesco, Mamet, Pinter, Lanford Wilson, and Sam Shepard. In recent years it has played host to such successful Off Broadway shows as *Fully Committed, Nunsense, The Telephone, Paternity, Blown Sideways through Life,* and many others. Call a week to a month in advance. The atmosphere is very casual and easygoing for ushers.

Classic Stage Company (CSC)
136 E. 13th St. (between Third and Fourth Avenues)
(212) 677-4210, ext. 56
housemanager@classicstage.org
www.classicstage.org
Ushers per performance: 3

For more than thirty years, CSC has built a reputation for reinventing classic works of the theater—some well known, others less so. They have attracted a loyal following by working with some of the best-known actors, directors, and writers from New York, Hollywood, and around the country. E-mail for ushering reservations a week to a month in advance of the performance.

The Culture Project
49 Bleecker St. (at Mulberry Street)
(212) 925-1806
www.cultureproject.org
Ushers per performance: 1

Since its inception in 1996, this theater company has been presenting award-winning and often star-studded productions that bring the national political conversation to the New York stage. Some of its most noteworthy productions include *The Exonerated, Bridge and Tunnel, My Trip to Al-Qaeda,* and many others. Call anytime from a few days to a few weeks in advance to make a reservation, depending on the popularity of the show.

Encores
City Center
West 55th St. (between Sixth and Seventh Avenues)
(212) 247-0430
mkt@nycitycenter.org
www.citycenter.org
Ushers per performance: 6–9

Presenting series of highly produced staged readings of musicals with star performers, Encores is considered one of the hottest tickets in town. Call far in advance to put your name on a list of volunteers to hawk CDs and other paraphernalia in the lobby to get into the shows. Warning: There is a waiting list about 12 miles long to get on the list, so be patient.

Here Performance Art Cafe

145 Sixth Ave. (between Spring and Dominick Streets)
(212) 647-0202
www.here.org
Ushers per performance: 1–2

Here is a downtown art center that brings together theater, performance art, music, dance, and visual art into one complex. With an ever-changing rotation of productions of all sorts in their three theaters and intriguing work on the walls and floors of their gallery. Here always presents something worthwhile to see. Call the box office manager a couple of days to a week in advance to reserve an ushering slot.

Irish Arts Center

553 W. 51st St. (between Tenth and Eleventh Avenues)
(212) 757-3318
info@irishartscenter.org
www.irishartscenter.org
Ushers per performance: 1–2

The Irish Arts Center presents a full season of productions by and about the Irish experience, as well as playing host to many imports from Ireland. Call to add your name to the list of volunteer ushers, and they will call when they need you.

Irish Repertory Theatre

132 W. 22nd St. (between Sixth and Seventh Avenues)
(212) 255-0270
www.irishrep.org
Ushers per performance: 2

This company has built a strong reputation for presenting the works of (believe it or not) Irish and Irish-American writers, both classical and contemporary. They have two theaters, and you may usher in either of them.

Call at least two weeks in advance for an ushering reservation, more if you need a specific date.

The Joyce Theater
175 Eighth Ave. (at 19th Street)
(646) 792-8355
www.joyce.org
Ushers per performance: 8

The leading theater for dance companies, the Joyce plays host to practically every major company from around the country and the world. They begin taking ushering reservations two weeks before each performance.

The Lamb's Theatre
130 W. 44th St. (between Sixth Avenue and Broadway)
(212) 575-0300, ext. 21
www.lambstheatre.org
Ushers per performance: 3

Designed by noted architect Sanford White in 1904, this building has played a leading role in the development of the American theater, not least serving as the original home to the Lambs, America's oldest theatrical club. It was here that Lerner met Lowe (*My Fair Lady, Camelot*), that Mark Twain wrote his first play, and that Richard Rodgers set to work on a new musical called *Away We Go* (later renamed *Oklahoma!*). The upstairs residences were once home to the likes of John Wayne, Fred Astaire, and John Philip Sousa. These days, their two Off Broadway theaters have been host to such shows as *Smoke on the Mountain, Dames at Sea, Beau Jest,* and *The Countess.* Call for ushering reservations.

Lucille Lortel Theater
121 Christopher St. (between Hudson and Bleecker Streets)
(212) 924-2817, ext. 207
ushers@lortel.org.
www.lortel.org
Ushers per performance: 3

This venerable Off Broadway theater has been the home of many major productions over its fifty-plus-year history, such as *Cloud 9, Steel Magnolias, Three Penny Opera, As Bees in Honey Drown,* and many others. Call anywhere from a few days to a few weeks in advance to make an ushering reservation, depending on the popularity of the show.

Manhattan Theatre Club (MTC)
City Center (theater and box office)
131 W. 55th St. (between Sixth and Seventh Avenues)
311 W. 43rd St., eighth floor (administrative offices)
(212) 247-0430, ext. 240
www.manhattantheatreclub.com
Ushers per performance: 4

MTC is a major producer of new plays, many of which end up transferring to larger commercial Broadway theaters, including *Proof, The Tale of the Allergist's Wife, Ain't Misbehavin',* and many others over the years. See them before they move, because you can't usher for them once they hit the Great White Way. To get an ushering reservation, e-mail them at least a few weeks in advance with your name, the production you are interested in, and a few dates you can make. They will e-mail you back with details. You can also volunteer-usher at their Broadway theater, MTC at the Biltmore. See their listing in the Broadway section for more details.

MCC Theater
Lucille Lortel Theater
121 Christopher St. (between Hudson and Bleecker Streets)
(212) 727-7722
www.mcctheater.org
Ushers per performance: 3

MCC is a small but popular Off Broadway company that has made a name for itself by producing such plays as the Pulitzer Prize–winning *Wit* and has worked with such actors as Calista Flockhart, Bridget Fonda, Thomas Gibson, Kyra Sedgwick, Marisa Tomei, Allison Janney, and Lili Taylor over its twenty-plus-year history. Make ushering reservations a week or two before performances begin. Slots fill up quickly.

Mint Theater Company
311 W. 43rd St., third floor (between Eighth and Ninth Avenues)
(212) 315-0231
www.minttheater.org
Ushers per performance: 1–2

This small, well-respected company concentrates on rediscovering lost classics from the nineteenth and twentieth centuries. Recent productions have included *The Voysey Inheritance, House of Mirth,* and *Mr. Pim Passes By.* Ushering slots do get filled quickly; call Mon through Fri noon to 6 p.m.; two to three weeks before performances begin to be assured of a reservation.

The New Group Theater
410 W. 42nd St. (between Ninth and Tenth Avenues)
(212) 244-3380
housemananger@thenewgroup.org
www.thenewgroup.org
Ushers per performance: 2

This high-profile company has staged many productions that have won all the awards and transferred to long runs on Broadway and at major Off Broadway theaters, including *Avenue Q, This Is Our Youth, Ecstasy, Another American Asking and Telling,* and others. Email two weeks in advance for ushering reservations.

New World Stages
340 W. 50th St. (between Eighth and Ninth Avenues)
(646) 871-1730
volunteer@newworldstages.com
www.newworldstages.com
Number of ushers: 1–2 per show, per theater

From the ashes of the World Wide Cinema (what used to be every cheap bastard's favorite $2 movie theater) comes a complex of seven state-of-the-art Off Broadway theaters. The theaters are owned and operated by the Dodgers, a producing organization that has been responsible for many of Broadway's biggest hits over the last twenty or so years. Since opening the doors to the theater complex they have played host to such productions as *Altar Boyz, Naked Boys Singin,* and the *Gazillion Bubble Show.* To make an ushering reservation, e-mail them two weeks ahead of the date you want. Check out their ushering rules and procedures on their website.

New York Theatre Workshop (NYTW)
79 E. 4th St. (between Second Avenue and Bowery)
(212) 780-9037
www.nytw.org
Ushers per performance: 6

NYTW produces some of the most daring and artistically challenging productions of any Off Broadway theater; it was the original producer of such Broadway hits as *Rent* and *Dirty Blond*. Ushering slots can be reserved anywhere from the day of a performance to three weeks in advance, depending on the popularity of the show. Be sure to get on their ushering mailing list, and they will send you reminders for each new show. They also throw in free coffee or tea at the concession stand for ushers.

The Pearl Theatre Company

131 W. 55th St. (between Sixth and Seventh Avenues)
(212) 598-9802
info@pearltheatre.org
www.pearltheatre.org
Ushers per performance: 4

One of the few true classical repertory companies remaining in New York. Their seasons concentrate on the works of Shakespeare, Chekhov, Coward, the Greeks, and other Dead European White Men. Their productions are almost never startlingly original, but almost always respectably done. E-mail the theater in advance for ushering reservations, specifying three dates in order of preference.

Performance Space 122

150 First Ave. (at East 9th Street)
(212) 477-5829
housemanager@ps122.org
www.ps122.org
Ushers per performance: 2

The longtime home of experimental and cutting-edge theater and dance, P.S. 122 continues to host many well-known and emerging performance artists, including Eric Bogosian, John Leguizamo, and Karen Finley. Send an e-mail the week of the performance to book an ushering slot in one of their two theaters.

Playwrights Horizons

416 W. 42nd St. (between Ninth and Tenth Avenues)
(212) 564-1235
usher@playwrightshorizons.com
www.playwrightshorizons.org
Ushers per performance: 4

Playwrights produces a season of new plays and musicals by well-known and up-and-coming playwrights, many of which transfer to larger Off Broadway or Broadway theaters. Past productions have included *Driving Miss Daisy, The Heidi Chronicles, Once on This Island,* and James Joyce's *The Dead.* The theater maintains a large list of ushers and send out mailings before each show begins performances. You have to be a real go-getter to get one of these coveted ushering slots. First you need to get on their e-mail list by sending them an e-mail (address above) with the words "Add to list" in the subject line. Then they will send out a mass e-mail telling you (and thousands of others) when they will be accepting reservations. On that day, you had better call first thing in the morning, because they usually fill all of their slots within hours.

Rattlestick Playwrights Theatre
224 Waverly Place (off Seventh Avenue at 11th Street)
(212) 627-2556
info@rattlestick.org
www.rattlestick.org
Ushers per performance: 1

This up-and-coming Off Broadway theater has begun to build a strong name for itself by producing contemporary playwrights. Past productions have included *Down South, Whale Music,* and *Killers and Other Family.* Call early in the run to snag an ushering slot. The theater also offers a schedule of free play readings; check their website for details.

The Roundabout Theatre Company
111 W. 46th St. (between Sixth and Seventh Avenues)
(212) 719-9393, ext. 523 (usher hotline)
www.roundabouttheatre.org
Ushers per performance: 6

The Roundabout Theatre Company has closed down shop at the Gramercy Theater and moved its Off Broadway productions into the old American Place Theatre. Expect a season chock-full of classics, small-scale musicals, and new plays with cast lists punctuated with star names. Sign up for an ushering slot at the theater on Mon, Tues, Thurs, or Fri from 10 a.m. to 5 p.m.

Second Stage Theatre
307 W. 43rd St. (at Eighth Avenue)
(212) 787-8302
jschleifer@2st.com
www.2st.com
Ushers per performance: 4

Hailed in past years by the *New York Times* as "the season's most indispensable theater," Second Stage produces a season chock-full of theater heavyweights like August Wilson, Stephen Sondheim, Edward Albee, and many others. To make a reservation, e-mail your full name and requested dates to the above address. They start taking requests three weeks before preview performances begin, and slots can fill up quickly, depending on the popularity of the show.

The Signature Theater Company
Peter Norton Space
555 W. 42nd St. (between Tenth and Eleventh Avenues)
(212) 244-7529
housemanager@signaturetheatre.org
www.signaturetheatre.org
Ushers per performance: 4

The Signature Theater Company specializes in highly regarded productions focusing each season on the works of a single American playwright. Past seasons have included works by Arthur Miller, Edward Albee, Maria Irene Fornes, and Sam Shepard. Call at least two weeks in advance; ushers are booked for performances one month in advance. Free coffee, tea, and hot chocolate for ushers!

SoHo Playhouse
15 Vandam St. (between Spring and Prince Streets)
(212) 691-1555
www.sohoplayhouse.com
Ushers per performance: 1

This theater has been home to such productions as *Killer Joe, Grandma Silvia's Funeral, The Divine Sister,* and others. Make reservations a few days to a week in advance by calling the box office noon to 7 p.m., Tues through Sat.

Theatre Row

410 W. 42nd St. (between Ninth and Tenth Avenues)
(212) 714-2442
www.theatrerow.org

This space is the home of six state-of-the-art Off Broadway theaters—the Acorn, the Beckett, the Clurman, the Kirk, the Lion, and the Studio. These spaces are used by many of New York's A-list theater companies, many of whom, though not all, use volunteer ushers. To find out if you can volunteer-usher for a particular show, you need to contact the production company for that show. Call the Theatre Row administrative offices (listed above) to get the contact information for the various companies. For best results you may want to stop by sometime close to showtime and ask about ushering at that specific theater.

The Vineyard Theatre

108 E. 15th St. (between Union Square East and Irving Place)
(212) 353-3366, ext. 226 (usher hotline)
housemanager@vineyardtheatre.org
www.vineyardtheatre.org
Ushers per performance: 2

The Vineyard produces and develops new works by many major figures in the American theater. They have brought to life such shows as *Fully Committed,* the Pulitzer Prize–winning *How I Learned to Drive,* and *Middletown.* Make ushering reservations by phone or e-mail one to three weeks in advance.

Women's Project at the Julia Miles Theater

424 W. 55th St. (between Ninth and Tenth Avenues)
Administrative offices: 55 West End Ave.
(212) 765-1706
info@womensproject.org
www.womensproject.org
Ushers per performance: 6

Dedicated to producing and developing the talents of women playwrights, over its twenty-plus-year history this theater company has been among the first to work with such artists as Eve Ensler, Maria Irene Fornes, Anna Deavere Smith, Liz Diamond, Tina Landau, and Joyce Carol Oates, among others. Call the office or e-mail them to get on their ushering list. Two weeks before a performance, you'll receive an e-mail that will tell you how to make reservations for that show. Also look for the free series of readings they hold once a year, usually around Nov.

The Wooster Group
The Performing Garage
33 Wooster St. (between Broome and Grand Streets)
(212) 966-9796
www.thewoostergroup.org
Ushers per performance: 2–6

Founded in the early 1970s by Jim Clayburgh, Willem Dafoe, Spalding Gray, and others, this company remains one of the premier experimental theater groups in the world. Their productions regularly tour internationally, but you can see one for free at the Performing Garage where it all started by reserving a slot as a volunteer usher. The ushering slots go fast, so call far in advance to nab one.

York Theatre Company
St. Peter's Church
619 Lexington Ave. (at 54th Street)
(212) 935-5820
boxoffice@yorktheatre.org
www.yorktheatre.org
Ushers per performance: 2

For more than thirty years, York has produced such award-winning musicals as *The Grass Harp, Pacific Overtures, She Loves Me, Company, 110 in the Shade, Sweeney Todd, Carnival,* and *Merrily We Roll Along.* Many of its productions have made the move to Broadway or larger Off Broadway theaters. Call

---

Off the Menu
If there's an Off Broadway show that you're interested in seeing and the theater isn't on this list, just ask at the box office if they use volunteer ushers for that show. There are always new venues popping up, and nontraditional performance spaces being used for new shows. Staff are very much used to answering this question. Nine times out of ten, they will say yes and tell you how to go about making a reservation.

---

two weeks ahead to make ushering reservations. The theater also presents free staged readings of new musicals on a regular basis. Call or check their website for the schedule.

CHEAP **SEATS**

Truth be told, the following listings are not exactly my idea of bargains. I mean, if you have to put out some actual cash for something, what's the point? But the rest of the world thinks these are good deals, so I'd be remiss if I didn't include this information. Here are a few worthy organizations that can get you good seats in loads of Broadway and Off Broadway theaters and concert halls for a minimum of cash.

Audience Extras (AE)
61 Lexington Ave., Suite 1A (between 25th and 26th Streets)
(212) 686-1966
www.audienceextras.com
The Catch: $85.00 yearly membership fee, and $30.00 personal reserve fund toward the $3.50 service charge per ticket.

Play by Play
312 W. 36th St. (between Seventh and Eighth Avenues)
(212) 868-7052
www.play-by-play.com
The Catch: $99 yearly membership, plus an $8 processing fee and $4 service fee per ticket, and a personal reserve fund.

Theater Extras
(914) 304-4093 or (212) 802-7277
www.theaterextras.com
The Catch: $99 annual membership, and $4 service charge per ticket.

TheaterMania Gold Club

915 Broadway, Suite 1406
(212) 352-0255, ext. 114
www.theatermania.com/Gold

The Catch: $99.00 yearly membership fee, and a $4.50 service charge per ticket.

These four companies exist for the sole purpose of getting living, breathing bodies into the seats of concert halls and theaters around the New York region. When a production needs a crowd—either because critics will be reviewing the production that night, or because it is early in the run and they want a full house to gauge audience response—producers turn to these guys to "paper the house" (translation: fill the seats). The bulk of the tickets offered are for Broadway, Off Broadway, and edgier Off-Off Broadway, theaters, but you can also often snag tickets for classical concerts at such venues as Lincoln Center and Carnegie Hall, as well as major cabaret performances, pop concerts and sporting events (yes, even Mets and Yankees tickets!). Each company operates slightly differently, but here is the basic model that they all follow. You pay a yearly membership fee that ranges between $85 and $99. Once you are a member, you have access to their list-

---

Standing Room Only

Dying to see that boffo Broadway hit, but you don't have the hundred bucks for the ticket or can't wait the six months until one becomes available? Standing room is what you're looking for. Many, but not all, Broadway theaters sell standing-room tickets. They're available only on the day of the performance and only if the show is completely sold out. It will cost you somewhere between $15 and $25 for the honor of standing to watch the show. The good news is that you'll have a great view: Standing room is directly behind the orchestra seating. And if you get tired, keep your eyes peeled for an empty seat for the second act. Check with the specific box offices for details.

---

ing of available productions through their website, where you can reserve one or two tickets for anything available. They generally offer anywhere from ten to forty offerings at any given time for performances taking place that day or over the next week or two. You will be charged a service fee of $4.50 for each ticket you reserve. Audience Extras and Play By Play will have you maintain a balance in a fund that these service fees are deducted from, while Theater Extras and TheaterMania Gold Club will charge the service charges to your credit card. This is a great way to expose yourself to an amazing array of performances without a whole lot of financial risk. If you use your membership for at least two or three a performances a year, it will easily pay for itself.

TKTS Booth

Theater Development Fund (TDF)
Duffy Square (47th Street and Broadway)
South Street Seaport; 186 Front St. (at John Street)
Downtown Brooklyn; 1 MetroTech Center (at Jay Street and Myrtle Avenue Promenade)
(212) 221-0013
www.tdf.org

The Catch: Sells tickets for 25, 35, or 50 percent off ticket price plus a $3 service charge per ticket.

"We'll get tickets at the booth" has been the cry of many a spontaneous theatergoer for more than twenty-five years. The TKTS booth sells tickets to Broadway, Off Broadway, music, and dance events the day of the performance at 25, 35, or 50 percent off the ticket price (plus a $4 service charge per ticket). They post the available shows outside the booth on boards, which change throughout the day. They accept credit cards, cash, and traveler's checks. As a rule, you can be sure you won't find tickets available to the newest, hottest show. The lines can be long, particularly on weekends and holidays. The tickets, however, are for some of the best seats in the theaters. Both the Duffy Square and South Street Seaport locations are open seven days a week; the Downtown Brooklyn location is open Tue through Sun.

JUST **PLAIN** FREE **THEATER**

American Academy of Dramatic Arts
120 Madison Ave. (between 30th and 31st Streets)
(212) 453-5340
www.aada.org

Some of the most legendary stars of stage and screen have trained at this institution, including Lauren Bacall, Spencer Tracy, John Cassavetes, Grace Kelly, Cecil B. DeMille, Danny DeVito, Colleen Dewhurst, Anne Bancroft, Ron Leibman, Jason Robards Jr., Kirk Douglas, and many others. To date, academy alumni have received nominations for more than seventy-two Oscars, sixty Tonys, and 211 Emmys. From Sept through Feb, the Academy Company—made up of third-year students—presents a season of free productions. Here's a chance to say you saw them when. Click on "Company Performances" on the website or call for dates and schedules.

Boomerang Theatre Company
Center Stage/NY
48 W. 21st St., fourth floor (between Fifth and Sixth Avenues)
(212) 501-4069
www.boomerangtheatre.org

This up-and-coming Off-Off Broadway company presents a series of readings of new plays. Also be sure to catch their summer season of free Shakespeare in the parks and public spaces around New York City.

52nd Street Project
500 W. 52nd St. (at Tenth Avenue)
(212) 333-5252
www.52project.org

The 52nd Street Project is a program through Ensemble Studio Theater that creates short theater pieces by or for the children of Hell's Kitchen in collaboration with professional theater artists. While these may not be Broadway productions, they are surprisingly well put together and offer an evening that is always full of laughter, original music, and a lot of talent (community and professional).

HB Playwrights Foundation

124 Bank St. (between Greenwich and Washington Streets)
(212) 989-6540
www.hbplaywrights.org

Established by acting legends Herbert Berghoff and Uta Hagen in 1965 as an offshoot of their renowned (and low-cost!) acting school, the theater presents four productions a year (always free) and has featured many well-established writers, actors, and directors. In recent years the company has given birth to such productions as *Mrs. Klein, Collected Stories,* and others that have moved to larger pay-for-your-ticket venues. The best way to find out about the performances is to call the office during business hours and ask to be added to their mailing list.

The Juilliard School

60 Lincoln Center Plaza (Broadway and 65th Street on plaza level)
(212) 769-7406 (box office)
(212) 799-5000, ext. 251 (drama division)
www.juilliard.edu

The Catch: You must call to get on the drama division's mailing list to get their calendar of events.

See tomorrow's stars of stage and screen today. This is considered the pre-eminent conservatory for actors in the country, and the school presents a full schedule of productions throughout the school year featuring students at every level of development. Often productions are put together by well-known directors—both faculty members and guest artists. All performances in the fall and early spring are free, though tickets are required and go fast. Call to put your name on the drama division's mailing list to get the calendar of free performances. Every spring they remount all of these productions for a Spring Repertory, but they charge for those tickets ($15). To get the free tickets, line up at the box office on the day they become available, usually two weeks before the performances begin; otherwise you'll probably be sold out of the event. You can also line up an hour before the show to try to get in on a standby basis. Performances by the music division are also free, though not those by the dance and opera departments.

New Dramatists

424 W. 44th St. (between Ninth and Tenth Avenues)
(212) 757-6960
www.newdramatists.org

New Dramatists is an organization devoted to developing playwrights, both up-and-coming and established, along with their material. They conduct an ongoing series of readings and workshops of new plays, musicals, and screenplays staffed with many leading actors and directors from the New York theater scene. Performances take place throughout the week (Mon through Fri) in the late afternoon or evening. All readings are free, and almost all are open to the public. Check the website or call for a calendar of events.

The New School For Drama

151 Bank St. (between Washington Street and the West Side Highway)
(212) 229-5859
www.newschool.edu/drama

From the end of Jan through May, The New School For Drama presents Random Acts, with graduating MFA (masters of fine arts) students performing in original one acts written by students in the playwriting program. All performances are free, but reservations are required.

New York Shakespeare Festival/The Public Theater

425 Lafayette St. (at Astor Place)
(212) 539-8500
www.publictheater.org

From the people who bring you Shakespeare in Central Park every summer come other free theater events throughout the year. Every spring and fall they hold a two-week festival of readings and workshops called New Work Now!; many of the pieces presented here have later ended up on their main stage, including the plays *Stop Kiss, References to Salvador Dali Make Me Hot, The Capeman,* and others. The Public also offers cheap rush tickets to each and every performance on the day of the event. Check their website for the details about these and many other free events that pop up throughout the year.

New York University Graduate Acting Program
721 Broadway (between Waverly and Washington Streets)
111 Second Ave. (between 6th and 7th Streets)
(212) 998-1921
www.gradacting.tisch.nyu.edu

The Catch: Only second-year productions are free.

One of the most respected graduate acting programs in the country has a distinguished alumnus list that boasts the likes of Billy Crudup, Camryn Manheim, Marcia Gay Harden, Barry Bostwick, Tony Kushner, and many others. See full productions of classics and contemporary plays mounted by the second-year students (they charge for the third-year student productions). Tickets are available one week before performances begin and sell out very quickly for these intimate performance spaces. Check the website or call for schedule and details.

Rattlestick Theatre Company
224 Waverly Place (off Seventh Avenue at 11th Street)
(212) 627-2556
www.rattlestick.org

Rattlestick annually offers a three-week festival of readings of new plays and works in progress every summer. Call or check their website for a schedule and details.

Theatreworks USA
Chelsea Studios
151 W. 26th St. (between Sixth and Seventh Avenues)
(212) 924-5877
www.theatreworksusa.org

Theatreworks USA is unquestionably the leading producer of professional theater for young audiences. Each year their wonderful productions tour to every corner of the country and reach over four million people. And every summer they present their newest production for free to New York audiences. Not-for-profit groups such as summer camps can reserve blocks of tickets, and individuals need to line up at the theater, where they distribute a limited number of tickets on a first-come, first-served basis. For more information check their website or call the number above.

Shows with Suggested Donations

Here are some other companies that bring the Bard and other works to a neighborhood near you. All the performances are free, but some of these companies are not shy about passing the hat at the end of the night. Call or check their websites for shows, times, and specific locations:

Circus Amok; politically minded circus performances in public parks throughout the five boroughs every June; (718) 486-7432; www.circus amok.org.

CityParks Theater; various companies present Shakespeare and other productions as well as performance workshops in parks throughout Manhattan and Brooklyn in July and Aug; (212) 360-8290; www .cityparksfoundation.org.

Gorilla Rep; Shakespeare plays that change locations with each scene; Riverside Park just north of 79th Street; www.gorillarep.org.

Hudson Warehouse; Riverside Park; (212) 560-6579; www.hudson warehouse.net.

Inwood Shakespeare Festival; Inwood Hill Park and other parks; (917) 918-0394; www.moosehallisf.org.

New York Classical Theatre; West 103rd Street and Central Park West; (212) 252-4531; www.newyorkclassical.org.

Shakespeare in the Park(ing Lot); Ludlow Street (between Delancey and Broome Streets); www.drillingcompany.org.

Theater for the New City; political street theater in parks throughout the five boroughs; (212) 254-1109; www.theaterforthenewcity.net.

York Theatre Company

St. Peter's Church
619 Lexington Ave. (at 54th Street)
(212) 935-5824
www.yorktheatre.org

York Theatre Company presents a varied schedule of free staged readings of new musicals at various times throughout the week. Call or check their website for schedule and details.

FREE **WILL(IAM):** FREE **THEATER** IN **THE** PARKS

Shakespeare in Central Park

New York Shakespeare Festival/The Public Theater
Delacorte Theater
Turtle Pond (mid-park at West 81st or East 79th Street)
(212) 539-8500
www.publictheater.org

The granddaddy of all Shakespeare in the Park festivals, Shakespeare in Central Park is now in its seventh decade of free performances in Central Park. They present star-studded productions each summer (at least one of which is always a Shakespeare play). They start handing out the free tickets at 1 p.m. each day at the Delacorte in Central Park and from 1 to 3 p.m. at the Public Theater (425 Lafayette St. between East 4th Street and Astor Place). In recent years they have also started handing out tickets in various locations throughout the five boroughs; call for details. These tickets are always in demand, so plan to spend a while on line. But don't let that deter you: This event attracts a great cross section of people, and waiting on line is often as much fun, if not more, than the show itself. If you don't have the time to wait, take a chance and stop by the Delacorte box office at 7:30 p.m., when they release many reserved tickets.

MUSIC:
OF FREE I SING

*"I'll open my case, and I might catch a coin,
but all ears may listen for free."*

—STEVE FORBERT "GRAND CENTRAL STATION,
MARCH 18, 1977"

New York is awash in free music, from almost any street corner or subway platform to clubs, bars, churches, parks, and concert halls. Any season, any day of the year, you can find the strains of any style of music: classical, rock, jazz, country, folk, experimental, world, ethnic . . . if you can hum it, you can find it somewhere in New York for free. Particularly during the summer months, you can hardly turn around without being enticed into another amazing performance at one of the many free concert series all over the city. This being New York, these venues attract top-name artists whom you'd usually have to pay top dollar to see. And I'm not talking about one great show a summer; this goes on week after week, all summer long. One thing to be aware of when attending free shows at many bars and clubs is they do often have a one-, two-, or more-drink minimum, which could add up to a tidy sum. Check out the prices before you order, too; sometimes even a Coke could cost as much as $5.

ROCK, **POP,** FOLK & **ALTERNATIVE**

The Back Fence
155 Bleecker St. (at Thompson Street)
(212) 475-9221
www.thebackfenceonline.com

The Catch: They charge admission on Saturday night only.

Straw on the floor, free peanuts at the bar, and free classic rock, country, and folk rock six nights a week.

Dempsey's Pub
61 Second Ave. (between 3rd and 4th Streets)
(212) 388-0662
www.dempseysnyc.com

Grab your penny whistle and uilleann pipes and come on down to Dempsey's every Tues for a traditional Irish music *seisun* (jam session) at 8 p.m. Musicians and listeners welcome.

Hank's Saloon
46 Third Ave. (at Atlantic Avenue)
Brooklyn
(718) 625-8003
www.hankssaloon.com

This Brooklyn down-home dive saloon is the twang mecca of New York. You will find free live country, rockabilly, and rock music seven nights a week. Don't miss the free pool every Tuesday. Once a month, on Monday, you can channel your inner Patsy Cline when they host New York's only country music karaoke night with a live band. No cover, no minimum.

Lakeside Lounge
162 Avenue B (between 10th and 11th Streets)
(212) 529-8463
www.lakesidelounge.com

A honky-tonk bar with a band in the back room late nights. It's free, but sometimes you get what you pay for. They book some good rock bands who try their damnedest to play above the roar of the crowd. No cover, no minimum.

The Living Room
154 Ludlow St. (between Stanton and Rivington Streets)
(212) 533-7237
www.livingroomny.com

The Catch: One-drink minimum per act, loosely enforced.

On-the-House Bands

Oh My Rockness, www.ohmyrockness.com, is the go-to website for comprehensive listings for every free indie rock show in New York City. These folks cull though hundreds of show listings every week and post them on their website for you to check out anytime you want to catch a show. Many of the listings also include in-depth reviews and information on the bands as well as the venues. They also list shows that you have to pay your way into, but if you simply hit the handy-dandy "Free Shows" tab, you can have access to the hundreds of free shows going on every week.

One of the top destinations in New York for an eclectic mix of singer-songwriters, indie-rock, and acoustic music acts every night that attracts a fun and attentive audience. Norah Jones often performed here before she took over the music world, and she still occasionally stops by for an unannounced set or two. They will occasionally charge an admission, but the vast majority of performances are free, though they charge a one-drink minimum per set and ask for a $5 suggested donation. They also have a smaller second room upstairs with free music every night.

Paddy Reilly's Music Bar
519 Second Ave. (at 29th Street)
(212) 686-1210

The Catch: Free shows/no minimum Sunday through Thursday nights (except some Tuesdays).

The definitive home of Irish music in New York. You'll find everything from Irish rock to traditional Irish music *seisun* on the schedule. Musicians are always welcome to join in on the *seisun*.

Parkside Lounge
317 E. Houston St. (at Attorney Street)
(212) 673-6270
www.parksidelounge.net

The Catch: Two-drink minimum that they do try to enforce—but "we're not gonna trow ya out if ya don't drink."

A local bar complete with pool table, pinball games, and a hip jukebox, along with a snazzy back room with live shows every night. You'll find a lot of local rock/alternative/blues bands most nights, as well as comedy. The lounge also hosts happy hour seven days a week. Most, though not all, shows are free (except for the two-drink minimum.)

Postcrypt Coffeehouse
Columbia University
Basement of St. Paul's Chapel
116th Street and Broadway
(212) 854-1953
www.columbia.edu/cu/postcrypt/coffeehouse

This is one of the great hidden treasures of New York City. Since 1964, every Friday and Saturday night during the school year, this small performance space (only about twenty-five seats) has been filled with the sounds of some of the top names in folk and acoustic music. Past performers have included David Bromberg, Jeff Buckley, Shawn Colvin, Ani DiFranco, John Gorka, Patty Larkin, Lisa Loeb, Ellis Paul, Martin Sexton, Tony Trischka, Suzanne Vega, Jerry Jeff Walker, and Dar Williams. No place in the city presents this music in a more pure form. Here acoustic means acoustic—no mikes, no nothing. Postcrypt always brings in a crowd that is serious about hearing the music. They also serve cheap beer and brownies, but best of all, the popcorn is always free.

The Red Lion
151 Bleecker St. (between Thompson Street and LaGuardia Place)
(212) 260-9797
www.redlionnyc.com

The Catch: Free shows Sunday through Thursday nights.

A full schedule of rock bands attracts a very young crowd.

JAZZ & BLUES

Arthur's Tavern
57 Grove St. (off Seventh Avenue South)
(212) 675-6879
www.arthurstavernnyc.com

The Catch: Two-drink minimum per act loosely enforced.

Since 1937, Arthur's Tavern has been serving up a variety of music for every taste: straight-ahead jazz, New Orleans–style jazz, real Chicago blues. On Monday nights for more than forty years, it's been home to the Grove Street Stompers Dixieland jazz band. Stop by any time of night; there's always something going on. Never a cover.

Take a Free Ride!

After a night on the town, **Right Rides'** mission is to get women home safe. This all-volunteer organization gives free rides home to women on Saturday nights from midnight to 3 a.m. (technically Sunday morning). The service is only for women, only on Saturday nights, and they will only take you home. At the moment, Right Rides currently serves forty-five neighborhoods across the Bronx, Brooklyn, Manhattan, and Queens. To catch a ride home, give them a call at (718) 964-7781 between midnight and 3 a.m. any Saturday night, and they will try to have a car to you within twenty minutes. For more information and a detailed map of their service area, check out their website, www.rightrides.org.

55 Bar

55 Christopher St. (between Seventh Avenue South and 8th Street)
(212) 929-9883
www.55bar.com

The Catch: Early shows on Friday and Saturday nights are always free.

Since 1919, this Prohibition-era dive has been presenting top-of-the-line jazz, funk, and blues. Stop in for the early show any Friday or Saturday night (6 to 9 p.m.) for a hot set of music with no cover, no minimum, and no attitude. They charge $3 to $5 for their other performances, but there is always free popcorn.

Groove

125 MacDougal St. (at West 3rd Street)
(212) 254-9393
www.clubgroovenyc.com

The Catch: Free admission only Sunday through Thursday.

Live rhythm and blues, funk, and hip-hop.

Parlor Jazz at Marjorie Eliot's

555 Edgecombe Ave., Studio 3F (between 159th and 160th Streets)
(212) 781-6595

Underground Music

For years the platforms of the New York City subway system have been the place to hear a varied, eclectic mix of music from all parts of the world played by some of the most talented (and sometimes not-so-talented) musicians around, all playing their hearts out for a handout. And for just as long, the police and MTA wished these folks would stop clogging up the subway's platforms and tunnels. They tried everything from ticketing to arresting offenders to get rid of them. It didn't work. The musicians stayed, and the quarters kept being tossed.

Finally, though, someone smart at the MTA persuaded the city to give in to the old adage "If you can't beat 'em, join 'em" and organized the **MTA Arts for Transit Music Under New York (MUNY)** program. So now you'll find jazz bands, folksingers, didgeridoo players, steel drummers, tap dancers, break-dancers, blues singers, salsa, and, of course, the ever-present Ecuadorian pan flute bands playing throughout the MTA system. MUNY holds auditions every spring at Vanderbilt Hall in Grand Central Station (open to the public) and has twenty-three locations where there are more than 150 performances every week. Some of the most popular sites are Grand Central Terminal, Penn Station, Times Square Station, 42nd Street (Sixth and Eighth Avenue stations), Grand Central Shuttle, Columbus Circle Station, Union Square, and Astor Place. Performances take place throughout the day and into the late night. For more information check out www.mta.info/mta/aft or call (212) 878-7452.

Of course, you'll still find plenty of other musicians littered throughout the system. My personal favorite is singer-songwriter **Kathleen Mock** (www.mockmusic.com), whose haunting melodies and beautifully resonant voice ring out in stations around the Upper West Side and Williamsburg and Park Slope in Brooklyn. When you're waiting for that late-night train to finally arrive, you'll be glad these folks are there to help you through the long wait.

Occasionally you come across one of those events that you feel privileged to have been a part of. Well, that's exactly what goes on every weekend at Ms. Marjorie Eliot's North Harlem apartment. Marjorie graciously welcomes you into her living room, hallway, kitchen, and anyplace else you can find some space to listen to some of the purest, sweetest, swingin'est jazz you will hear anywhere and for any price. And here, of course, there isn't any price. The music begins at 4 p.m. on Sun. Every week Ms. Eliot brings together an ensemble of guest musicians and fifty or more of her closest friends for an afternoon of joyful music. And anyone who attends quickly becomes one of those dear friends. The atmosphere is so warm and comfortable, and the music played so intimately, you'll think you're sitting in a friend's living room listening to some of your favorite tunes—which, in fact, you are.

St. Nick's Jazz Pub
773 Saint Nicholas Ave. (corner of 149th Street)
(212) 283-9728
http://stnicksjazzpub.net

The Catch: A posted three-drink minimum, but it is basically never enforced.

This nondescript Harlem pub is the home of the city's hottest jam session every Monday night starting at 9:30 p.m. But the swinging doesn't end on Monday; every night of the week some of the best players around take to the stage, including many top-name surprise guest appearances by the likes of Wynton Marsalis, Savioun Glover, Olu Dara, James Carter, and others. There is a sign on the tables saying they charge a cover and a three-drink minimum, but they basically never enforce it.

CLASSICAL **MUSIC**

Brooklyn Heights Music Society
157 Montague St. (between Henry and Clinton Streets)
info@brooklynsymphonyorchestra.org
www.brooklynheightsorchestra.org

This well-respected community orchestra is made up of a mix of amateur, student, retired, semiprofessional, and professional musicians. They present an array of symphony, orchestral, and chamber concerts in libraries, churches, and temples around Brooklyn. You are also welcome to bring your own bassoon, tuba, or triangle and join in on their open rehearsals every Monday evening. Check their website for the schedule or e-mail them for more information. Performances and rehearsals are always free, but they will be happy to accept your donation.

Brooklyn Queens Conservatory of Music
58 Seventh Ave. (at Lincoln Place)
Park Slope, Brooklyn
(718) 622-3300
www.bqcm.org

The conservatory is one of the country's oldest community music schools. They offer a full schedule of free concerts that run the gamut from children's recitals to professional-level classical and jazz performances. Sometimes there's a charge for guest performers and the larger concerts, but most shows are free.

Carnegie Hall Neighborhood Concert Series
Locations throughout the five boroughs
(212) 247-7800
www.carnegiehall.org

For more than thirty-five years, the distinguished hall has presented more than eighty concerts a year (Sept through Apr) in neighborhoods throughout the five boroughs in libraries, churches, and community centers. The series presents a mix of classical, jazz, pop, and folk music; all shows are free and open to all. For schedule and location information, call or click on the "Explore & Learn" menu at their website.

The Interchurch Center
475 Riverside Dr. (between 119th and 120th Streets)
(212) 870-2200
www.interchurch-center.org

This interdenominational center for all faiths offers free concerts every Wed at 12:05 p.m., Sept through May. Performances last about thirty minutes;

the programs range from string quartets to woodwind ensembles, traditional African folk music to Celtic songs and dances, medieval to jazz, vocal soloist to choir, piano to organ, and emerging artists to established professionals.

The Juilliard School
60 Lincoln Center Plaza (Broadway and 65th Street on the plaza level)
(212) 799-5000
www.juilliard.edu

The Catch: Free tickets go quickly.

See the leading artists of tomorrow, today. This is the preeminent conservatory for classical musicians in the country, and they present a huge array of classical, chamber music, and jazz concerts by students and faculty throughout the year. Most of the performances are free, though some require tickets. To get tickets for these events, stop by the box office on the day they become available; otherwise you may be sold out of the event. You can also line up an hour before the show to try to get in on a standby basis. Venues are throughout Lincoln Center and the Juilliard School, and events are scheduled in the afternoon and evening all week long. Check the website or pick up a copy of the performance schedule at the box office. Performances by the drama division are also free, though not those by the dance and opera departments.

Manhattan School of Music
120 Claremont Ave. (between 121st Street and Seminary Row)
(212) 749-2802
www.msmnyc.edu

The MSM presents a full schedule of free classical and jazz concerts by students, faculty, and visiting artists, and master classes.

Mannes College of Music
150 W. 85th St. (between Columbus and Amsterdam Avenues)
(212) 580-0210
www.mannes.edu

Mannes offers a full schedule of free orchestral, chamber music, and jazz concerts throughout the school year.

NYU Department of Music and Performing Arts Professions
35 W. 4th St., Suite 777 (at Greene Street)
(212) 998-5424
www.steinhardt.nyu.edu/music

Students and faculty present a full schedule of classical, chamber, jazz, and musical theater concerts along with their calendar of talks and workshops, all free and open to the public.

Trinity Church
74 Trinity Place (Broadway at Wall Street)
(212) 602-0800
www.trinitywallstreet.org

The Catch: $2 suggested contribution, but nothing required.

The Concerts at One series offers classical, jazz, and popular music performances every Thursday afternoon. You can also catch lunchtime performances at their sister church nearby, St. Paul's Chapel (Broadway and Fulton Street), every Mon at 1 p.m. Both of these national landmarks are steeped in American history and worth a look anytime.

OUTDOOR **SUMMER** CONCERTS

During the summer months New York is the Mecca, Medina, Jerusalem, and Emerald City of free music. Almost any open green space transforms into a concert hall for an amazing array of established stars and cutting-edge performers of practically every genre of music. Many of these venues have become quite popular over the years—which means you should be sure to show up early to claim your space on the lawn or in the stands.

BAM Rhythm & Blues Festival
MetroTech Center (between Flatbush Avenue, Jay, Johnson, and Willoughby Streets)
Downtown Brooklyn
(718) 636-4100
www.bam.org
Thurs at noon, June through Aug.

Brown-bag it over to Brooklyn for this hot festival of legendary stars. Don't be misled by the name of the festival: In the past the festival has lined up a varied roster of top-name performers such as Dr. John, the Robert Cray Band, Los Lobos, Steel Pulse, Burning Spear, and others.

Bryant Park
Sixth Avenue between 41st and 42nd Streets
(212) 768-4242
www.bryantpark.org

Known mostly for the hugely popular film series on Monday nights, the park also hosts a great deal of concerts and performances throughout the summer. You will find the likes of the B52s, Carly Simon, the Beach Boys, and other big-name groups performing in the park for the TV show *Good Morning America*. The park also hosts classical, jazz, and Broadway performances in the afternoon and evening. Check the website for the extensive schedule.

Celebrate Brooklyn
Prospect Park Bandshell (Prospect Park West and 9th Street)
Park Slope, Brooklyn
(718) 855-7882
www.celebratebrooklyn.org
June through Aug.

Brooklyn's popular free series presents a star-studded schedule of everything from free films and spoken word and dance performances to rock, jazz, Latin, folk, and world music performances.

Central Park SummerStage
Rumsey Playfield
72nd Street, mid-park
(212) 360-2777
www.summerstage.org
June through Aug.

If New York is the Promised Land of free concerts during the summer, this is the Wailing Wall. The schedule runs the entire length of the summer, with performances almost every night of the week and a wildly varied schedule that runs the gamut from opera to hip-hop, from world to tween pop. You're likely to find names you're familiar with—like Joan Jett, Counting Crowes, David Byrne, or the Indigo Girls—and just as likely to be wowed by performers whose names you never would have come across if not for SummerStage's daring programming. There are also evenings devoted to spoken word and dance. Seating is on a first-come, first-served basis; for some of the more popular shows, the line starts hours before the gates open.

Cool Music for Warm Summer Days
1 Battery Park Plaza (between Pearl and Bridge Streets)
(212) 407-2429
www.rivertorivernyc.com
Wed at 12:30 p.m.

Local musicians of every sort (Dixieland, folk, rock, classical, and more) entertain the lunchtime crowd every Wed (downtown) and Thurs (uptown).

El Museo del Barrio
1230 Fifth Ave. (at 104th Street)
(212) 831-7272
www.elmuseo.org
Thurs at 6 p.m., June through Aug.

Every Thursday evening the museum turns on the heat (and the volume!) with an exhilarating Latin concert series. Spotlighting both local favorites and international stars performing in a surprising variety of styles within the Latin music world, including hip-hop, Cuban surf, rock, reggae, *bachata*, and, of course, salsa.

Free Concerts in Parks
Neighborhood parks throughout Brooklyn, the Bronx, and Manhattan
(212) 360-2777
www.cityparksfoundation.org
June through Sept.

The undisputed champ of free events, the City Parks Foundation stages more than 1,100 free performances throughout the year in parks throughout the five boroughs, with the bulk of the events taking place between June and Sept. They offer everything from free concerts, theater, dance, hip-hop, and Latin events; the Charlie Parker Jazz Festival; SummerStage; as well as a huge amount of kids' events. Check out their website for a detailed schedule; they are sure to have something fantastic going on practically every day of the summer. And as if that weren't enough, the City Parks Foundation also offers a full schedule of free tennis, golf, and track and field lessons for kids in these parts all summer long.

Harlem Meer Performance Festival
Charles A. Dana Discovery Center
Central Park (110th Street and Central Park North)
(212) 310-6600
www.centralparknyc.org
Sun at 4 p.m., June through Sept.

Upper Central Park makes a beautiful backdrop for this free concert series showcasing established and emerging jazz, Latin, dance, and gospel artists.

Harlem Week/Harlem Jazz and Music Festival
Throughout Harlem and Manhattan
(212) 862-7200
www.harlemdiscover.com
End of July to Aug.

What started out as a one-day event has grown into a monthlong celebration of African-American life in America. The festival hosts many concerts throughout the month in different locations around Harlem and Manhattan, as well as films, lectures, sporting events, street fairs, and more. Most events are free. Check the website for this year's schedule.

Jazzmobile
154 W. 127th St. (between Lenox and Seventh Avenues)
(212) 866-4900 or (212) 866-3616 (concert hotline)
www.jazzmobile.org
Various times and locations around the five boroughs.

Since 1964, Jazzmobile has been bringing the music to the people by presenting a lineup of world-class musicians in parks, libraries, schools, and street corners all around New York and the surrounding areas. They also offer free Saturday workshops and master classes for students age seven and up at PS 197 in Harlem, which have included such jazz legends as Max Roach, Branford Marsalis, and Donald Byrd. Check the website for details.

Madison Square Park

Between Madison and Fifth Avenues from 23rd to 26th Street
(212) 538-1884
www.madisonsquarepark.org
June to Aug.

Taking the lead of Bryant Park, Madison Square Park has become a destination for endless free activities in a spectacular green setting during the summer. The free concerts take place on various evenings and Saturday afternoons during the summer. The evening series includes an eclectic array of well-known artists such as Lucy Kaplansky, James Hunter, and the Regina Carter Quintet, and Saturday afternoons are filled with music from up-and-coming folk and blues performers. The park also hosts a summer reading series with literary heavyweights, children's activities, and many other unique events throughout the year. Check out their website for schedules and details.

Martin Luther King Jr. Concert Series

Wingate Field (across the street from Kings County Hospital)
Winthrop Street (between Brooklyn and Kingston Avenues)
(718) 222-0600
www.brooklynconcerts.com
Mon, July and Aug.

The Best of the Fests

During the summer months the entirety of downtown Manhattan can be summed up by three words and one punctuation mark: It's a festival! From the Hudson River, around Battery Park, up to the South Street Seaport, and everywhere in between, there are literally hundreds and hundreds of free concerts, performances, and events scheduled from June to September as a part of these downtown fests. While many of the specific venues and concert series are listed in this chapter, the scope of these festivals is ever expanding. You owe it to yourself and your ever-contracting entertainment budget to check out their websites or nab a copy of their festival guides.

Downtown NYC River to River Festival, www.rivertorivernyc.org

Hudson River Festival, www.hudsonriverpark.org

Seaport Music Festival, www.seaportmusicfestival.com

Stars of gospel, soul, funk, and jazz perform at this summer concert series. Performers have included Mighty Clouds of Joy, George Clinton, Stephanie Mills, the O'Jays, Chaka Khan, Hezekiah Walker, and the Gap Band.

Met in the Parks
Parks throughout the five boroughs
(212) 362-6000
www.metoperafamily.org
June.

For three weeks in June, the world-renowned Metropolitan Opera Company sheds the pomp and pretense of the opera hall and presents concert performances to the masses in Central Park and other parks throughout the five boroughs. Check the website for schedule and locations.

Music at Castle Clinton
Battery Park
(212) 835-2789
www.rivertorivernyc.com
July 4 and Thursday evenings in July and early Aug.

The season opens with a large open-air concert in Battery Park on the Fourth of July weekend, drawing thousands of listeners; then the shows move into the smaller space at Castle Clinton. Tickets are required (free, but limited) for the Castle Clinton shows and given out on a first-come, first-served basis at 5 p.m. on the day of the show. Past performers have included Crash Test Dummies, Taj Mahal, Mark Cohen, Billy Bragg, Emmylou Harris, Sonic Youth, and Junior Brown.

Naumburg Orchestral Concerts
Naumburg Bandshell, Central Park (mid-park at 72nd Street)
(212) 501-7809
www.naumburgconcerts.org
Tuesday evenings, late June to Aug.

This may not be the biggest or most well-known outdoor concert series, but having presented free concerts in Central Park since 1905, it is the oldest continuous series of such concerts anywhere in the country. The series regularly includes performances by the New York Chamber Symphony, Empire Brass, and others. Check their website for a schedule of concerts.

New York Philharmonic
Concerts in the Parks
(212) 875-55900
www.nyphil.org
July.

For more than thirty-five years, the Philharmonic has brought millions of people into the parks for what they call "Priceless Music Absolutely Free." With guest musicians and conductors, they present two programs of classical and popular music in city parks throughout the five boroughs and always cap the evening off with a spectacular fireworks display.

The Pool Parties
Williamsburg Waterfront
Williamsburg, Brooklyn
www.thepoolparties.com
Sun, in July and Aug.

Brooklyn's favorite abandoned pool plays host to a wild and rocking concert series every Sunday during July and Aug. This indie-rock fest attracts fans from all over the city and beyond and encourages music lovers to join in on the fun, which is by no means limited to the stage. The goings-on include a 30-foot Slip 'n' Slide, hula hoops, a dodgeball court, and even water volleyball. The concerts are free, but reservations are encouraged. Check out their website for more details and to make reservations.

River & Blues
Battery Park City Parks
Robert F. Wagner Jr. Park (at Battery Place)
(212) 267-9700
www.bpcparks.org
Thursday evenings, July and Aug.

Bring a picnic dinner and enjoy the spectacular sunset views of the lower Hudson while you enjoy these jazz, blues, funk, and fusion performances. Past performers have included Hiram Bullock, John Hammond, and Howard Fishman.

Seaside Summer Concert Series
Asser Levy Park (at West 5th Street and Surf Avenue)
Brighton Beach, Brooklyn
(718) 222-0600
www.brooklynconcerts.com
Thursday evenings, July and Aug.

Head out to the heart of Brooklyn and travel back in time to this series that features many of the biggest names in music and comedy from the 1950s, 1960s, 1970s, and 1980s (golden oldies, disco, rock, and stand-up comedy). In past years they have featured appearances by Gladys Knight, Jay Black and the Americans, Pat Benatar, the Temptations, David Brenner, the Village People, and others.

South Street Seaport
Pier 17 (at Fulton and South Streets)
(212) SEA-PORT (732-7678)
www.southstreetseaport.com
Tues through Sun at noon and 5:30 p.m., May through Sept.

Starting with a huge Cinco de Mayo Festival and running throughout the spring and summer, the South Street Seaport presents lunchtime and after-work concerts in every style of music, from country, folk, and rock to gospel, jazz, and Latin. The performers often include well-known acts as well as up-and-coming artists. Many summer weekends are also filled with full-day music, sports, and other festivals. Any day you can count on running across your fair share of jugglers, mimes, magicians, and other buskers to keep you entertained. Monday is the only day they don't schedule any official programs. Call or check the website for up-to-date information.

Summer in the Square
Union Square (14th to 17th Streets between Park Avenue and
University Place)
(212) 460-1200
www.unionsquarenyc.org
Thurs, June through Aug.

Stop by the park for a midweek jolt of music. Every week brings something completely different, including jazz, classical, blues, Brazilian, and theater, and free yoga classes, dance performances, and children's shows. Check their website for the schedule.

FILM:
CHEAP SHOTS

Mugger: "Don't make a move. This is a stick-up.
Your money or your life! . . .
Look, bud, I said your money or your life!"

Jack Benny: "I'm thinking it over."

Now that World Wide Cinemas is a distant memory (what most cheap New Yorkers used to lovingly refer to as "the $3 theater") and prices are more than $10 a ticket, there has never been a greater need to find places to see movies without spending the moolah. If you've ever been among the throngs of people camped out at Bryant Park on a summer Monday evening, you know what I mean. Well, Bryant Park is only the beginning of the cheap cinema offerings throughout the city. From outdoor screenings under the stars during the summer to bars, libraries, and even theaters throughout the year, here is your list of where to get your fix of free flicks.

FREE **FLICKS**

Anthology Film Archive
32 Second Ave. (at 2nd Street)
(212) 505-5181
www.anthologyfilmarchives.org

The Catch: You must be an Anthology member.

For those of you on the lookout for something other than what you will find at your local multiplex, Anthology is definitely the place for you. This world-renowned institution specializes in collecting, preserving, and exhibiting American independent, experimental, and avant-garde films and video, as well as some classics from Hollywood and European filmmakers. If you are willing to shell out the $60 yearly membership fee, you are entitled to attend all of their Essential Cinema screenings, which happen at least once a week, for free. Without the membership you would pay $9 for each screening. The membership also gets you into any of their other screenings for $6.

Barbès
376 9th St. (corner of Sixth Avenue)
Park Slope, Brooklyn
(347) 422-0248
www.barbesbrooklyn.com
www.brooklynindependent.com
First Mon of the month, 7 p.m.

This intimate Park Slope performance space hosts an incredibly eclectic variety of shows every week, mostly music, but on the first Monday of the month they turn on the projector for the Brooklyn Independent Film Series. The free series focuses on the kind of films that you are not going to be seeing at your local multiplex, including features, documentaries, and shorts. The filmmakers are often present at the screenings for Q and A's following the films. Every other night, watch a variety of independent films and documentaries often followed by live music. Most shows are free, though they do pass the hat!

Bryant Park Summer Film Festival
West 40th to West 41st Streets (between Fifth and Sixth Avenues)
(212) 512-5700
www.bryantpark.org
Mon at nightfall, June through Aug.

This is the granddaddy of all free film screenings in New York. It has become incredibly popular, and as a result you need to get there mighty early if you have any hope of claiming a piece of the greenery for your own. They start letting people onto the lawn at 5 p.m. Since HBO foots the bill for this event, you can be sure you'll get a preview of something coming soon to a friendly cable network near you. There is always a cartoon before the feature, and then you can join the crowd dancing to the HBO trailer just before the film begins (don't ask me why). The features on the huge screen range from cinema classics (*Goldfinger, Rear Window, The French Connection*) to kitschy favorites (*Viva Las Vegas, The Wild One*).

Casa Italiana Zerilli-Marimò
24 W. 12th St. (between Fifth and Sixth Avenues)
(212) 998-8730
www.nyu.edu/pages/casaitaliana

This NYU institution hosts four to five free screenings of classic and contemporary Italian films throughout the school year. The films are just a small part of their full schedule of exhibitions, performances, and talks on all things Italian. All events are free and open to the public.

Celebrate Brooklyn

Prospect Park Bandshell (Prospect Park West and 9th Street)
Park Slope, Brooklyn
(718) 855-7882
www.celebratebrooklyn.org
Most Fridays at 7:30 p.m., July and Aug.

Brooklyn's popular free series presents everything from free films, to spoken-word and dance performances, to live rock, jazz, Latin, folk, and world music. Classic and silent films are often accompanied by live contemporary music and performers.

Czech Center at Bohemian National Hall

321 E. 73rd St. (at 83rd Street)
(646) 422-3399
www.bohemiannationalhall.com

The Czech Center hosts a series of classic and contemporary Czech films with English subtitles at the Bohemian National Hall throughout the year.

Deutsches Haus

42 Washington Mews (near University Place)
(212) 998-8660
www.nyu.edu/deutscheshaus
Selected Fridays at 6:30 p.m., and other times.

This cultural center for all things German regularly holds free film screenings. Recent series have focused on film versions of Kafka's novels, gay films in early German cinema, and the films of Marlene Dietrich, as well as contemporary films from Germany. Most screenings are held on Friday evenings, but there are others scattered throughout the week on their schedule. Often films are accompanied by lectures and live performances. Call or check the website for schedule and details.

French Institute/Alliance Française

Florence Gould Hall
55 E. 59th St. (between Madison and Park Avenues)
(212) 355-6160
www.fiaf.org
Tuesday afternoons and evenings.

The Catch: You must be a French Institute member.

While not exactly free, for fans of French films this is a pretty worthwhile deal. If you're a member of the French Institute ($95 for a single or $150 for a family), you can attend the weekly Crossing the Line screenings every Tuesday for free. This usually consists of a double feature, often of recent popular favorites as well as classics and lesser-known films. All films are shown in French with English subtitles.

Instituto Cervantes

211–15 E. 49th St. (between Second and Third Avenues)
(212) 308-7720
http://nuevayork.cervantes.es
Wed at 7:30 p.m.

For lovers of Spanish and Latin American films or English-language films that deal with those parts of the world, there is no better destination than the weekly film series put together by the Cervantes Institute. They also offer free panel discussions, lectures, and a great library (see page 191). For more information on other activities, call or check their website.

Iris & B. Gerald Cantor Film Center at NYU

36 E. 8th St. (between Broadway and University Place)
(212) 998-4100

Every week during the school year, the center holds many screenings of international films, Hollywood hits, and student films. Some events are lim-

---

Who Wants to Be a Moviemaker?

Do you ever find yourself walking out of a movie thinking I could do better than that? Or do you just know you could be the next Scorsese, if you knew where to start? Well, here's your chance to put your money (or should I say time?) where your mouth is. By volunteering your time at the **Downtown Community Television Center** (87 Lafayette St., between White and Walker Streets; 212-966-4510; www.dctvny.org), you are able to take classes and use their equipment and facilities free of charge. You must, however, commit to approximately sixteen hours a week doing administrative or production work in exchange for the free ride. For more information see the chapter titled "Education: Cents-Less Smarts."

---

ited to NYU students; others are free and open to the public. Call or drop by for a schedule.

Monday Movie Series
All Saints Parish Hall
707 Washington St. (at 7th Street)
Hoboken, New Jersey
www.allsaintshoboken.com
Mon at 6:30 p.m., July and Aug.

Just on the other side of the Hudson, you can escape the heat of the city with this series of classic Hollywood films shown in the air-conditioned Parish Hall. They even throw in free seltzer and popcorn.

Movies Under the Stars
Pier A Park (1st Street and Frank Sinatra Drive)
Hoboken, New Jersey
(201) 420-2207
www.hobokennj.org
Wed at 8 or 8:30 p.m., June through Aug.

For the cost of a ride on the Path train ($1.50), hop over to Hoboken, where they show many recent hits and blockbusters in this summer series.

Movies with a View
Empire-Fulton State Park (between the Brooklyn and
Manhattan Bridges)
(718) 802-0603
www.brooklynbridgepark.org
Thursday nights, July and Aug.

In the shadow of the majestic Brooklyn Bridge, this film series screens Hollywood and independent films, many of which have been shot in, are about, or are made by people from Brooklyn. The evening always starts off with a live DJ spinning some tunes to set the mood, and they also provide free valet parking for your bicycle.

The Museum of Modern Art (MoMA)
11 W. 53rd St. (between Fifth and Sixth Avenues)
(212) 708-9400
www.moma.org
Free on Fri, 4–8 p.m.

The museum has two movie theaters that are free with admission to the museum—and on Target Free Fridays, that's free, too. They show classic and contemporary independent and art films. Call for the latest schedule and details.

Ocularis

Galapagos Art and Performance Space
16 Main St. (between Water and Plymouth Streets)
Dumbo, Brooklyn
(718) 222-8500
www.galapagosartspace.com

Ocularis runs a number of art film series in Williamsburg, Long Island City, and Astoria throughout the year. The screenings are in conjunction with institutions like P.S. 1 Contemporary Art Center, the Asia Society, the African Film Festival, and others. They show documentaries, experimental and

---

Everyone's a Critic

Here's your chance to let Hollywood know what you think. Many major film studios run private screenings of soon-to-be-released films. They're hoping to gauge response, figure out how to market the movie, learn what changes might be needed, or simply see if the movie's any good. There's no way to necessarily get on a list to see these previews, because they want a random sampling of people, but they are constantly going on, and there are ways to increase your chances of getting an invitation.

You'll often find people handing out screening passes in front of multiplexes (particularly Loews Lincoln Square–Broadway between 67th and 68th Streets). If you see someone handing out passes, don't be afraid to approach and ask for one. These folks are paid by the number of people they can get to show up at the screenings. If you promise to show up, they want you. They are usually (though not always) looking for people between the ages of seventeen and thirty-four, but they don't check IDs. And they won't let anyone involved in the entertainment industry into the screenings. If that's you, when they ask what you do for a living, remember to embrace your inner accountant.

---

avant-garde films, and contemporary and emerging-artist flicks, as well as features from around the world (in other words, you are not going to see *Terminator 3* here). Screenings are often accompanied by live music and dance. Some films are free, others are not; check the website for a detailed schedule.

River Flicks

Pier 46, Hudson River and Christopher Street
Pier 54, Hudson River and 14th Street
(212) 732-7467
www.hudsonriverpark.org
Wed, dusk at Pier 54 (films for grown-ups).
Fri, dusk at Pier 46 (films for kids).
July and Aug.

Every Friday night grab the kids and take them down to Hudson River Park for some of the best family films ever put to celluloid. Whether it is animated features like *Shark Tales* or *Shrek,* live-action comedies like *Back to the Future* or *Daddy Day Care,* or classics like *Willy Wonka and the Chocolate Factory* (an annual event!), the whole family is sure to have a great time. Or you can get a sitter for the little ones every Wednesday night and make your way up to Pier 54 to catch some adult films. All right, don't get crazy, these are all films rated PG-13 or R, like *Fast Times at Ridgemont High, Clerks,* and *Gladiator.* Whenever you decide to go, the films are all free, and even the popcorn is on the house.

Riverside Park South

Pier 1 (Hudson River between 70th Street)
(212) 408-0219
www.riversideparkfund.org
Wednesday evenings at dusk, July and Aug.

As the development of the Hudson River waterside continues to spread uptown, the free opportunities are following. One of the highlights is Movies on the Hudson, held at this park between 65th and 72nd Streets. Grab a blanket and picnic under the stars while you catch a fun selection of cinema classics and Hollywood blockbusters such as *Chicago, Who's Afraid of Virginia Woolf?, Dirty Rotten Scoundrels,* and *Fiddler on the Roof.* The park also hosts a full schedule of other free events every week, including yoga and Pilates classes, concerts, lots of kids' events, and free kayaking.

Socrates Sculpture Park's Outdoor Cinema

32–01 Vernon Blvd. (at Broadway)
Long Island City, Queens
(718) 956-1819
www.socratessculpturepark.org
Wed at 7 p.m., July and Aug.

Since the borough of Queens is one of the most culturally diverse place on the face of the planet, with communities from almost every country in the world, you can say this festival is both a local and an international one. Each week the series chooses a film that represents a community in Queens (Greek, Cuban, Korean, Brazilian, Indian, etc.). They fill out the evening with live music and dance performances from the country and have local restaurants provide the regional cuisine. The performances and film are free, but you will have to pay for the food. Films have included *Zorba the Greek, Buena Vista Social Club, Central Station,* and *House Party.*

Sony Wonder Technology Lab

550 Madison Ave. (at 56th Street)
(212) 833-7858
www.sonywondertechlab.com
Sat at 2 p.m. (twice a month).

The Sony Wonder Technology Lab screens recent and some less recent Hollywood favorites (*The Wedding Planner, Ghostbusters, House of Flying Daggers, Muppets from Space*) on their amazing high-definition screen. They accept reservations the week of the film and give out any remaining tickets at 1:45 p.m. Throughout the week they also offer free screenings geared toward kids age six and younger (*Elmo, Sesame Street,* etc.) followed by fun kid-friendly workshops. Check their website or call for the schedule of screenings. Get there early and enjoy the four floors of interactive activities—everything's free.

BETTER **THAN** THE **BOOK**

Public Libraries
www.nypl.org/branch/events
www.queenslibrary.org
www.brooklynpubliclibrary.org

Many public libraries throughout Manhattan, Brooklyn, Queens, Staten Island, and the Bronx show regularly scheduled films every week. These films could include black-and-white classics from the 1930s and 1940s, documentaries, foreign films, and recent features. Here's a list of the branches with screenings on a regular basis; call or check the websites to confirm schedules.

Manhattan Branches
Chatham Square Library, 33 E. Broadway (between Catherine and Market Streets); (212) 964-6598; the third Thurs of the month at 5 p.m.

Donnell Library Center, 20 W. 53rd St. (between Fifth and Sixth Avenues); (212) 621-0618; Wed at 2:30 p.m.

58th Street Library, 127 E. 58th St. (between Lexington and Park Avenues); (212) 759-7358; Fri at 2 p.m.

Jefferson Market Library, 425 Sixth Ave. (at 10th Street); (212) 243-4334; Mon at 6 p.m.

Mid-Manhattan Library, 455 Fifth Ave. at 40th Street; (212) 340-0849; every Wed at 6:30 p.m.

Ottendorfer Branch, 135 Second Ave. (at St. Marks Place), (212) 674-0947; every other Fri at 3 p.m.

St. Agnes Library, 444 Amsterdam Ave. (between 80th and 81st Streets); (212) 877-4380; Wed at 2 p.m.

Yorkville Library, 222 E. 79th St. (between Second and Third Avenues); (212) 744-5824; Fri at 3 p.m. (twice a month).

Brooklyn Branches

Bay Ridge, 7223 Ridge Blvd. (at 73rd Street); (718) 748-5709; every Mon at 1:30 p.m.

Brighton Beach, Brighton First Road (near Brighton Beach Avenue); (718) 946-2917; every other Mon at 1:30 p.m.

Central Library, Grand Army Plaza (Flatbush Avenue and Eastern Parkway); (718) 230-2100; Fri at 6 p.m. (feature films), Tues at 7 p.m., twice a month (documentaries), and other times; call for schedule.

Mapleton, 1702 60th St. (at 17th Avenue); (718) 256-2117; Thurs at 3 p.m.

Sheepshead Bay, 2636 E. 14th St. (at Avenue Z); (718) 368-1815; Tues at 1:30 p.m.

Wakefield Branch, 4100 Lowerre Place (at East 229th Street); (718) 652-4663; Mon at 5 p.m.

Bronx Branches

Baychester Library, 2049 Asch Loop North; (718) 379-6700; call for details.

Queens Branches

Flushing, 41-17 Main St. (at Kissena Boulevard); (718) 661-1200; every Thurs at 2:00 p.m.

Fresh Meadows, 193-20 Horace Harding Expressway (at 193rd St.); (718) 454-7272; every second Mon at 2:00 p.m.

Staten Island Branches

New Dorp Branch, 309 New Dorp Lane (at Clawson Street); (718) 351-2977; Sat at 2 p.m.

TELEVISION TAPINGS:
PUBLIC ACCESS

Alien: "On this cable system, we receive over one million channels from the farthest reaches of the galaxy."
Bart: "Do you get HBO?"
Alien: "No, that would cost extra."

—THE SIMPSONS

After Hollywood, New York is home to the most small-screen shows. While Los Angeles is the place to be if you want to see tapings of sitcoms, the kinds of programs that are based in New York have a mix of everything, including talk shows, game shows, variety shows, comedies, and courtroom shows. It's possible to get tickets to many of these shows the week of the taping, but many of the more popular shows have long waiting lists and require you to request tickets from a couple of months to up to a year in advance. All television tapings are free, but be warned that some do require a substantial commitment of time. The upside is that there's usually a very funny comedian working the crowd trying to keep you entertained while you sit around waiting for the official fun to begin.

The audience is an important part of the show, so they want to keep you lively for when they need you to hoot, holler, and applaud wildly. And one of the best ways they have found to keep you interested is through bribery. Often these shows offer giveaways for the audience. You could receive anything from key chains and T-shirts to Broadway tickets and books.

The Colbert Report
513 W. 54th St. (between Tenth and Eleventh Avenues)
(212) 586-2477
www.comedycentral.com
Tape days: Mon through Fri at 7:30 p.m.

The Daily Show's Stephen Colbert tackles the issues of the day, and hurts them. Reserve tickets through the website, though they do go fast. You can also show up at the studio at 7 any night to try for standby tickets.

The Daily Show with Jon Stewart
733 Eleventh Ave. (between 51st and 52nd Streets)
(212) 586-2477
www.comedycentral.com
Tape days: Mon through Thurs, 5:30–7:30 p.m. (arrive by 4).

Jon Stewart is an Emmy Award–winning news satire and comedy talk show. Reserve tickets months ahead through the website. You must be at least eighteen years old. You can also try your luck on the day of the show by showing up early and hoping for some no-shows.

Good Morning America
West 44th Street and Broadway
(212) 930-7855
www.abcnews.go.com/GMA
Tape days: Mon through Fri, 7–9 a.m.

Hang out with Diane Sawyer and the GMA gang in their Times Square studio as they talk about world events, chat with celebrities, and tell you the best way to clean your dust bunnies. Send for tickets through the website about a month in advance. Plan to arrive at 6 a.m.; the show is on the air from 7 to 9. You can also always join the crowd on the street outside the studio.

Late Night with Jimmy Fallon
NBC Studio
30 Rockefeller Plaza (49th Street, between Fifth and Sixth Avenues)
(212) 664-3056
www.latenightwithjimmyfallon.com
Tape days: Tues through Fri, 5:30–6:30 p.m.

Join Jimmy Fallon for his late-night interviews. Call the ticket request line for reservations two to three months in advance. Standby tickets are given out at 9 a.m. at the NBC Studio lobby on a first-come, first-served basis. Standby tickets do not guarantee you'll get into the show; it will depend on how many people with reserved tickets fail to show up at the taping later that day.

The Late Show with David Letterman
The Ed Sullivan Theater
1697 Broadway (between 54th and 55th Streets)
New York, NY 10019
(212) 975-1003 (general info)
(212) 247-6497 (standby tickets)
www.lateshowaudience.com
Tape days: Mon through Thurs at 5:30 p.m. (4:15 arrival time), and again on Thurs at 7 p.m. (5 arrival time).

It's the top ten list, viewer mail, Stupid Pet Tricks, Paul, Dave, and you, all together in a very chilly studio (bring a sweater!). For advance tickets, fill out an application at their website or in person at the theater (Mon through Fri 9:30 a.m. to 12:30 p.m. or Sat and Sun 10 a.m. to 6 p.m.). They will call you if they have tickets available for the day you requested, but be prepared to answer a David Letterman trivia question when they call (Who runs the Hello Deli? Name a recent Top Ten category? Who is Dave's announcer?) or you are out of luck. Send for tickets at least two months in advance. To get standby tickets on the day of the taping, call the standby phone line at 11 a.m. You have to be pretty lucky and persistent to nab one of these rare tickets, but give it a shot; there isn't an in-person standby line.

Live with Regis and Kelly

7 Lincoln Sq. (at 67th Street and Columbus Avenue)
(212) 456-3054
http://bventertainment.go.com/tv/buenavista/regisandkelly
Tape days: Mon through Fri at 9 a.m. (arrive at 8).

Regis tries not to lose it, Kelly tries to understand it, and Gelman tries to keep it all together on this morning chat show. For advance tickets, send a postcard with your name, address, phone number, the date for which you would like tickets, and the number of tickets requested (limit four per person). Send ticket requests to Live Tickets, Ansonia Station, P.O. Box 230777, New York, NY 10023. Requests can take up to a year to be filled. To try for standby tickets on the day of taping, arrive at the studio as early as 7 a.m.; tickets are given out on a first-come, first-served basis.

Martha

221 W. 26th St. (between Seventh and Eighth Avenues)
(917) 438-5999
www.marthastewart.com/martha
Tape days: Tues at 10 a.m., Wed and Thurs at 10 a.m. and 2 p.m.

Martha loosens up the apron strings on her morning talk show, which includes lots of celebrity guests, audience participation, and, of course, a few tips on everything from homemade apple pies to handmade xylophones. The tickets can be hard to come by, and they can be had only through the website. Check it often for when new dates are available. For standby tickets the day of, get there two hours before showtime and bring your knitting to work on while you wait on line.

The Maury Show

New York's Hotel Pennsylvania
401 Seventh Ave. (between 32nd and 33rd Streets)
(866) 996-2879
www.mauryshow.com
Tape days: Wed, Thurs, and Fri at 8:30 a.m. (arrive by 8:15 a.m.).

Maury Povich presents a lively audience-participation talk show. You can request tickets on the website anytime up until the day of taping. If you don't have tickets, they say you can always come to the studio the day of the taping; they'll probably be able to get you in.

The People's Court

401 Fifth Ave., eighth floor (at 37th Street, between Fifth and
Madison Avenues)
(888) 780-8587
tickets@peoplescourt.com
www.peoplescourt.com
Tape days: Tues and Wed at 10 a.m. and 2 p.m. (be prepared to stay for
three hours).

Judge Marilyn Milian presides over this courtroom reality show. Call or e-mail for tickets any time up until the day of taping.

Rachael Ray Show

222 E. 44th St. (between Second and Third Avenues)
www.rachaelrayshow.com
Tape days: Tues, Wed, and Thurs at 11:30 a.m. and 4 p.m.

The perky anti-Martha, Rachael Ray cooks and chums it up with celebrities on her daytime talk show. Tickets are in high demand for the show, so be prepared to wait up to a year for your tickets to show up. To try for tickets, fill out a form at their website. To try for day-of-the-show standby tickets, show up at 10 a.m. (for the 11:30 show) or 2:30 p.m. (for the 4 show), grab a standby voucher, and keep your fingers crossed.

Saturday Night Live

NBC Studio
30 Rockefeller Plaza (49th Street, between Fifth and Sixth Avenues)
(212) 664-3056
www.nbc.com/snl
Tape days: Sat, Sept through June.

The original late-night comedy sketch show, with popular guest stars and top-of-the-charts musical guests. They run a lottery every Aug to give away tickets for the upcoming year of shows. Check the website for details. You may have better luck getting standby tickets, which are distributed every Sat at 7 a.m. at the NBC Studio lobby on a first-come, first-served basis. Standby tickets do not guarantee you'll get into the show; it will depend on how many people with reserved tickets fail to show up later for the dress rehearsal at 8 p.m. or the live show at 11:30.

The View

320 W. 66th St. (off West End Avenue)
(212) 456-0900
www.abc.go.com/daytime/theview
Tape days: Mon through Fri at 11 a.m. (plan to arrive by 9:30 a.m.).

Barbara and the gals talk about everything from terrorism to bra sizes. Fill out a ticket request form at the website. Tickets will be sent for dates about four to six months from the date they are received. They often have room for you the day of the show, however: Stop by the studio between 8 and 9 a.m. to stand in line. These tickets are distributed on a first-come, first-served basis. You must be at least eighteen years old to attend.

Who Wants to Be a Millionaire

30 W. 67th St. (at Columbus Avenue)
(212) 456-1494
www.millionairetv.com
Tape days: Tues and Wed at noon and 3 p.m.

Meredith Vieira is the host with the most (money, that is). Fill out their ticket request form at their website. And when you attend a taping, you can also audition to get into the "hot seat" yourself. You must be at least eighteen to attend.

COMEDY:
CHEAP JOKES

"I've been asked to say a couple of words about my husband, Fang. How about 'short' and 'cheap'?"

—PHYLLIS DILLER

I could say that the price of comedy shows in New York is no laughing matter, but that would be too obvious, so I'll just say the cost of laughing in the city is no joke (sorry, couldn't resist). Suffice it to say, yucks cost bucks (okay, I'm done). But you can have the last laugh by stopping in at one of these free comedy nights. Many feature newcomers taking their first shots at stand-up or are opportunities for more established comics or improv troupes to try out new material—or more likely a combination of the two. The schedules do change from time to time, so be sure to call to confirm information before showing up.

Magnet Theater
254 W. 29th St. (between Seventh and Eighth Avenues)
(212) 244-8824
www.magnettheater.com
Sat at midnight

Every Sat the Magnet Theater attracts all kinds of funny folks to their Magnet Mixer, when veteran improvisers join forces with students and any Joe off the street who wants to take part in these one-of-a-kind improv free-for-alls. They also offer free improv classes once a month and other free shows regularly. Check their website for the schedule and details.

The People's Improv Theater
154 W. 29th St. (between Sixth and Seventh Avenues)
(212) 563-7488
www.thepit-nyc.com
Wed at 7, 8, 9:30., and 11 p.m.; Mon, Tues, and Thurs at 11 p.m.

The People's Improv Theater (aka the PIT) is one of the top spots for improv and sketch comedy in New York, and they top the list of Cheap Bastard–friendly (aka free) shows offered every week. The jackpot of jollies happens every Wednesday night with four free shows starting at 7 p.m., when owner and improv master Ali Farahnakian takes to the stage for a full hour of wackiness, along with some guest performers. At 8 and 9:30 p.m. their top improv teams take each other on for an all-out comedy competition, and anyone is welcome to join in on the fun as they top off the evening with an improv jam at 11 p.m. There is always a full house for these Wednesday-night shows, so plan on turning up early to grab a seat. The free laughs keep on coming every Mon, Tues, and Thurs night at 11, when they offer other improv jams and stand-up open mic.

Upright Citizens Brigade

307 W. 26th St. (at Eighth Avenue)
(212) 366-9176
www.ucbtheater.com
Sun at 9:30 p.m., Wed at 11 p.m., and Fri at midnight.

UCB is one of New York's leading comedy improv troupes and the only one that gives it away for free. They host three freewheeling performances every week. Wednesday night is School Night, a late-night set of stand-up comedy hosted by Justin Purnell with guest appearances by some of the city's best comedians (www.ucbschoolnight.com). On Sunday nights, don't miss Asssscat 3000 for improvisation at its purest, with guest performers from such shows as *Saturday Night Live, Late Night with Jimmy Fallon, The Daily Show with Jon Stewart,* and others. Every Friday night at midnight they host their outrageous version of an open mic night that includes sketch and stand-up comedy. They don't take reservations for these shows, so get there a couple of hours early to grab tickets. They always have a full house for these shows, and the evening is well worth the effort.

DANCE:
FREE EXPRESSION

"Dancing: The highest intelligence in the freest body."

—ISADORA DUNCAN

Maybe it's because New Yorkers are always on their feet—racing along the sidewalks, crammed together in the subways, or trudging up a five-story walk-up—that it seems as if everyone in New York dances in one way or another. Or perhaps it's the palpable energy of the city that draws dancers from every corner of the planet. Whatever the reason, New York is like a dance itself, and its clubs, public spaces, and studios abound with opportunities for you to strut your stuff without unstuffing your bank account. If you prefer to watch, New York is home to some of the world's leading dance companies and conservatories, so the talent on display at no cost is unrivaled anyplace in the world.

WATCHING **IT**

Celebrate Brooklyn
Prospect Park Bandshell (Prospect Park West and 9th Street)
Park Slope, Brooklyn
(718) 855-7882
www.brooklynx.org/celebrate
June through Aug.

Brooklyn's popular free series regularly commissions new works by local and internationally recognized dance companies and presents dance concerts throughout the summer schedule. Their calendar also includes free films, readings, and music of every genre.

Central Park SummerStage
Mid-park (enter at East or West 72nd Street)
(212) 360-2777
www.summerstage.org
June through Aug.

Free performances are staged throughout the summer, from big names to the cutting edge in music, opera, dance, spoken word, and more. This is a very popular venue; claiming a spot on line early is recommended. Dance performances are presented most Friday evenings.

Dancing in the Streets
545 Eighth Ave., Suite 1830 (between 37th and 38th Streets)
(212) 625-3505
www.dancinginthestreets.org

This organization commissions and presents all forms of dance and movement performances throughout the city. All productions are site-specific
performances in various parks, open spaces, and indoor spaces. Most performances are free.

The Joyce Theater
175 Eighth Ave. (at 19th Street)
(646) 792-8355
www.joyce.org

The Catch: Work as a volunteer usher to see the performances for free.

The leading theater for dance companies, the Joyce plays host to practically
every major company from around the country and around the world. Call to
set up dates to be a volunteer usher and see the show for free. They begin
taking reservations two weeks in advance.

The Kitchen
512 W. 19th St. (between Tenth and Eleventh Avenues)
(212) 255-5793
usher@thekitchen.org
www.thekitchen.org

The Catch: Work as a volunteer usher to see the performances for free.

Although its location has moved farther uptown in recent years, the Kitchen
remains firmly downtown in ethos. For the last thirty-plus years, it has been
home to such nontraditional, uncategorizable performers as Philip Glass,
Laurie Anderson, Bill T. Jones and Arnie Zane, Eric Bogosian, David Byrne
with the Talking Heads, Meredith Monk, Brian Eno, John Lurie, Robert Mapplethorpe, Cindy Sherman, and many others. Performances strive to combine
music, dance, video, spoken word, and any other forms an artist feels like
playing with at the moment. E-mail about two weeks in advance to reserve
a spot as a volunteer usher.

Lincoln Center Out of Doors Festival

65th Street and Broadway
(212) 875-5000
www.lincolncenter.org
Throughout Aug.

This eclectic performance, music, and dance festival every August features leading modern, ethnic, and cutting-edge dance companies, as well as music from around the world in almost every genre and a great selection of children's performances.

Movement Research

Dance Theater Workshop
219 W. 19th St. (between Seventh and Eighth Avenues)
Judson Memorial Church
55 Washington Sq. South
(212) 598-0551
www.movementresearch.org
Mon at 8 p.m. at Judson Memorial Church, Sept through June.
Every other Tues at 7 p.m. at Dance Theater Workshop, Sept through June.

Movement Research presents free modern, improvisational, and adventurous dance performances every Monday night at Judson Memorial Church and works in progress every other Tues at their Open Studio performance at Dance Theater Workshop. Both series attract many of the most highly regarded and up-and-coming downtown dance artists.

New York University

Tisch School of the Arts—Graduate Dance School
111 Second Ave., third floor (between 6th and 7th Streets)
(212) 998-1980
www.dance.tisch.nyu.edu
Oct through May.

The graduate dance department offers free contemporary dance performances throughout the school year, often with notable guest choreographers.

DOING **IT**

Dance Tango
www.dancetango.com

Dance Tango presents a calendar of Tango events around the city. Check the website for free tango lessons and dancing to live and recorded music.

Midsummer Night Swing at Lincoln Center
65th Street and Broadway
(212) 875-5000
http://new.lincolncenter.org
Late June through July.

Yes, you too can be a dancer at Lincoln Center. Beginning in late June and running through July, the plaza at this famed performance center turns into the best dance floor in New York City. Every night they present top names from every sort of dance music, including American regional, Latin, Caribbean, African, ballroom, rhythm and blues, and, of course, swing! You can pay your way onto the official dance floor ($17), which is usually pretty overcrowded, but the savvier folks spread out on the vast plaza to Savoy shuffle to their heart's content. Dance lessons begin at 6:30 p.m., dancing at 7:30 p.m.

MoonDance
Hudson River Park
Pier 54, Hudson River at 14th Street
(212) 627-2020
www.hudsonriverpark.org
Sunday evenings, July and Aug.

Swing, tango, and cha-cha away every Sunday night under the stars with live music from New York's hottest bands. Free lessons begin at 6:30 p.m., and the dancing keeps going until 10.

Sandra Cameron Dance Center

199 Lafayette St. (between Broome and Kenmore Streets)
(212) 431-1825
www.sandracameron.com
The last Fri of every month.

This popular dance studio offers classes to the masses in swing, salsa, ballroom, and tango. Stop in for one of the monthly guest nights and get a free introductory swing and salsa class, some hot dance performances, and open foxtrot, swing, salsa, and ballroom dance sessions. There's even free wine and cheese!

SO **YOU** WANT **TO** BE **A** DANCER: **WORK-STUDY** DANCE **CLASSES**

New York is the place to be if you hope to join those tapping feet on 42nd Street—but it's not a cheap dream to pursue. Group dance classes can cost as much as $15 per hour. But fear not, there are ways for you to make it to the Great White Way without spending such a great green amount. Many of the leading dance studios around New York offer scholarships, internships, or work-study options in exchange for free classes, or to greatly reduce the cost of classes.

Broadway Dance Center

322 W. 45th St. (between Eighth and Ninth Avenues)
(212) 582-9304
www.broadwaydancecenter.com

The Catch: Reduced rate of $5 per class in exchange for work-study hours.

The Broadway Dance Center hosts classes in jazz, ballet, tap, modern, tumbling, and aerobics with leading teachers from Broadway and around the world. They run an extensive work-study program that's open to dancers at any level. Students work in various positions around the studio (front desk, cafe, office, boutique, or cleaning crew). For each work-study hour worked, you earn one class at a discounted rate of $7 instead of the regular rate of

$20 per class. No audition is required, but you must apply, interview, and make a four- to six-month commitment to a work-study schedule.

Movement Research
Dance Theater Workshop
219 W. 19th St. (between Seventh and Eighth Avenues)
(212) 598-0551
www.movementresearch.org

Movement Research classes are more likely to win you a chance to work on an Off-Off Broadway performance art piece than a part in a Broadway musical. If that's your type of dance, this is absolutely the place for you. They offer a full schedule of classes and workshops in contact improvisation and modern and postmodern techniques, as well as other classes that defy simple definition but combine all kinds of movement influences from around the world. Work-study students are expected to work about ten hours a week in exchange for unlimited free classes. Hours and assignments are flexible and could include registering students for morning or weekend classes, working on the tech crew during performances, running light errands, or distributing flyers. Call to schedule an interview; no audition required.

Peridance
126 E. 13th St. (between Third and Fourth Avenues)
(212) 505-0886
www.peridance.com

Peridance offers classes in ballet, jazz, tap, yoga, hip-hop, and an emphasis on all forms of modern. They have various work-study positions where you can get a free class for every hour and half you work. Stop by to fill out an application; no audition required.

Steps on Broadway
2121 Broadway (between 74th and 75th Streets)
(212) 874-2410
www.stepsnyc.com

The Catch: $15 registration fee required.

Steps on Broadway offers classes in all styles and levels. They accept all levels of dancers into the work-study program, but you must be committed to training and be willing to work eight to ten hours a week. Work-study students work at the registration desk or in their administrative offices, clean studios, or help prepare for performances. Depending on your specific job, you will be able to take all the classes you want either for free or $3 each (regularly $15 per class). Call to set up an interview.

The West Side Dance Project

260 W. 36th St., third floor (between Eighth and Ninth Avenues)
(212) 563-6781
www.westsidedanceproject.com

This small dance studio offers classes in jazz, ballet, and tap. They have auditions a couple of times a year for their scholarship program. You don't necessarily need to be a "dancer" to win one of these positions. They look for people who are pursuing careers in the musical theater and are hoping to improve their dance skills. Scholarship winners are required to work one three-hour shift at the front desk a week and must take at least five hours of dance classes a week.

MAGIC:
CHEAP TRICKS

"Money disappears like magic."

—ARABIC PROVERB

You might think the closest you can get to seeing a free magic show in New York is watching how quickly people's money disappears when they play three-card monte, but you'd be wrong. There is a thriving world of magic in this city, and even with nothing up your sleeve, you can be entertained by many of the finest magicians in the world without spending a single quarter (not even that one you have hidden behind your ear). Just stop into any of the handful of magician supply shops around the city to be dazzled at the magic counter, or visit during one of their weekly free performances.

Fantasma Magic
421 Seventh Ave., second floor (between 33rd and 34th Streets)
(212) 244-3633
www.fantasmamagic.com
Sat at 2 and 4 p.m.

Just wandering through this wonderfully magical store, playing with all the unusual items, and strolling through the free Houdini Museum could be enough entertainment for a day. But every Sat it gets even more entertaining when they offer free magic shows at 2 and 4 p.m. They also have plans to offer free magic lessons, juggling lessons, and balloon sculpting classes in the future. Call for details.

Society of American Magicians
Goldman Auditorium
1425 Madison Ave. (at 98th Street)
www.magicsam.com
First Fri of the month at 8 p.m.

This is the oldest and most prestigious magicians society in the world. Their monthly meeting brings together an array of talent from those trying to break into the business to masters of the art. And wherever there are magicians, there is magic. Once they take care of their secret magician business, they often open up the meetings to the public with free magic shows. Check their website for a schedule and information.

Old Dogs and New Tricks

How do you make a burrito disappear? Stop by the downstairs dining room at **Maui Tacos** (330 Fifth Ave., between 32nd and 33rd Streets; 212-868-9722) any Saturday afternoon from 2 to 5 p.m. Since 1938, a group of professional and amateur magicians has been gathering (only recently at Maui Tacos) to perfect new tricks, exchange ideas, sample some exotic salsas, take full advantage of the free refills on the sodas, and try to slip something past their hardest audience—each other. There is no formal show here, just a chance to see some amazing artists working on their craft in an informal, one-on-one setting. And the tacos are pretty tasty, too. Over the years, the group has migrated to various eateries. If you don't find them at Maui Tacos, call the folks at **Tannen's** (212-929-4500). They should know where to find them.

Tannen's Magic Studio

45 W. 34th St., Room 608 (between Fifth and Sixth Avenues)
(212) 929-4500
www.tannenmagic.com

Well, they won't tell you how they're done, but everyone behind the counter at Tannen's is a bona fide magician and can show you any trick in the house. And there are thousands of tricks in the place. Of course, the only way to find out the secrets behind the magic is to buy the tricks, but they will demonstrate any one of them for free. There are no shows at this store, but just spend some time around the counter, and you're sure to catch a trick or two.

SECTION 2:

Living in New York

FOOD:
ON THE HOUSE

"The remarkable thing about my mother is that for thirty years she served us nothing but left-overs. The original meal has never been found."

—CALVIN TRILLIN

Fast food, gourmet food, exotic food, health food, breads, cakes, wings, hors d'oeuvres, hot dogs, canapés, sushi, Italian, Mexican, Chinese, food, food, food. Anything you desire, it's in New York, and it's better than anywhere else in the world. But for free? Yes indeed. Wander through the many gourmet markets and selected specialty stores around the city, and you'll find a delightful (and filling) selection of samples to chow down on. Make your way to any number of bars and restaurants that set out some grand and some not-so-grand spreads during happy hours. And if you must spend money, you can shop at some fancy joints for pennies, if you know when to go.

HAPPY **HOURS**

Many bars, pubs, and restaurants around the city offer some kind of free food during happy hours. What you'll find at these places runs the gamut from basic bar food to sumptuous buffets. For the most part you are expected to buy a drink to partake of the eats, but there are usually all kinds of discounts on the drinks as well during happy hours. And hey, if you don't drink or don't feel like footing the bill for a martini, no one says you can't just order a club soda. Be sure to leave the bartender a nice tip though. Yes, in New York, even Cheap Bastards should remember to tip. While I have included here only those places that have a long history of offering free eats, policies do change from time to time.

EAST SIDE

Ashton's
208 E. 50th St. (at Third Avenue)
(212) 688-8625

Offering more than just the chip-and-dip fare, this friendly Irish pub always provides something substantial to chow down on during happy hour. Mon through Fri, 5 to 7 p.m.

McCormack's Public House

365 Third Ave. (between 26th and 27th Streets)
(212) 683-0911

McCormack's Public Hours offers free food from 5 to 7 p.m. every Fri. The Irish pub usually serves appetizers like skins or wings (though one night they put out some kind of black sausage thing—mmm-mm). Also, they broadcast international rugby games.

Nevada Smiths

74 Third Ave. (between 11th and 12th Streets)
(212) 982-2591
www.nevadasmiths.net

This Irish pub and soccer haven offers a buffet of wings and sandwiches every Friday afternoon starting at 5:30 p.m.

One Fish Two Fish

1399 Madison Ave. (at 97th Street)
(212) 369-5677
www.onefishtwofish.com

Stop by this jam-packed uptown seafood restaurant to pick at the appetizers they set out at the bar every Mon, Tues, Thurs, and Fri from 4 to 6 p.m. Though if you really want to dig in, make sure to show up on a Wednesday for ladies' night (half-price drinks for ladies!) or on Thursday evening, when they pull out all the stops with a large buffet of appetizers and other delicious goodies.

Pig 'n Whistle on 3rd

922 Third Ave. (between 55th and 56th Streets)
(212) 688-4646
www.pignwhistleon3.com

This low-key Irish pub sets out a small buffet of a couple of tasty selections like chicken fingers, mini pizzas, poppers, or wings. Mon through Fri, 5:30 to 7:30 p.m.

Playwright Irish Pub

27 W. 35th St. (between Fifth and Sixth Avenues)
(212) 268-8868
www.playwrightirishpubnyc.com

This lively Irish pub and horse racing mecca (you can even place your bets from the bar!) sets out a buffet of tasty finger food Mon through Fri from 5 to 8 p.m.

Rodeo Bar

375 Third Ave. (at 27th Street)
(212) 683-6500
www.rodeobar.com

A fun and casual Tex-Mex bar/restaurant with barrels full of freshly roasted peanuts all around. At happy hours (Mon through Sun, 4 to 9 p.m.) they supply a small buffet of munchies (wings, nachos, potato skins, and the like). Every night they have live rockabilly or country music and never charge a cover. Yee-ha!

Rolf's

281 Third Ave. (at 22nd Street)
(212) 477-4750

This German restaurant sets out free finger sandwiches at the bar at 6 p.m. until they're gone seven nights a week. Be sure to check out all of the over-the-top Christmas decorations.

The Watering Hole

106 E. 19th St. (between Park Avenue and Irving Place)
(212) 674-5783
http://wateringholenyc.com

This small bar packs a big gastronomic wallop by setting out an extensive free buffet every Mon through Fri for the after-work crowd. But you better be quick: The grub is only out from 3 to 7 p.m., and it goes fast.

WEST SIDE

Channel 4
58 W. 48th St. (between Fifth and Sixth Avenues)
(212) 819-0095

This stylish Irish bar and restaurant sets out a nice spread of appetizers—wings, spring rolls, quesadillas—Mon through Fri from 5 to 7 p.m.

Charley O's Bar & Grill & Bar
713 8th Ave. (at 45th Street)
(212) 977-0025

This Broadway-district hangout sets out a small buffet of appetizers Mon through Fri from 3 to 6 p.m.

D. J. Reynolds
351 W. 57th St. (between Eighth and Ninth Avenues)
(212) 245-2912

Try your luck at this quiet and friendly Irish pub. Every Thurs and Fri from 5 to 8 p.m., they set out something different. It might be a hearty snack of wings or chicken nuggets, or you could end up with a substantial meal of steak or chicken Marsala over pasta.

Kennedy's
327 W. 57th St. (between Eighth and Ninth Avenues)
(212) 759-4242

This Irish pub puts out a bit of bar food—wings or meatballs—Mon through Fri, 4:30 to 7 p.m. or until it's gone. Good for a nibble, but it probably won't fill you up.

Langan's
150 W. 47th St. (between Sixth and Seventh Avenues)
(212) 869-5482

This makes a great pretheater stop. Mon through Fri, 5 to 8 p.m., you'll find chips and salsa at the bar and a small buffet of bar food, which could include wings, mozzarella sticks, meatballs, or other tasty munchies.

O'Flaherty's Ale House

334 W. 46th St. (between Eighth and Ninth Avenues)
(212) 581-9366

This theater-district Irish pub satisfies its starving-actor clientele with free shepherd's pie or pasta Mon and Tues nights at about 10:30 p.m. Don't worry—you don't have to recite any Shakespeare to partake. They also have free live music seven nights a week (acoustic, rock, and Irish).

O'Reilly's Townhouse

21 W. 35th St. (between Fifth and Sixth Avenues)
(212) 502-5246

This lively Irish pub with a busy after-work crowd sets out a free buffet of shepherd's pie, pasta, or wings Mon through Fri from 5 p.m. "till it's gone."

Peter's Restaurant

182 Columbus Ave. (between 68th and 69th Streets)
(212) 877-4747

This comfortable upscale restaurant treats its upper West Side customers to a sampling of its Asian-influenced American menu at their bar Mon through Fri from 5 to 8 p.m.

Pig 'n Whistle

165 W. 47th St. (between Sixth and Seventh Avenues)
(212) 302-0112

Just down the block from Langan's, this makes a great pre-theater stop as well. Mon through Fri, 5 to 8 p.m., chow down on chips and salsa at the bar and a buffet of appetizers.

Rudy's Bar and Grill

627 Ninth Ave. (at West 44th Street)
(212) 974-9169
www.rudysbarnyc.com

Look for the Big Pig outside to find the place and "pig out" on the free hot dogs. This is a real neighborhood joint. The franks are always available (1 to 10 p.m.), but don't try asking for one without ordering a drink first.

The Sun Room

123 W. 57th St. (between Sixth and Seventh Avenues)
(212) 664-1589

The saying goes, God works in mysterious ways. Well, one mystery I have no desire to see solved is the Sun Room. Sponsored by the Calvary Baptist Church, this is by all outward appearances your everyday Starbucks-style coffeehouse, complete with cozy couches, reading material, and, of course, coffee and snacks. Now, while you may not be able to get your Caramel Macchiato here, you will save enough money to fill your own coffers because everything in the shop is completely free. Okay, you are thinking, what's the catch? Do I have to listen to a sermon while I sip my coffee? No, you do not. Born out of the aftermath of September 11, 2001, the cafe strives simply to be a "refuge from the noise." There is no proselytizing going on here, and everyone is welcome to stop in and get a drink, have a nibble, and relax. Of course, if you do have some crisis of faith that a strong cup of joe won't solve, they will be happy to talk it over with you. Otherwise, no catches.

Sing for Your Supper

Here are a couple of places to stop by and lend a hand or join in on some chanting and get yourself a full meal.

Food Not Bombs NYC, Tompkins Square Park; (212) 254-3697; www.abcnorio.org. The artists collective/punk rock club ABC No Rio serves up free vegetarian meals in Tompkins Square Park every Sun at about 3:30 p.m. This meal is generally meant for the homeless, but they always need volunteers to help in food preparation—and, of course, they'll feed you, too. Stop by ABC No Rio at about 1 p.m. to help cook (156 Rivington St., between Clinton and Suffolk Streets).

Sri Sri Radha Govinda Manir, 305 Schermerhorn St. (between Nevins and Bond Streets), Brooklyn; (718) 855-6714; www.radhagovinda.net. This is the main New York Hare Krishna temple, and it's very large and well attended. They offer free vegetarian feasts on Sunday nights at about 8. All are welcome, and there's no need to shave your head.

Just free coffee, tea, cookies, muffins, and more every Tues through Thurs from 11 a.m. to 4 p.m.

DOWNTOWN, EAST AND WEST VILLAGE

Crocodile Lounge
325 E. 14th St. (between First and Second Avenues)
(212) 477-7747

No two words in the English language evoke quite as much joy as the words free pizza, and while it may not be the best pie New York has to offer, the Crocodile Lounge's free pizza certainly does go down well with a mug of cold beer. They will ask you to lay down a few bucks for a drink to get your free, fresh-baked 8-inch pie.

Cucina di Pesce
87 E. 4th St. (between Second and Third Avenues)
(212) 260-6800
www.cucinadipesce.com

This Italian restaurant sets out free mussels at the bar every day from 4 to 8 p.m., as well as all appetizers for half price.

11th Street Bar
510 E. 11th St. (between Avenues A and B)
(212) 982-3929

This East Village hangout serves free wings on Fri, 4 to 8 p.m.

The Thirsty Scholar
155 Second Ave. (between 9th and 10th Streets)
(212) 777-6514

The Thirsty Scholar sets out a free load of wings, rings, or whatever the kitchen happens to have available from about 6 p.m. until whenever it's gone. Mon through Fri, 6 to 8-ish p.m.

Ty's Bar
114 Christopher St. (between Bleecker and Hudson Streets)
(212) 741-9641

On the second Tues of every month, get yourself a hearty meal and shake the hand of some of New York's bravest (and gayest) as this gay saloon plays host to the monthly gathering of the gay firemen and EMS organization, Fire-FLAG/EMS. All are welcome. The buffet opens at about 8:30 p.m.

BROOKLYN

The Brazen Head
228 Atlantic Ave. (between Court Street and Boerum Place)
Boerum Hill, Brooklyn
(718) 488-0430
www.brazenheadbrooklyn.com

This local Brooklyn bar is heaven for fans of microbrews and darts, and, of course, for Cheap Bastards! Monday nights they serve free wings and things when they welcome dart players of all skill levels from far and wide for an open dart night. Sunday afternoons they roll out the free bagel buffet for your brunching pleasure.

Hank's Saloon
46 Third Ave. (at Atlantic Avenue)
Brooklyn
(718) 625-8003

Free live country/rock/rockabilly music Wednesday through Sunday nights at this hardcore Brooklyn dive. On Sunday and Monday nights, don't miss the free barbecue. You never know what they'll be serving up; some weeks it could be a mighty fine spread, others it might be hockey-puck hamburgers and shriveled hot dogs. No cover, no minimum.

FREE **SAMPLES:** A **SAMPLING**

New York City is overrun with gourmet markets, farmers' markets, and specialty stores that charge an arm and a leg for anything from a leg of lamb to overpriced olives from around the world. These markets, however, are also gold mines of free samples. You can get a taste of almost anything, from gourmet breads, cakes, and cookies to olive oils, cheeses, and exotic fruits.

Agata & Valentina

1505 First Ave. (at 79th Street)
(212) 452-0690
www.agatavalentina.com

One of New York's premier gourmet markets, Agata & Valentina often sets out a wide variety of samples of everything from smoothies and cheeses to bread and sometimes even pizzas. But when, oh, when will they set out some tasty tidbits from their incredible-looking desserts and pastries? You will find the best selection of samples on the weekends.

Aji Ichiban

167 Hester St. (between Mott and Elizabeth Streets)
(212) 925-1133
1721 Broadway (between 54th and 55th Streets)
(212) 571-3755

This Chinese candy store offers some truly unusual, intensely flavorful delicacies. You'll find signs all over the store encouraging you to try such unusual fare as the dried curry squid, mini roasted crabs, and preserved chili olives. There are tamer selections of chocolates, biscuits, and gummy candies as well.

Balthazar Bakery

80 Spring St. (between Crosby Street and Broadway)
(212) 965-1785
www.balthazarbakery.com

The Catch: It's not easy to get away without buying something.

Considered one of the best bakeries in the city (and one of the most expensive), Balthazar always offers something to snack on at the register. It's a very small place, so it isn't easy to get away without buying something so you don't look like a Cheap Bastard. If you're willing to brave the stares from behind the counter and from those on line, dive right in—their treats are delicious. But if you are willing to lay down a few bucks, stop by after 8 p.m., when they slice the prices on all baked goods by 40 percent and offer deals on their prepackaged sandwiches and salads.

Black Hound New York

170 Second Ave. (between 10th and 11th Streets)
(212) 979-9505
www.blackhoundny.com

The delectable treats displayed artistically in the window will beckon you into this fine bakery, but the rich rewards are the generous individually wrapped samples of their goods (or should I say goodies!) placed throughout the store. Stop in often!

Chelsea Market

75 Ninth Ave. (between 15th and 16th Streets)
(212) 243-6005
www.chelseamarket.com

The former home of the Nabisco Company and the birthplace of the Oreo cookie, Chelsea Market is a sumptuous marketplace of gourmet shops. Sample breads, brownies, gourmet butters, cookies, and fruit. Selections are particularly abundant on weekends, when you can also sample some fine wines (Fri and Sat). They even supply free Wi-Fi.

Eli's

1411 Third Ave. (at 80th Street); (212) 717-8100
431 E. 91st St. (between York and First Avenues); (212) 987-0885
www.elizabar.com

Stop by these dreamy gourmet markets often to gorge yourself on the generous samples in their bakeries and to ogle at the tantalizing displays. But be warned: While the fresh food is awfully inviting, the prices are ridiculously steep.

Gourmet Garage
453 Broome St. (at Mercer Street)
(212) 941-5850
www.gourmetgarage.com

At these gourmet markets, you can sample from the olive bar, cheeses, and other gourmet treats from time to time. Check their website for information on the other five NYC locations.

Greenmarket Farmers Market
Union Square, 17th Street and Broadway
(212) 788-7476
www.cenyc.org

New York has many official farmers' markets (forty throughout the five boroughs), which attract a wide variety of upstate and Long Island farmers to the city to sell their wares. The hands-down best market for samples of everything from heirloom tomatoes and organic apples, beans, and peppers to fresh bread, cakes, and jams is the Union Square market, held every Mon, Wed, Fri, and Sat. Call or check the website for information on other markets around the city.

Jefferson Market
450 Sixth Ave. (between 10th and 11th Streets)
(212) 533-3377

Browse the goodies at this West Village market; look for bakery, cheese, and deli samples.

Murray's Cheese Shop
257 Bleecker St. (at Cornelia, between Sixth and Seventh Avenues);
(212) 243-3289
Grand Central Station, 73 Grand Central Terminal
(43rd Street at Lexington Avenue);
(212) 922-1540
www.murrayscheese.com

Murray's is considered to be one of the finest cheese shops in the world, and you are welcome to sample any cheese in the world at either one of their shops. They often have samples out for you to dip into, but feel free to ask for a bit of anything they have. Their helpful and extraordinarily knowledgeable staff will happily slice off for you a bit of whatever you request. Stop by to meet cheese-makers from all over the world and sample their goods. Check their website for an up-to-date schedule of tastings.

Pommes Frites

123 Second Ave. (between 7th and 8th Streets)
(212) 674-1234
www.pommesfrites.ws

Specializing in "authentic Belgian fries," they offer free samples that consist of about six large fries and your choice of two gourmet dipping sauces. The samples are great little snacks, with no pressure to buy.

Soutine Bakery

104 W. 70th St. (between Columbus Avenue and Broadway)
(212) 496-1450
www.soutine.com

A neighborhood favorite, Soutine is a tiny bakery that always sets out something sweet to nibble on. Primarily known for creating sophisticated wedding cakes, Soutine also turns out fluffy croissants, sugar-coated fruit, and dark chocolate meringue cake.

Todaro Bros.

555 Second Ave. (between 30th and 31st Streets)
(212) 532-0633
http://todarobros.com

Since 1961, Todaro Bros. have stuffed this cramped store with imported Italian olive oils, pastas, and fresh mozzarella. Stop in this gourmet market to sample cheeses, olive oils, bread, and more.

Tonnie's Minis

120 W. 3rd St. (near McDougal Street)
(212) 473-2002
http://tonniesminis.com

This little cupcake of a shop hands out cupcake shots—the smallest, cutest, tastiest samples of their full-size cupcakes.

Two Little Red Hens
1652 Second Ave. (between 85th and 86th Streets)
(212) 452-0476
www.twolittleredhens.com

Like a little bit of country in the city, this adorable bakery serves up a delicious selection of cakes, cookies, and pastries. The store always has a generous selection of treats out for your sampling pleasure.

Union Market
754–756 Union St. (at Sixth Avenue)
Park Slope, Brooklyn
(718) 230-5152
288 Court St. (between Degraw and Douglass Streets)
(718) 709-5100
www.unionmarket.com

This gourmet market in Brooklyn sets out some tasty samples in their deli, and you can always grab an olive or marinated mushroom or two at their olive bar. They also set out samples of olive oil, cookies, and cheeses as well.

Vosges Haute-Chocolat
132 Spring St. (between Wooster and Greene Streets)
(212) 625-2929
1100 Madison Ave. (at 83rd Street)
(212) 717-2929
www.vosgeschocolate.com

You will always find some delicious and exotic chocolates set out on the counter of this wonderfully original chocolate store. The combinations of sweet and spice that they put together somehow manage to melt in your mouth and explode with flavor at the same time.

Whole Foods Market
250 Seventh Ave. (at 24th Street)
(212) 924-5969
www.wholefoodsmarket.com

These health food mega-markets are often, though not always, great destinations to fill up on samples of everything from delicious organic fruits and vegetables to fresh baked goods and exotic teas and coffees. Your best bet is to stop by on the weekend or during lunch hour, but you will almost always find something to nibble on somewhere in the store. Check out their website for information on their other NYC-area locations.

Williams-Sonoma
10 Columbus Circle (between 58th and 60th Streets)
(212) 832-9750
www.williams-sonoma.com

The New York flagship location for this purveyor of all things cooking is equipped with a huge kitchen itself. The staff is almost always dishing up something tasty to try. They also hold cooking demonstrations every day at 2 p.m. on everything from carving skills to cupcake decoration.

EAT **LATE,** EAT **CHEAP!**

Hey, eating late may not be very good for the size of your waist, but it can do wonders for the size of your wallet. If you must spend money—and, of course, I generally do frown on that—then drop by one of these places to eat for half price (after the specified times). These shops, restaurants, gourmet markets, and health food stores all have a policy of cutting their prices at the end of the day to get rid of that day's fresh sandwiches, salads, and other assorted taste delights.

Amish Market
731 Ninth Ave. (between 49th and 50th Streets)
(212) 245-2360
www.amishfinefood.com

This market often slices prices on their precut sandwiches at about 6 p.m. on most evenings. The store closes at 10 p.m. Remember to ask at the register whether or not you have to pay full price. They also have great olive bars for sampling and occasionally cheeses and desserts for you to taste. Additional locations are at 53 Park Place between West Broadway and Church

Street (212-608-3863) and 240 E. 45th St. between Second and Third Avenues (212-370-1761).

Café Amrita
301 W. 111th St. (between Eighth and Manhattan Avenues)
(212) 222-0683

Stop by this relaxed Harlem coffeehouse after 4:30 every day for half-price muffins, scones, and other delicious baked goods.

Café Angelique
68 Bleecker St. (between Broadway and Lafayette Street)
(212) 475-3500
www.cafeangelique.com

This delightful little Parisian bakery and cafe slashes the prices in half every night on their sandwiches and pastries from 7 until they close at 8 p.m. A second location is at 49 Grove St. (212-414-1445).

The City Bakery
3 W. 18th St. (between Fifth and Sixth Avenues)
(212) 366-1414
www.citybakerycatering.com

This gourmet cafe and bakery turns out some of the city's most scrumptious pastries—the problem is a single one of them can easily run you $5. But if you stop by after 3:30 in the afternoon, you might just be lucky enough to snag a whole box of treats (four to six per box) for the ludicrously low price of $5. They don't offer these every day, just when they have a surplus of sweet delights. They often run two-for-one specials late in the day on their artistic tarts. Also, if you are a chocoholic and have never tried their hot chocolate, it is worth spending the money to try it once. The cup is rich enough to warrant its rich price tag—$4.50 with the homemade marshmallow.

Integral Yoga Natural Foods
229 W. 13th St. (between Seventh and Eighth Avenues)
(212) 243-2642
www.integralyoganaturalfoods.com

This natural food store has an extensive salad bar including all kinds of beans, vegetables, tofu creations, and other green and brown edibles. They sell off generous platters of leftovers from the day at greatly reduced prices ($2.25 for a small and $4.25 for a large) starting at 6 p.m. Mon to Fri and at 5:30 on weekends.

News Cafe
107 University Place (between 12th and 13th Streets)
(212) 353-1246

A newsstand/sandwich shop that slashes the prices on its tasty sandwiches, wraps, salads, and baked goods at 7 every night. Feel free to sit and read the newspapers and magazines from around the world while eating your cheap dinner (try not to get any dressing on the papers, though). The cafe closes at 10 p.m. every night.

Todaro Bros.
555 Second Ave. (between 30th and 31st Streets)
(212) 532-0633
http://todarobros.com

At this gourmet market they sell off their leftover fresh sandwiches for half price from 8 to 10 p.m. every night.

Zabar's
2245 Broadway (between 80th and 81st Streets)
(212) 496-1234 or (800) 697-6301
www.zabars.com

At this world-famous marketplace for gourmet cheeses, deli, coffee, baked goods, and more, they often cut the prices on prepared sandwiches, depending on how much is still left at the end of the day. They make the decision at about 6 p.m. They close at 7:30 p.m. Mon through Fri and 8 p.m. on Sat.

WINE TASTINGS:
CHEAP DRUNK

"I like best the wine drunk at the cost of others."

—BERGEN EVANS

Not only do the wine shops of New York offer you a chance to try some of the finest wines and spirits from around the world, but you can also end up learning a heck of a lot about the fruits of the vine. You'll find two types of wine-tasting situations at stores around the city. One is the local shop that uncorks a bottle or two for customers to try (and hopes you'll buy). The other, more desirable situation is when a vintner or wine distributor brings out an entire line of wines for the public to sample. You get to try more wines, the staff are usually very knowledgeable and eager to teach you about the wines without pushing you to buy anything, and you can usually depend on their bringing something tasty along "to cleanse the palate" between wines. All this can be true about the local shop, but you're just as likely to find a guy with a bottle saying, "Here, try some of this stuff, I hear it's good." Most shops offer a discount on whatever is being tasted that day, so if you're inspired to lay down some cash, this will lighten the blow.

EAST SIDE

Ambassador Wines & Spirits
1020 Second Ave. (at 54th Street)
(212) 421-5078
http://ambassadorwines.com

This local shop holds tastings Thurs through Sat, 4 to 8 p.m. They're strong on French, Italian, and German wines.

Beekman Liquors
500 Lexington Ave. (between 47th and 48th Streets)
(212) 759-5857
www.beekmanliquors.com

This sophisticated local shop hosts a full schedule of tastings throughout the week. In addition to the many varieties of wine offered, they often pour various spirits as well. Their events are most consistently held on Thursday and Friday evenings from 4 to 7 p.m., but check their website for many additional chances to imbibe on other evenings.

Best Cellars

1291 Lexington Ave. (between 86th and 87th Streets)
(212) 426-4200
www.bestcellars.com

This is a great no-nonsense yet know-it-all place to go to check out some great-tasting wines. The very knowledgeable staff serves up some delightful, inexpensive wines on weekday evenings from 5 to 8 p.m.; on Sat from 2 to 4 p.m. and they usually pair the wine with food prepared by local chefs.

Cork & Bottle

1158 First Ave. (between 63rd and 64th Streets)
(212) 838-5300

This small, low-key wine and spirits spot has a fair selection of both Old World and New World wines. The store may lack variety compared with bigger shops, but it compensates for its friendly customer service. The store offers occasional tasting, usually on Fri at 5 p.m.

Crush Wine Co.

153 E. 57th St. (between Lexington and Third Avenues)
(212) 980-9463
www.crushwineco.com

Crush may very well be the Holy Grail of wine shops in New York City for anyone interested in tastings. They give you what you want—loads of high-quality wines to taste—when you want it—anytime! Step into the comforts of the tasting room at this sleek and modern shop, and you will always find a diverse selection of six bottles opened and ready for you to gulp down. And it doesn't stop there; they also play host to a variety of larger tastings and events (some of which are not free), when they crack open even more bottles by specific vineyards or varietals and often include generous spreads of cheese and gourmet food. Check their website for a schedule of classes and events.

Ehrlich Wines & Spirits

222 Amsterdam Ave. (at 70th Street)
(212) 877-6090
www.ehrlichwines.com

One of the oldest wine shops in the city, Ehrlich Wines & Spirits carries a hefty selection of domestic and imported wine. Many of the staff are even

Brooklyn Brew

If your tastes are more Michelob then merlot, you will definitely want to hop over the bridge to the borough that once was the home to as many as forty-eight breweries. While many of these are gone, the thirst for beer is still strong in Brooklyn. **Bierkraft** is a Park Slope gourmet market with a vast selection of beers from every corner of the world (more than 650 brands), and they are not afraid to give it away. Every Tuesday night at 7, anyone can stop in for their semiformal beer tastings. No tuxedos required, but a real interest in the art and craft of beer making is. This is a sit-down affair in which a master brewer will lead you through a tasting of five or so handpicked beer and food pairings. You can also stop by anytime to try their house brew of the day. The staff master brewer is known for his batches of unfamiliar beers that can be anything from a Belgian triple to an English mild. Bierkraft is located at 191 Fifth Ave. (between Sacket and Union Streets); (718) 230-7600; www.bierkraft.com.

The **Brooklyn Brewery** in Williamsburg has brought the fine art of mass-produced beer to Brooklyn, and every Saturday it is on display for all to see. The brewery offers free tours and samples of their brews. For more information see page 216.

And Williamsburg's thriving art galleries, a decidedly more downscale scene than its richer Manhattan counterpart, hand out free bottles of beer at exhibit openings. For a selection of Williamsburg's galleries, see pages 243–245.

sommeliers. The best thing is nearly everyday from 5 to 8 p.m., except Monday, this small corner shop opens a bottle or two for sampling.

86th Street Wine & Liquor

306 E. 86th St. (at Second Avenue)
(212) 396-3535

Plenty of bargain wines and a knowledgeable staff make this unassuming corner wine store a neighborhood favorite. On Saturdays, the wine store opens up a couple of bottles for tastings from 5 to 8 p.m.

Mister Wright Liquors
1593 Third Ave. (between 89th and 90th Streets)
(212) 722-4564
www.misterwrightfinewines.com

This large store cracks open a few bottles for tasting on Thurs, Fri, and Sat from 4 to 7 p.m.; you might even catch a special tasting on Mon and Tues. It could be anything from cheap (or shall I say inexpensive?) to fine wines. Check their website for a full calendar of upcoming tastings.

Union Square Wine & Spirits
140 Fourth Ave. (at 13th Street)
(212) 675-8100
www.unionsquarewines.com

This posh shop is always pouring something wonderful and unusual for you to try. Every week (Thurs and Fri, 6 to 8 p.m.; Sat, 2 to 5 p.m.) they play host to a number of distributors, vintners, and sommeliers from around the city and the world who pour their selections for you to sample in the lavish upstairs salon. From time to time they also collaborate with local restaurants to provide food to match the wines.

Windsor Court Wine Shop
474 Third Ave. (between 32nd and 33rd Streets)
(212) 779-4422

Tucked away in the Kipps Bay neighborhood, Windsor Court carries a strong selection of Australian, French, and Italian wines, as well as some domestic. The store pours wines every Thurs, Fri, and Sat, 5 to 8 p.m., Sept through May.

WEST **SIDE**

Acker Merrall & Condit Co.
160 W. 72nd St. (between Columbus Avenue and Broadway)
(212) 787-1700 (store)
(212) 875-0222 (wine workshop)
www.ackerstore.com

America's oldest and finest wineshop (if they don't say so themselves) is a great place to head any Sat from 2 to 5 p.m. to sample some of their "finest" wines. This is a great chance to learn a few things from their knowledgeable staff or visiting vintners. They also run **The Wine Workshop**, which holds a full schedule of seminars and classes on the finer points of wine. They charge a pretty penny for these workshops, but they do use volunteers as pourers in the classes, which allows you to attend them for free. Call The Wine Workshop to add your name to the list, and they will call you when they have an opening (see page 150 for more information).

Best Cellars
2246 Broadway (between 80th and 81st Streets)
(212) 362-8730
www.bestcellars.com

Like its sister shop on the East Side, Best Cellars is an excellent spot to check out great tasting wines. The tastings, held weekday evenings (5 to 8 p.m.) and on Sat (2 to 4 p.m.), are often accompanied by food prepared by local chefs.

Candlelight Wines
2315 Broadway (between 83rd and 84th Streets)
(212) 877-7085

Candlelight Wines stocks a fair selection of domestic and imported wines, mostly under $25. From 1 to 5 p.m. every Saturday, from Sept through June, the cozy store up a couple of bottles and sets out some cheese and crackers for you to nosh while you taste.

Chelsea Wine Vault
75 Ninth Ave. (between 15th and 16th Streets)
(212) 462-4244
www.chelseawinevault.com

This great wine find is located in the Chelsea Market. They offer four full days of tastings, of everything from Beaujolais and bubbly to scotches and other spirits. Stop by Thursday and Friday evenings from 4 to 7 p.m. and Saturday and Sunday afternoons from 1 to 5 p.m. Don't miss their once-a-year Open House Anniversary celebration. This is a wonderful event that happens on a Sat in early Nov; you'll find more than fifty wines for sampling, free catered hors d'oeuvres, and free introductory wine classes.

Columbus Wines & Spirits
730 Columbus Ave. (between 95th and 96th Streets)
(212) 865-7070

This local shop offers tastes from a few inexpensive bottles on Sat from 4 to 7 p.m. They sometimes offer a selection of kosher wines to sample on Fri.

86th Street Corner Wine & Liquor Company
536 Columbus Ave. (at 86th Street)
(212) 496-1769

In a pretty small space, this store stocks a decent selection of wine. The best part is that there are free tastings on Thurs, Fri, and Sat, 4 to 8 p.m.

International Wines & Spirits
2903 Broadway (at 113th Street)
(212) 280-1850

This store packs its shelves with a well-rounded selection of wines. Come for tastings on Fri and Sat, 4 to 7 p.m.

Morrell & Company Wine & Spirits Merchants

1 Rockefeller Plaza (at 49th Street, between Fifth and Sixth Avenues)
(212) 688-9370
www.morrellwine.com

This fancy (and expensive) wine store brings in distributors to hawk their line of wines every Sat, 2 to 5 p.m.

Ninth Avenue Vintner

669 Ninth Ave. (between 46th and 47th Streets)
(212) 664-WINE (9463)
www.ninthavenuevintner.com

A friendly community shop that brings in vintners to show off their wines most Fridays and Saturdays, 5 to 8 p.m. They have a nice selection of Long Island wines.

67 Wines & Spirits

179 Columbus Ave. (at 68th Street)
(212) 724-6767
www.67wine.com

Corkscrew U

Don't know your Asti Spumante from your elderberry wine? Take a class. There are many courses offered throughout the city that will let you expand your choice of wines beyond twist-off or cork. Most of these are one-day seminars on wines from specific regions of the world, but some are in-depth courses exploring every aspect of the wine, from seeds to sipping. And you can take the classes for free by volunteering to be a "pourer" for these classes. Basically all that's involved is showing up for the class an hour or so early, setting out the glasses and class materials for the paying students, pouring the wines that are used in the classes, and staying a little while after the class ends to load the glasses in the dishwasher. While the class is on, you're able to fully participate and taste all the wines used. See the chapter titled "Education: Cents-Less Smarts" for more details on classes at the New School Culinary Arts Program and The Wine Workshop.

A fine store for fine wines and every bit of wine paraphernalia you could ever imagine. Make your way up to the second-floor kitchen area and get an education in wines by sampling vintages of different countries, regions, types, and styles Tues through Sat, 4 to 7 p.m. They often have cooking demonstrations or at least something tasty to nibble along with the wines. Check their website for a listing of weekly events.

DOWNTOWN **EAST**

Astor Wines & Spirits
399 Lafayette St. (at East Fourth Street)
(212) 674-7500
www.astoruncorked.com

New York's largest wine store offers tastings grouped by region or type, giving you the opportunity to try everything from Dom Perignon to the wines of New Zealand and South Africa; from moderately priced to fine wines. The friendly staff offers samples in a no-pressure-to-buy atmosphere. Be sure to cleanse your palate with the gourmet breads and cheeses that often accompany the wines. The store offers tastings Wed, Thurs, and Fri, 6 to 8 p.m., and on Sat, 3 to 5 p.m. Check the website for a calendar of events.

DOWNTOWN **WEST**

Burgundy Wine Company
143 West 26th St. (between Sixth and Seventh Avenues)
(212) 691-9092
www.burgundywinecompany.com

The folks at this specialty shop like their Burgundy, and they also like to share it. You can stop in any day they are open, and you will have a chance to sample a bottle or two of their favorite wines. They crack open a bottle for you to sip every night from 5 to 7 p.m. and on Saturday from 11 a.m. to 7 p.m. They make a point of making Wednesday evenings a particularly good night to stop in, mostly because they want a good excuse to goof off from work. They always have at least three bottles open, some cheese, and often some live jazz to get you in the mood.

Sea Grape Wine & Spirits

512 Hudson St. (between Christopher and West 10th Streets)
(212) 463-7688
www.seagrapewines.com

This small neighborhood shop stocks a broad selection of wines, complete with amusing descriptions. They host tastings every Thurs, 5:30 to 8:30 p.m.

HAIR, BEAUTY & MASSAGE: FREE-STYLE

*"You'd be surprised how much it costs
to look this cheap."*

—DOLLY PARTON

Just because your bank account is running low doesn't mean you can't look and feel like a million bucks. In fact, looking good and feeling good can look and feel a whole lot better the less you pay to get that way. And in New York anything you need or want done can be had for nothing or very little: haircuts, coloring, highlights, facials, makeovers, manicures, and massage. The most common places to look for free or cheap services are salons with training programs, beauty and barbering schools, and manufacturers testing new products.

PRODUCT **TESTING** CENTERS

Here's your chance to be the first on your block to try out the newest products that some of the leading hair care manufacturers are developing. These companies are in the final stages of testing these items and want your opinion. Fear not: These creams, colors, mousses, and gels have all gone through a battery of tests already and are safe for you to use. In other words, you won't end up with a head full of green hair (unless, of course, that's what you want). You should know, though, that they won't be able to customize colors for your hair. You will be able to choose your colors, but they must be selected from the standard set of colors prepared for the shelves of any local store.

Clairol Product Evaluation Salon
345 Park Ave., lobby (between 51st and 52nd Streets)
(646) 885-4200 or (646) 885-4201

The services they offer and the products they test include hair coloring, highlights, relaxers, conditioners, styling mousses, and gels. All services are free and performed by licensed and skilled stylists. You must stop by first to apply—Mon through Thurs from 9:30 to 11 a.m. or 1:30 to 4 p.m. All men and women age eighteen or older may participate. The services they provide at any given time depend on the products being tested. The most common and consistent service offered is hair coloring. Once you're accepted onto the models' panel, you're welcome to come back in once a month for treatments.

L'Oréal Technical Center

575 Fifth Ave., second floor (at 47th Street)
(212) 984-4008

The Catch: Women must have shoulder-length or shorter hair (but not too short).

This is the product evaluation salon for all L'Oréal coloring and hair care products. Stop by Mon through Thurs from 10 a.m. to 4 p.m. for an evaluation and patch test. If they accept you into the program, they will color your hair every four weeks. They occasionally use men as well (long hair not necessary) but primarily seek women.

Redken Testing Center

435 Hudson St. (between Morton and Leroy Streets)
(212) 885-1317

They test all the new Redken products in development and can offer you quite a few fantastic services in the process. They offer coloring services and blow-outs, as well as perms and straightening. Stop by any Wednesday or Thursday afternoon from 2 to 4 p.m. for an evaluation. Then they will set you up for an appointment. Once you get a treatment, you can set up follow-up appointments every five weeks.

HAIR **SALONS**

These are some of the most exclusive (and expensive) salons in the city, and they all have training programs for fully licensed hairstylists who are receiving further instruction in specific styles or techniques. This makes it a low-risk situation: You can feel reasonably confident you won't end up with an accidental Mohawk at these salons. The only catch is that you are sometimes required to spend two to three hours at the salon when you are modeling for a class. Many of the salons that offer free services can be picky about whom they use as models; women are generally used more than men, and longer hair gets you an appointment quicker than shorter hair. All the salons listed below offer free cuts and/or colorings.

Bumble & Bumble

415 W. 13th St., sixth floor (between Greenwich and Washington Streets)
(866) 728-6523
www.bbumodelproject.com

The Catch: For free cuts and styling, models must have long enough hair to have at least 2 to 3 inches cut off.

This salon has a large training program. To get a free cut or style, you'll need to be chosen as a model for one of their professional seminars held on a regular basis. To apply to be a model, fill out their pre-evaluation form on their website or show up to their model call every Monday evening from 5:30 to 6:30 p.m. You can qualify as a cut model, style model, or color model (though you can only be a color model once you have been a cut model). They are looking for models who are willing to see a real change in their style—no trims here. You can even earn Hairmiles—a "frequent styler club" where you can earn points and prizes for coming back for more appointments once you have been approved as a model. If you aren't chosen as a model, you can still schedule a low-price cut or color from a staff apprentice for $10 to $20 on Mon from 10 a.m. to 4 p.m.

Crops for Girls

154 Orchard St. (between Stanton and Rivington Streets)
(212) 677-2772
www.cropsforgirls.com

The Catch: To get a free cut, you have to go from long hair to very short or let Michael do whatever he wants with your hair.

This salon specializes in short haircuts for women. It may be funky, it may be conservative; you never know what it may end up being. But you know it will be very short and Michael Giovan, the owner, will cut it himself. Call to make an appointment. If you are not quite willing to let Michael have his way with your hair, you can always pay for a cut and have it your way since his rates are darn reasonable (especially the $30 student discount!). Women only.

Dramatics NYC

158 E. 23rd St. (between Third and Lexington Avenues)
(212) 460-5709
www.dramaticsnyc.com

Show up any Mon at 10:30 a.m., and maybe you will be picked by one of the instructors for a free cut. This small chain of New York salons caters to a young, energetic, and on-the-go crowd, and they train all of the new stylists for their salons at this location. If you do not get picked for that class, they will call you back for another class.

Face Station

855 Lexington Ave. (between 64th and 65th Streets)
(212) 249-8866
www.facestation.com

This bustling Upper East Side salon offers free cuts and colors by their assistants most weekdays from 10 a.m. to 7 p.m. Give them a call a few days ahead to schedule an appointment.

Jeffrey Stein Salon

685 Third Ave. (at 43rd Street); (212) 557-0005
1336 Third Ave. (at 76th Street); (212) 772-7717

Jeffrey Stein has seven salons around the city, but these two offer free cuts for hair models on Wednesday mornings (43rd Street) and on Tues (76th Street). They offer cuts to men and women, depending on what skills and styles they're working on. Call one to two weeks in advance to set up an appointment.

Matrix Global Academy

435 Hudson St. (between Leroy and Morton Streets)
(917) 606-9500
www.matrix.com/academy

Fancy Places at Not-So-Fancy Prices

These salons all run training programs and charge reduced rates for stylish cuts given by their students. These appointments are generally easier to get than the free ones:

Carsten Institute, 41 Union Sq. West (Broadway and Fifth Avenue); (212) 675-4884; Tues through Sat from 8:30 a.m. to 1:30 p.m.; $20 cuts; $35 color.

Cutler Salon, 115 E. 57th St. (between Park and Lexington Avenues); (212) 308-3838; 465 W. Broadway (between Prince and Houston Streets); (212) 674-2210; Tues, Wed, and Thurs; $15. They hold trainings twice a year, where they offer free cuts to hair models. Check their website for times (www.cutlersalon.com).

Minardi Beauty Focus, 29 E. 61st St., fifth floor (between Fifth and Madison Avenues); (212) 308-1711; Wednesday afternoons; $30 cut and style (also use models for coloring classes some Monday nights—free coloring, but you must stay for the entire five-hour class).

Miwa Alex Hair Salon, 24 E. 22nd St. (between Broadway and Park Avenue); (212) 228-4422; Tuesday mornings; $25.

Parlor, 102 Avenue B (between 6th and 7th Streets); (212) 673-5520; www.parlorhairsalon.com; Mon, 9:30 a.m. to 3 p.m.; $15 cuts and style.

Paul Labrecque Salon, 171 E. 65th St. (at Third Avenue); (212) 595-0099; Mon; $25 for cuts; coloring and highlights also available, but pricey.

This huge and stylish salon is a training facility owned and operated by Matrix, the supplier of endless products to every salon from Super Cuts to the super-high-end salons. The academy trains licensed and experienced hair stylists in the latest products, techniques, and styles. They use models

The Redken Exchange, 565 Fifth Ave. (between 46th and 47th Streets); (212) 984-4703; www.redkensalon.com. Stop by Thurs at noon for a consultation, and they'll schedule you for a color and/or cut by a professional learning new techniques. It could take two weeks to a month to get an appointment. $15 for services. Occasionally they offer free services to test new products.

Salon Ishi, 70 E. 55th St. (between Madison and Park Avenues); (212) 888-4744; Wednesday evenings; $20 for cuts or color.

Scott J. Salons & Spas, 242 E. 86th St. (between Second and Third Avenues); every Wednesday morning; 257 Columbus Ave. (at 72nd Street); some Wednesday mornings; (212) 769-0107; www.scottj .com; $10 cuts/$20 color.

Shige Kosuda Salon, 141 E. 55th St. (between Lexington and Third Avenues); (212) 759-2397; Tues and Wed; $10.

Vidal Sassoon, 90 Fifth Ave. (between 14th and 15th Streets); (212) 229-2200; 730 Fifth Ave. (at 56th Street); (212) 535-9200; show up at 6 p.m. on Wed for a consultation, and they will schedule an appointment for you the following week; $20–$40 (depending on how far into the program the student is).

Younghee Salon, 64 N. Moore St. (between Greenwich and Hudson Streets); (212) 334-3770; http://youngheesalon.com; Wed; $15.

during their training events, giving you a chance to get free coloring services (they will also trim and style your hair as well). To be a model, you need to stop by and fill out a short application, and they will take a picture of you. They will call you when they can schedule an appointment for you.

Oscar Bond Salon Spa

42 Wooster St. (between Grand and Broome Streets)
(212) 334-3777
www.oscarbondsalon.com

Slick SoHo style is served up at this salon. Stop by Mon through Thurs from 10 a.m. to 4 p.m. and let them know you are interested in being a hair model. They will give your hair the once-over and let you know if they have a class coming up that they can use you in. If they use you in the class, all the services are free.

Riccardo Maggiore Salon

136 E. 57th St., second floor (at Lexington Avenue)
(212) 586-6482
www.riccardomaggiore.com

Class models get free cuts and/or coloring during the Tuesday classes. Call to put your name on the list.

Salon de Quartier

1032 Second Ave. (between 54th and 55th Streets)
(212) 688-5460
206 Smith St. (between Butler and Baltic Streets)
Cobble Hill, Brooklyn
(718) 246-7244
www.salondequartier.com

This high-energy salon offers free cuts by assistants whenever they hold classes (about once a month at the Brooklyn location and every now and then at the Manhattan salon). Call or stop by to leave your name, and they will call you when they are scheduling appointments.

Salon Ziba

200 W. 57th St. (between Broadway and Seventh Avenue)
(212) 767-0577
www.salonziba.com

Salon Ziba holds separate cut and color trainings once a month. Call to put your name on the list, and they will call you when they need a model for the classes, which are generally held on weekday mornings. The appointments for cuts are free and include wash, cut, style, and blow-dry, but they do charge $10 for the color appointments ($15 for highlights), which do not include a blow-dry. Also, they are very strict about appointment times. Be there on time or you are out of luck.

Tony & Guy Hairdressing Academy (TIGI)

673 Madison Ave., second floor (at 61st Street)
(212) 702-9771 or (800) 256-8585
http://toniguy.com

Hair stylists come from all over the country to take part in the classes and continuing education at this hotshot salon. On Thurs, Fri, and Sat, services can cost you up to $300, but if you are able to nab an appointment during their class hours Sun through Wed, not only is your service free, but they will even throw in three free products. Stop by on Fri at 6 p.m. for a consultation, and they will set up an appointment for you in the next week or two if they can use you in one of the classes. All appointment times are in the morning. They are looking for men and women who are willing to make a "noticeable change" in their styles or colors, so no "a little off the top" here. Once you are registered with them, you can call back for more appointments every month or so. These stylists are all experienced professionals, so you can pretty much depend on quality services here.

BEAUTY **SCHOOLS**

These schools are training folks to sit for their state licensing exams, so the amount of experience and skill fluctuates greatly from student to student. You do take on some risk of a coif catastrophe when you put your head in their hands. In fact, they usually have you sign a release to this effect before you get your haircut. The students are supervised, but the level of supervision varies from place to place. The better you describe what you'd like done, the happier you'll be with your results.

American Barber Institute

252 W. 29th St. (between Seventh and Eighth Avenues)
(212) 290-2289
www.abi.edu

The Catch: A low fee is charged for work done by students.

They offer haircuts for $5, but you might get lucky and find their "flyer guy" handing out flyers for even cheaper cuts at 29th Street and Eighth Avenue. Stop by anytime Mon through Fri from 9 a.m. to 6:30 p.m. for a cut.

Atlas Barber School
34 Third Ave. (between 9th and 10th Streets)
(212) 475-1360
www.atlasbarbersch.com

The Catch: They charge a fee for services performed by students.

This must be the minor-league farm system for Astor Place Haircutters (world renowned for their quick clipper cuts at $12 a snip). If you're in the market for one of those maybe neat, maybe funky, anything-you-can-do-with-a-clipper-in-ten-minutes-cuts, this is the place for you. It will run you $5 a buzz.

Aveda Institute
233 Spring St. (between Sixth Avenue and Varick Street)
(212) 807-1492
www.aveda.com

The Catch: They charge a fee for services performed by students.

This upscale beauty school offers hair, facial, and spa services by students using Aveda's organic products. Prices are a bit steeper than at other beauty schools, but still pretty cheap by New York standards (haircut $20; coloring $25 to $60). You can also be a model for Aveda classes and receive services for free. Call (212) 367-0339 for details. It is best to try to book appointments four to six weeks in advance.

Christine Valmy International School for Esthetics
437 Fifth Ave., second floor (between 38th and 39th Streets)
(212) 779-7800
www.christinevalmy.com

The Catch: They charge fees for services provided by students.

Many of the students who train here go on to work at some of the most exclusive (and expensive) spas in New York, but while they are in school it won't cost you much to let them poke and prod at your face. A one-hour facial will run you $30 during the day, $42 evenings and Sat.

Empire Beauty School
22 W. 34th St. (between Fifth and Sixth Avenues)
(212) 967-1717
www.empire.edu

The Catch: They charge a low fee for services performed by students.

Okay, this place isn't too swanky, and the cuts won't be cutting edge, but if you're in the market for a basic cut, style, color, or manicure, it certainly is cheap. Their most consistent clientele are old ladies and recently released convicts, which makes for a very interesting waiting room! The fees are $8 for a shampoo and cut, manicure $5, and lip, chin, or eyebrow wax $5. All work is performed by students. Additional locations are at 38–15 Broadway at Steinway Street, Astoria, Queens (718-726-8383) and 2384 86th St. at Twenty-fourth Avenue, Bay Ridge, Brooklyn (718-373-2400).

New York International Beauty School
500 Eighth Ave. (between 35th and 36th Streets)
(212) 868-7171
www.nyibs.com

The Catch: They charge a low fee for services performed by students.

The Beauty School salon offers cut-rate services starting at $5. Senior students perform such services as styling, cuts, perms, coloring, and hair relaxing while being supervised by licensed instructors. Stop by Mon through Thurs from 9 a.m. to 2 p.m., Fri until noon, and Sat until 1 p.m.

MASSAGE

Quintessence Reiki
Spring Wellness
636 Broadway (at Bleecker Street)
(917) 570-8013 or (212) 388-9817
reikimaster.michael@gmail.com

This is not your Uncle Ike's idea of a massage. Reiki works with the energy of the universe (*rei*) and the body's energy (chi); the practitioners only lightly touch you during a session. The results can be surprisingly relaxing, calming, and healing. Lead by Reiki master Michael Stoltz, Quintessence holds free "Healing Circles" the first and third Wed of each month from 7 to 9 p.m., which consist of a guided meditation, a short hands-on session (so to speak) lasting between ten to twenty minutes, and a question-and-answer discussion about the practice.

The Swedish Institute for Massage Therapy
226 W. 26th St. (between Seventh and Eighth Avenues)
(212) 924-5900 or (877) 406-7933
www.swedishinstitute.com

The Catch: They charge low fees for massage therapy performed by students.

Over the Counter

Whenever you're in need of some professional beauty assistance, stop by any makeup counter at the finer department stores and have a pro do the work for you. Try the counters at the following stores:

Macy's, 151 W. 34th St. (at Sixth Avenue); (212) 695-4400.

Bergdorf Goodman, 754 Fifth Ave. (at 58th Street); (212) 753-7300.

Saks Fifth Avenue, 611 Fifth Ave. (at 50th Street); (212) 753-4000.

Lord & Taylor, 424 Fifth Ave. (at 38th Street); (212) 391-3344.

Bloomingdale's, 1000 Third Ave. (between 59th and 60th Streets); (212) 705-2000.

All of the above offer free makeovers using their oh-so-pricey products. Of course, the hope is that you will then buy a load of $43 mascara, $59 lipsticks, and $94 skin-cleansing citrus retonifier—but that's up to you.

If you want a free massage, you'll have to start dating a massage therapist, and even then it's not a sure thing (we've all seen the Seinfeld episode). So when you need some good cheap hands-on massage, check out the P. H. Ling Clinic at the Swedish Institute. They have two options for low-cost massage. The Stress Reduction Clinic is open to all (but slots fill up quickly) and offers a package of six relaxing and refreshing massages for $150. You register for a series of six one-hour massages, and each week you will receive either a Swedish or shiatsu session (based on therapist availability). No preferences for modality are taken; you take what you're given from week to week. The Therapeutic Massage Clinic is available to those who have a prescription from a doctor or chiropractor for treatment on a specific injury or condition. You must register for a package of twelve one-hour massages for $250. This series consists of twelve consecutive weekly sessions. Each patient will receive both Eastern (shiatsu) and Western (Swedish, sports massage, or the like) treatments throughout the twelve weeks. The work is performed by students in their final semester and supervised by faculty. Both clinics are offered three times a year and are very popular; applying for a slot as early as possible is advised.

MAKEUP

NYBS Creative Arts
336 W. 37th St., Suite 1430 (between Eighth and Ninth Avenues)
(212) 245-6371
www.nybsca.com

This makeup school is always looking for models for class (of any ethnicity). You may even get paid for your time. Call to set up an interview. Classes held in the afternoon, Mon through Fri.

REAL ESTATE:
THIS LAND IS YOUR LAND

"The best is the cheapest."

—BENJAMIN FRANKLIN

Yes, apartments in New York are just as ridiculously expensive as you've heard they are. With studio apartments the size of a closet going for more than $1,200 a month considered to be a steal—if you can find one—the price of four walls and a bed has really made living in Manhattan almost impossible. But even while the rents were continuing to skyrocket, I managed to find myself a spacious studio apartment in a desirable neighborhood for the unbelievable rent of $560 a month (and it just went up from $521). You might think I'm lucky, but I contend that all it takes for anyone to get such a deal is lots of patience and perseverance. There are thousands of apartments like this all around the five boroughs (and, yes, plenty in Manhattan) through the Mitchell-Lama and 80/20 programs. And these places can be yours without any exorbitant broker's fee, "key fee," or huge deposit.

All that's generally required to move in is the first month's rent and one month's rent as security. The secret is getting your name on as many waiting lists as you can for older buildings, and putting in as many applications as you can for new developments. This won't solve your apartment needs in the short term, though. Unfortunately, it can take between one and ten years for your name to come up (I waited three years), but don't let that stop you from putting your name on lists. Even if you're going through the I-don't-even-know-if-I'll-still-be-in-New-York-in-three-years syndrome, put your name on the lists. If you're still here, and you probably will be, you'll be happy you did. If you aren't, they'll just call the next lucky Cheap Bastard.

LOW-RENT, **NO-FEE** APARTMENTS

New York City Housing Development Corporation
110 William St. (between John and Fulton Streets)
(212) 227-5500 (administrative office)
(212) 863-5610 (affordable housing hotline)
www.nychdc.com

The Catch: Each building has various maximum income eligibility restrictions.

Everywhere you look in the city, there is a new building going up, and chances are that building is part of some program through the Housing Development Corporation (HDC) that makes it possible for us Cheap Bastards to get into some of the hottest real estate on the planet. The HDC has any number of programs to get you into these buildings, with such fun names as LAMP, New HOP, Mixed Income, 80/20, Taxable 80/20, New HOP 80/20, and CO-OPS (yes, you can even buy a co-op!), and they seem to be coming up with new programs (and catchy names) every day. But all the programs operate under the same basic premise: The HDC gives the developers certain tax breaks and low-interest loans if they make a portion of the apartments in the swanky new building available to low- and middle-income people (at low- and middle-level rents!). Each building and program has its own income restrictions (some of them up to as much as $150,000 for a family of four), and there are heaps of paperwork and interviews that you need to go through. The good news is, once you are in, you are in. You do not need to maintain a low income to remain in the apartments. They list all of the buildings currently accepting applications and those who will soon be accepting applications on their website. The competition can be pretty stiff for these apartments, so it is a good idea to apply to a number of buildings at one time. The time between application and move-in date can be any-where from a few months to a few years.

Housing Partnership Development Corporation

450 Seventh Ave., Suite 2401 (between 34th and 35th Streets)
(646) 217-3370
www.housingpartnership.com

The Catch: Must meet income requirements and limitations to qualify.

This is a chance to own a new home or condo in neighborhoods around the city with small down payments (as low as 5 percent) and many tax exemptions and incentives—and maybe even no closing costs. The mission of the Housing Partnership's New Homes/Neighborhood Builders program is to increase homeownership opportunities for moderate-income families who are priced out of the conventional real estate market. If you qualify, you can become the owner of a brand-new condo, single-family, or multifamily home. These homes or buildings are built from the ground up by reputable architects and contractors, come complete with many amenities, and are heavily subsidized by the city. There are developments in all five boroughs in such neighborhoods as Fort Green, Harlem, Coney Island, Bedford Stuyves-ant, Williamsburg, Crown Heights, Hunts Point, and others. Check out the website for a list of current projects.

At Your Service

Can't afford any New York City rents? Can't afford to raise a family in New York? Well then, how about raising a family and living in a penthouse duplex on Central Park West? Yes, it can be done. Get a position as a live-in nanny, butler, cook, or personal assistant to the upper crust of New York society and live way beyond your means.

The most common live-in job (particularly for women) is as a nanny. Besides room and board, nannies are paid between $400 and $800 a week for their child-care duties and some light housekeeping responsibilities (though some families try to push that part of the job description to the limit). Agencies and families are looking for at least a one-year commitment and some experience. The best way to look for a nanny position is through word of mouth, but there's no shortage of agencies to place you as well. Any reputable agency will not charge you a fee; any fees are paid by the families. Here are a few good places to start your search:

Professional Nannies Institute, 501 Fifth Ave., Suite 908; (212) 692-9510; www.profnannies.com.

A Choice Nanny, 850 Seventh Ave., Suite 706; (212) 246-5437; www.achoicenanny.com.

The Nanny Authority, (973) 466-2669; www.nannyauthority.com.

NY Nanny Center, 250 W. 57th St.; (212) 265-3354; www.nynanny.com.

Family Extensions, (203) 966-9944 or (800) 932-2736; www.familyextensions.com.

If taking care of somebody else's kids isn't your idea of a good time, there are many other live-in positions you can apply for. The rich and famous need you to do everything from cook for them to clean for them, teach their children, keep track of their personal calendars, and attend to their private aircraft. If your calling is to be a majordomo, valet, chauffeur, or housekeeper, try these agencies:

Lifestyle Resources, 23 W. 36th St., Suite 4B (between Fifth and Sixth Avenues); (212) 947-9792; www.sterlinglifestyle.com.

Domestic Placement Network, (805) 640-3608 or (877) 206-5262; www.dpnonline.com.

Mitchell-Lama Housing Companies

City-Sponsored Developments
Department of Housing Preservation and Development
100 Gold St. (between Frankfurt and Spruce Streets,
near the Brooklyn Bridge)
(212) 863-6500 (city-sponsored Mitchell-Lama)
(212) 863-5610 (affordable housing hotline)
www.nyc.gov

State-Sponsored Developments
NYS Department of Housing and Community Renewal (DHCR)
25 Beaver St. (between Broad and New Streets)
(212) 480-7343
www.dhcr.state.ny.us/Programs/Mitchell-Lama

The Catch: Applicants must meet income requirements, and waiting lists can be long.

There are 132 city-sponsored buildings and 269 state-sponsored buildings in the Mitchell-Lama program (many in the five boroughs), with a total of more than 110,000 units throughout the system. This program was created in the 1950s to provide affordable housing for low- and moderate-income families. The apartments in these buildings are larger than the average shoe boxes most New Yorkers call home, there are no broker's fees, and the rents are amazingly low. Get the lists of buildings with open waiting lists through the websites or call. You must apply to each building separately; there is no centralized waiting list. The waits could be anywhere from one to ten years, so apply early and to many buildings. The income requirements vary, depending on the building and the size of your household. Once you have an apartment, though, you are not required to maintain a low income level. You will need to submit your income tax forms to the building management each year, which adjusts your rent yearly according to state-mandated levels. Once you have exceeded a certain prescribed level of income, you'll be required to pay "market value"—still ridiculously cheap. Market value rents (the maximum you will pay) range from studio apartments for $521 to three-bedroom apartments with a terrace for $997 (these do vary somewhat from building to building).

CHILDREN & TEENS:
OLLI OLLI OXEN FREE

"Children are poor man's riches."

—ENGLISH PROVERB

New York is an amazing place for kids, and not just for those who can afford to go to the Manhattan Day School. Yes, at times it may seem like there are so many places to go, sights to see, things to do—and ways to drop a load of cash—that New York doesn't feel very kid friendly for a parent's wallet. Fear not. There are classes, movies, fun and games, readings, even health insurance, and tons of other fun and useful things for kids without Mom and Dad having to stop at the ATM. During the week, you can

Dial-a-Teacher

Can't find the capital of Uzbekistan? Stumped by the square root of the hypotenuse? Or just want to check that you spelled *Crispus Attucks* correctly? Then call up a teacher and get some help. The Dial-a-Teacher program, run by the United Federation of Teachers, has been helping out baffled students and parents for more than twenty years by fielding more than 2,000 calls a week. A staff of forty-five teachers fluent in Spanish, French, Haitian Creole, Italian, Greek, Hebrew, Chinese, and, yes, English stand at the ready to help you with your homework in any subject Mon through Thurs, 4 to 7 p.m., throughout the school year.

These folks won't just give you the answers to your questions; since these are all qualified teachers you're talking to, they will strive to reteach the ideas behind the questions, making sure you understand the answers. And if you have already finished your homework, they will be happy to check your work with you. Dial-a-Teacher also offers a battery of workshops for parents during the day or in the evening designed to make parents more aware of what their children are learning and teach them how to help their children more effectively at home.

Dial-a-Teacher can arrange to hold workshops at local schools or at their Manhattan headquarters. If you attend workshops at the Dial-a-Teacher offices, they will send a bus to pick you up, take you home, and even serve you breakfast and lunch! And yes, all help and workshops are free of charge. For homework assistance call (212) 777-3380. To find out more about workshops, call (212) 598-9205 or click on "parents" at the website www.uft.org.

fill out any day's schedule with the endless free after-school programs. And on weekends there is never a shortage of creative fun for the whole family in the major parks, museums, and other institutions throughout the city.

AFTER-SCHOOL **PROGRAMS**

Beacon Schools
Eighty locations throughout the five boroughs
The NYC Department of Youth and Community Development
156 William St. (between Ann and Beekman Streets)
(212) 788-6754
www.nyc.gov/dycd

Don't ever say New York City didn't give you anything! The eighty Beacon School programs are a gift to every student and parent in New York City. Spread throughout every school district in the five boroughs, the programs offer extensive after-school, evening, and weekend classes that are basically free day camp for students of all ages. Each program's activities vary, but they all generally include time for homework help and tutoring as well as lots of fun structured activities. Activities might include arts and crafts, sports, drama, music, dance, music, photography, martial arts, and computer classes as well as vocational training and health classes. Some classes and activities are offered to adults as well. Registration is required for all programs, but everything is free, even the snacks! To find the locations in your neighborhood, check the website.

New York City Recreation Centers
Forty-two locations throughout the five boroughs
(See Appendix D for locations)
Dial 311 or (212) NEW-YORK (from outside New York City)
www.nycgovparks.org

At every one of New York City's Public Recreation Centers, you will find a variety of after-school programs (Mon through Fri, 3 to 6 p.m.) for children ages six to fourteen. The programs at each location vary depending on the center's facilities and staffing, but all strive to incorporate the "Straight A's:

Athletics, Arts, and Academics." The schedules could include swim programs, sports instruction, computer classes, Internet access, homework help, arts and crafts, and classes in literacy, performing arts, visual arts, and much more. For schedules and more information, check with the local recreation centers.

ARTS & CRAFTS

The Art Shack
Hudson River Park
Hudson River at Chambers Street
(212) 766-1104
www.manhattanyouth.org

Spend a great afternoon creating all types of projects (painting, drawing, sculpting . . .) with fun teachers and fresh air. All materials are supplied. Weather permitting, Sat and Sun, noon to 5 p.m., May through Sept.

Choristers
St. John's In The Village
224 Waverly Place (between Perry and West 11th Streets)
(212) 243-6192
www.stjvny.org

Every Monday afternoon children of all religions and backgrounds gather together in the parish hall of St. John's In The Village to take part in this free music and voice-training program. The curriculum of this very serious program focuses on reading music, sight singing, ear training, and musicianship while learning the music of a wide variety of classical styles and periods (no contemporary or children's music here). Auditions are required, and once you are accepted into the program you must commit to a full schedule of classes (every Monday afternoon) and performances (one Sunday a month). While this is a church-run program, it is not a religious program at all.

Cooper-Hewitt, National Design Museum
2 E. 91st St. (at Fifth Avenue)
(212) 849-8353
www.cooperhewitt.org

The Catch: You must be a New York City high school student.

Through a program called Design Directions, high school students interested in any aspect of design (fashion, industrial, graphic, media, film, interior, architecture, urban planning, and so forth) connect with the vast professional resources in New York City. Programs include daylong workshops, after-school programs, design studio visits, and precollege preparation (college visits; application and portfolio workshops). All classes are free and open to all on a first-come, first-served basis.

Fools Co. Inc.'s New York School for Performing Arts
Various locations around Manhattan
(212) 307-6000
foolsco@nyc.rr.com
www.foolsco.org

The Catch: You must be between sixteen and twenty-one years old.

For more than twenty years, Jill Russell has been training young adults in all aspects of the performing arts through the Artsworker Apprentice program, which provides free weekly workshops in performance, movement, masks, puppetry, voice and diction, and more. The program is open to all with the desire to learn. No audition or previous experience is needed, but preregistration is required. Call or e-mail for more information.

Jazzmobile
PS 197
135th St. and Fifth Ave.
(212) 866-4900 (administrative office); (212) 866-3616 (hotline)
www.jazzmobile.org

The Catch: A one-time $80 registration fee is required.

Since 1969 Jazzmobile has been offering free Saturday music workshops and master classes for students age seven and older at PS 197 in Harlem with such musicians as Max Roach, Branford Marsalis, and Donald Byrd. Students need to have at least some basic music knowledge to participate, and they must register and have their skill evaluated to determine if they fit into the beginning, intermediate, or advanced classes. The classes run from Nov through Mar, and a one-time registration fee of $80 is required. In summer they also bring a lineup of world-class musicians to the parks, libraries, schools, and street corners of New York City and the surrounding areas. Check the website for details.

The Museum of Modern Art (MoMA)
Education Department
11 W. 53rd St. (between Fifth and Sixth Avenues)
(212) 708-9828 (high school programs)
(212) 708-9807 (family programs)
www.moma.org

MoMA is an absolute wonderland of free arts activities for everyone from toddlers to teens. The museum offers lively tours and special activities specifically targeted to this young audience (ages four through fourteen), as well as films, discussions with artists, and workshops. All of these family activities are scheduled on the weekends and include free admission to the museum for up to two adults and three children. Many of the programs offer tickets on a first-come, first-served basis at the museum the day of the event; others do require preregistration. For high schoolers the museum offers a number of eight-week and sixteen-week courses every year, which might include drawing, printmaking, or curatorial and museum work. Every Friday night starting at 4:45 p.m., high school students are invited to chow down on some free pizza and watch a great selection of classic, contemporary, and experimental films. Preregistration is required for the courses, but you can just show up for the movies. Check out the website for details.

New York University Program in Educational Theatre
Press Annex, 82 Washington Sq. East, Room 23 (at Washington Place)
(212) 998-5868
http://steinhardt.nyu.edu/music/edtheatre

The Catch: $110 materials fee.

Thirteen- to eighteen-year-old budding thespians take part in a free five-week intensive summer program called "Looking for Shakespeare." Throughout the session, students will work with a host of theater professionals to shape an original play based on the Bard's themes but taken directly from the participants' own lives. While working on the play, the performers receive coaching in playwriting, improvisation, acting, voice, and movement, culminating in a fully staged production for the public. Participants must interview and audition for the program, but no experience is necessary, just enthusiasm and energy.

Prospect Park Audubon Center
Lincoln Road and Central Drive in Prospect Park
(718) 287-3400
www.prospectpark.org/audubon

Nestled in the wilds of Brooklyn's sprawling Prospect Park, the Audubon Center offers a full roster of free activities for all nature-loving kids, from toddlers to teens. Wednesday afternoons, kids ages nine through thirteen can drop by and join the Green Team to learn about the natural wonders of the park and how to help conserve them. Friday afternoons, the Nestlings (ages three through five) have a fun afternoon full of storytelling, music, and crafts. And on the weekends you will always find special programs as well as regular crafts classes and bird-watching and nature tours for kids of all ages. Some programs require registration, but all are free. Call or check out the website for schedule and information.

The Public Theater's Shakespeare Lab Jr.
425 Lafayette St. (between East 4th Street and Astor Place)
(212) 539-8516
www.publictheater.org

One of New York's preeminent and leading purveyors of the Bard's work opens its doors to students for an intensive week of workshops and theater training. Students work on Shakespeare with professional actors, learn about the backstage workings of a professional theater, attend a performance at the Delacorte Theater in Central Park, and get a chance to perform themselves. The workshops are open to students entering the tenth grade and above. No audition is required, but you must register. Workshops run for one week throughout the month of Aug and are filled on a first-come, first-served basis.

The Wooster Group

The Performing Garage
33 Wooster St. (between Broome and Grand Streets)
(212) 966-9796
www.thewoostergroup.org

The Catch: You must be a twelve- to seventeen-year-old New York City student.

This edgy, experimental theater company offers a free three-week summer institute. Students get experience working alongside professional artists like company members Willem Dafoe and Kate Valk, as well as developing performance skills and creating original work. No prior experience is required; call for an application.

FILMS

The Museum of Modern Art (MoMA)

11 W. 53rd St. (between Fifth and Sixth Avenues)
(212) 708-9828 (Friday Night at the Movies
for High School Students)
(212) 708-9805 (family programs)
www.moma.org

The education department at MoMA presents Friday Night at the Movies for High School Students, a series of six classic and contemporary films in the spring and fall. Each series consists of films grouped under an intriguing theme (for instance, the irresistible villain: *Dr. Jekyll and Mr. Hyde, Psycho,* and *The Usual Suspects*) and is followed by talks with the film department curators of the museum. Hey, they even throw in free pizza and soda. No tickets or reservations are required—just show up! On Saturday and Sunday mornings the museum invites you to bring down the young'uns for special tours, activities, and screenings. They have programs targeted toward four-year-olds, five- to ten-year-olds, and eleven- to fourteen-year-olds. Some programs require preregistration (and fill up quickly!), and others are first-come, first-served on the day of the event. All of these programs include free admission to the museum for up to two adults and three children. Check the website for details.

River Flicks

Pier 46, Hudson River and Christopher Street (films for kids)
Pier 54, Hudson River and 14th Street (films for grown-ups)
(212) 627-2020
(212) 732-7467
www.hudsonriverpark.org

River Flicks shows great family-friendly films (all rated G or PG) screen on Pier 46 every Friday at about 8 p.m. (or when it gets dark) in July and Aug. In past seasons films have included *Mary Poppins, Little Shop of Horrors, Willy Wonka and the Chocolate Factory, Harry Potter,* and *Chicken Run.* They also present another series of films for grown-ups every Wednesday night at Pier 54. They set up some chairs on the pier for your comfort, and there's also plenty of room for you to bring a blanket and picnic under the stars while you watch. Of course, no movie is complete without the popcorn—and it's free, too.

FILMS AT *PUBLIC* LIBRARIES

Many public libraries throughout the city have regularly scheduled films and videos for children between the ages of three and ten every week. These programs usually run anywhere from thirty minutes to a couple of hours and consist of a few short films that could include vintage Disney cartoons, films of children's books, and rare children's classics as well as occasional

---

Nixing Netflix

Forget about spending almost $15 a month to rent videos on Netflix. Most local libraries have a large collection of children's videos and DVDs. Disney, cartoons, educational and full-length features, classics, and new releases—you'll find plenty on the shelves to please all tastes. You can borrow tapes for a week (three days in Queens). Watch out for the late fees, though: $1 per day at the NYPL, $2 per day in Brooklyn, and a whopping $3 per day in Queens.

---

feature-length films. For more details on times and programs check out the library websites: **www.nypl.org** (for the Bronx, Staten Island, and Manhattan), **www.queenslibrary.org,** or **www.brooklynpubliclibrary.org.** Below is a list of the branches with screenings for children every week. These schedules do change from time to time. Be sure to call the branch to confirm schedules.

Manhattan Branches

Aguilar Library, 174 E. 110th St. (between Third and Lexington Avenues); (212) 534-2930; Tues at 4 p.m.

Bloomingdale Branch, 150 W. 100th St. (between Columbus Avenue and Broadway); (212) 222-8030; call for schedule.

Columbus Library, 742 Tenth Ave. (between 50th and 51st Streets); (212) 586-5098; call for schedule.

Jefferson Market Library, 425 Avenue of the Americas (at 10th Street); (212) 243-4334; Tues at 3:30 p.m.

96th Street Library, 112 E. 96th St. (between Park and Lexington Avenues); (212) 289-0908; Wed at 10:30 a.m.

125th Street Branch, 224 E. 125th St. (between Second and Third Avenues); (212) 534-5050; call for schedule.

St. Agnes Library, 444 Amsterdam Ave. (between 81st and 82nd Streets); (212) 877-4380; Thurs at 4 p.m.

Yorkville Branch Library, 222 E. 79th St. (between Lexington and Third Avenues); (212) 744-5824; Wed at 4 p.m.

Bronx Branches

Bronx Library Center, 10 E. Kingsbridge Rd. (between Jerome and Morris Avenues); (718) 579-4244; Wed at 2 p.m.

Fordham Library Center, 2556 Bainbridge Ave. (at Fordham Road); (718) 579-4244; Wed at 3:30 p.m.

Grand Concourse Library, 155 E. 173rd St. (at Selwyn Avenue); (718) 583-6611; Fri at 4 p.m.

Melrose Library, 910 Morris Ave. (at East 162nd Street); (718) 588-0110; Tues at 4 p.m.

Morrisania Library, 610 E. 169th St. (at Franklin Avenue); (718) 589-9268; Thurs at 3:30 p.m.

Pelham Bay Branch, 3060 Middletown Rd. (at Jarvis Street); (718) 792-6744; call for schedule.

Tremont Branch, 1866 Washington Ave. (at 176th Street); (718) 299-5177; Wed at 3 p.m.

Westchester Square Library, 2521 Glebe Ave. (at St. Peter's Avenue); (718) 863-0436; Fri at 3:30 p.m.

Brooklyn Branches

Bay Ridge, Ridge Boulevard at 73rd Street; (718) 748-5709; Fri at 3:30 p.m.

Brower Park, St. Marks Avenue near Nostrand Avenue; (718) 773-7208; Mon at 2 p.m.

Central Library, Grand Army Plaza (at Flatbush Avenue and Eastern Parkway); (718) 230-2100; Sat at 11 a.m., films for the whole family.

Coney Island, Mermaid Avenue near West 19th Street; (718) 265-3880; call for schedule.

Flatbush, Linden Boulevard near Flatbush Avenue; (718) 865-0813; call for schedule.

Kings Bay, Nostrand Avenue near Avenue W; (718) 368-1709; Mon at 3 p.m.

Marcy, DeKalb Avenue near Nostrand Avenue; (718) 935-0032; call for schedule.

New Lots Library, New Lots Avenue and Barbey Street; (718) 649-0311; call for schedule.

Queens Branches
Central Library, 89–11 Merrick Blvd. (between Eighty-ninth and Ninetieth Avenues); (718) 990-0700; Wed at 10:30 a.m. (summer only).

Flushing Library, 41–17 Main St.; (718) 661-1200; Fri at 10:30 a.m. (summer only).

Queens Village, 94–11 217th St. (between Jamaica and Hillside Avenues); (718) 776-6800; Fri at 3:30 p.m.

Staten Island Branches
Stapleton, 132 Canal St. (at Wright Street); (718) 727-0427; Fri at 3:30 p.m.

SPORTS & GAMES

Battery Park City Parks
Rockefeller Park House (Hudson River and Chambers Street)
(212) 267-2020
www.bpcparks.org or www.hudsonriverfestival.com

The schedule is chock-full of regularly scheduled activities for kids from toddlers to teens (and plenty for adults as well!). Starting in May and running through Oct, their weekly schedule includes everything from soccer, inline-skating lessons, and gardening to drawing classes, concerts, and family dances. Check their detailed websites for schedule and locations.

Big City Fishing

Pier 26 (Hudson River at North Moore Street)
Pier 46 (Hudson River at Christopher Street)
Pier 64 (Hudson River and 24th Street)
Pier 84 (Hudson River and 44th Street)
Pier 95 (Hudson River at 56th Street)
(212) 533-park (7275)
www.hudsonriverpark.org

New York City and fishing? Not two things you would think go together. Well, the Hudson River is the cleanest it has been for almost a hundred years and the fish are abundant, so come on down and cast a line. The fishing is open to all, but mostly it's children who do the casting. If you're big enough to hold a rod, you're welcome to participate in this catch-and-release fishing. All equipment, bait, and instructions are provided free of charge. Programs are offered weekends from Memorial Day through Labor Day and weekdays in July and Aug.

The Center for Anti-Violence Education

421 Fifth Ave., second floor (between 7th and 8th Streets)
Park Slope, Brooklyn
(718) 788-1775
www.cae-bklyn.org

The Catch: Free for fourteen- to nineteen-year-old girls only.

Sign up for a free self-defense course or an after-school karate class for teen girls. The self-defense course lasts for five weeks and is offered five times a year; the karate class is taught throughout the school year. The form of karate they teach (Goju) uses a lot of spiritual and meditative exercises (along with the usual kicks, chops, and *hii-yaas!*) to build the girls' inner strength as well as outer. They also offer low-cost/sliding-scale classes for younger children (girls and boys) and adults.

The Charles A. Dana Discovery Center

Central Park at 110th Street and Lenox Avenue
(212) 860-1370
www.centralparknyc.org

Sitting majestically on the Harlem Meer at the north end of the park, the Dana Discovery Center offers a variety of free family programs and hands-on exhibits throughout the year. From Apr through Oct stop by any Tues through Sun from 10 a.m. to 4 p.m. and the center will provide you with poles, unbarbed hooks, bait, and instruction booklets for you to while away the hours with some catch-and-release fishing. The Dana Center also offers a variety of educational programs, nature exhibits, and jazz concerts (see page 39).

City Parks Youth Tennis, Track & Field, and Golf
Locations throughout the five boroughs
(718) 760-6999
www.cityparksfoundation.org

Each year thousands of kids who hope to be the next Andre Agassi or Anthony Kim take to the city parks to participate in one of the most extensive youth training programs anywhere in the world. Children ages five through sixteen can take part in three separate programs supported by the City Parks Foundation and receive free lessons in tennis, track and field, and golf. Each program varies slightly, but lessons, equipment, and tournaments are free. Sometimes the kids even have a chance to meet and learn from stars of the games.

Lasker Rink
Central Park (110th Street and Lenox Avenue)
(212) 348-4867
www.centralparknyc.org

The Catch: $5 registration fee required for each six-week session.

Two six-week sessions of (almost) free ice-skating lessons are available for children age eight to seventeen between Jan and Mar on Tues from 4 to 6 p.m. To take part you must preregister at the North Meadow recreation center (mid-park at 97th Street) and lay down your $5 registration fee for each six-week session. Skate rentals are provided free of charge. And, those registered for the classes have free entry into the rink any other time throughout the week, though you will have to pay for your skate rental ($5).

Learn to Play . . . Soccer, Baseball, Lacrosse, Basketball, Baseball
City recreation centers and parks throughout the five boroughs
(212) 360-3300
www.nycparks.org

These separate programs run by the City Parks Department offer girls and boys age thirteen and younger (and sometimes fourteen-year-olds) the chance not only to learn the basics of any of these sports but also to play and compete with other children throughout the city. Free and open to all, these leagues go on at different times of year and provide children with all the skills and equipment they need to enjoy the games. Call for schedules and locations.

Learn to Swim Program
City pools and recreation centers throughout the five boroughs
(212) 360-3300
www.cityparksfoundation.org or www.nycparks.org

Everybody in the pool! Free swimming instruction for children ages three through fourteen is available during the summer at all thirty-three city-run outdoor pools, and lessons continue throughout the year at city-run indoor pools and recreation centers. Recreation center memberships for children younger than age thirteen are free; for fourteen- to seventeen-year-olds it costs $5 to $10. (For more information on other city recreation center offerings, see the chapter titled "Fitness, Fun, & Games: Cheap Thrills." For complete listings of recreation center locations, see Appendix D.)

HEALTH **INSURANCE**

Child Health Plus
Mayor's Office for Health Insurance Access
Human Resources Administration
330 W. 34th St. (between Ninth and Tenth Avenues)
(800) 698-4543
www.nyc.gov/healthstat

This free or low-cost health insurance is available to New York City residents up to age eighteen. The cost of enrolling depends on your income and the size of your family. It's free for anyone whose income is below a certain level; if your income is higher, you may have to pay $9 or $15 per month per child. If your income is too high to qualify for these subsidized rates (around $50,000 a year for a family of four), you can still take part in the program, but you will have to pay full price for the plan (steep, but not thoroughly purse popping at about $150 a month). This is comprehensive coverage (including medical, vision, and dental) and a pretty amazing deal even if you aren't qualified to receive it for free.

MUSEUMS

Belvedere Castle/Henry Luce Nature Observatory
Central Park (enter at West 81st or East 79th Streets)
(212) 772-0210
www.centralparknyc.org
Hours: Tues through Sun, 10 a.m.–5 p.m.

Besides being a castle built high on a hill (a pretty desirable destination for any kid or adult), this is also the home of a nature observatory complete with your fair share of frogs, turtles, and birds and lots of hands-on exhibits. The urban park rangers who run the observatory also run guided tours (free!) on weekends. And if you prefer to explore the wilds of the park on your own, you can borrow a free Birding Kit from them. The kit is filled with useful stuff like a pair of binoculars, a field guide, a sketch pad, and colored pencils. Check out the website for tour schedule and details.

Brooklyn Children's Museum
145 Brooklyn Ave. (between St. Marks and Prospect Streets)
(718) 735-4400
www.brooklynkids.org
Free hours: Every third Thurs, 5–7:30 p.m.; every second and fourth Sat and Sun, 2–5 p.m.

For more than a hundred years, the world's first children's museum has been entertaining and enlightening kids with a mixture of hands-on exhibits and performances and an extensive collection of cultural objects and natural-history specimens. They fling the doors wide open for free entry every weekend for the early birds (11 a.m. to noon). During the summer their Free Fridays (5 to 7 p.m.) are not to be missed: In addition to full access to the museum, they always offer great musical performances for young and old alike on their rooftop.

Leffert's Homestead

Prospect Park (near Flatbush Avenue and Empire Boulevard)
(718) 789-2822
www.prospectpark.org
Hours: Thurs through Sun, noon–6 p.m.; extended hours during the
summer months.

This is one of the few surviving Dutch Colonial farmhouses in Brooklyn, and possibly the only children's historic house museum in the country. The house gives children a chance to explore American history and experience everyday life as it was in the little farming village of Flatbush through hands-on exhibits, storytelling, seasonal celebrations, and craft workshops. Activities are free and open to all.

Sony Wonder Technology Lab

550 Madison Ave. (at 56th Street)
(212) 833-8100
www.sonywondertechlab.com
Hours: Tues through Sat, 10 a.m.–5 p.m.; Sun, noon–5 p.m.

Start your visit off by meeting B. B. Wonderbot, the talking, all-knowing robot, and wind your way through four floors of interactive fun. Then walk out with your very own "Certificate of Achievement in the Advanced Program in Communication Technology." This is a very popular site; you're advised to make reservations by calling the above number at least a week in advance. They accept reservations only Tues through Fri from 8 a.m. to 2 p.m. You can get in without a reservation, but it could be a long wait in line. Also, don't miss a chance to attend their children's film screenings once a month in their amazing high-definition theater. Films for grown-ups are shown on Saturday afternoons twice a month.

STORES **FOR** THE **FUN** OF **IT**

There are a few stores around the city that are too amazingly fun to miss. Of course, the danger here is that you'll be tempted, pressured, or whined into spending some actual money. If you can think of these as incredible interactive museums (without gift shops!), then you'll have a great time playing with their "exhibits."

F.A.O. Schwarz
767 Fifth Ave. (at 58th Street)
(212) 644-9400
www.fao.com

They have crowned themselves "The Ultimate Toy Store"—and they live up
to the billing. Three huge floors of the newest, biggest, best, most state-of-
the-art (and most expensive!) toys and games to be found anywhere in the
world, and almost all of them are available for you to play with. Plenty of
costumed characters, roving magicians, and ridiculously friendly staff make
any visit a fun and memorable one.

Halloween Adventure
104 Fourth Ave. (at 11th Street)
(212) 673-4546
www.halloweenadventure.com

Make a day of walking around this store, playing with all the unusual nov-
elty items and gags, trying on the wild costumes, masks, and hats. And for
an extra little treat of tricks, head downstairs to the magic department,
where they are always demonstrating some amazing magic tricks, or maybe
even see a whole magic show at their theater, where they offer free magic
shows throughout the year (except during Oct).

NBA Store
666 Fifth Ave. (at 52nd Street)
(212) 515-6221
www.nba.com/nycstore

If you're a basketball fan, this place is a slam dunk. Of course, you'll find
every piece of NBA and WNBA paraphernalia you could imagine, but you
don't need to buy a thing to have a great time. Lots of free video games,
basketball carnival games, and even a full-size cushioned basketball court
make the spot worth a visit. They also host a full schedule of special events,
including in-store appearances and workshops by basketball greats and concerts. Check the website for a schedule of special events.

New York Doll Hospital
787 Lexington Ave. (between 61st and 62nd Streets)
(212) 838-7527

This trauma center for teddy bears and other cuddlies in critical condition is unlike any shop you've been in before. If you're prepared for piles of decapitated dolls, unstuffed animals, and just some of the oddest and rarest (and most different-looking) dolls anywhere, then stop by to see who has checked in recently. The doctor on call is sure to be the third-generation owner Irving Chais, a seemingly curmudgeonly fellow who turns kindhearted when kids come by to visit his patients.

Nintendo World

10 Rockefeller Plaza (48th Street, between Fifth and Sixth Avenues)
(646) 459-0800
www.nintendoworldstore.com

You and your kids will definitely make the "Wii" sound at this video game wonderland. Spread out over two levels, this store offers over 10,000 square feet of hands-on gaming entertainment. You can try out every game and system Nintendo has to offer, including the latest games for the Wii, DS, and Game Boy, as well as classics like Super Mario Brothers and Pokemon, at their more than fifty interactive game stations. Warning: Plan to spend plenty of time here, because it may be hard to drag yourself, eh . . . I mean your kids away from the games.

STORYTELLING

Bank Street Bookstore

610 W. 112th St. (at Broadway)
(212) 678-1654
www.bankstreet.edu/bookstore

Bank Street Bookstore is considered one of the best bookstores for and about children in the city. Every week you'll find many author readings, musical performances, and costumed characters for children, as well as discussions and presentations for parents. Events are scheduled at various times throughout the week. Call or check their website for details. Almost all events are free, though some require reservations.

Playtime!

From the countries that brought you Lego and Brio comes a chance to bring your children (age five and younger) for an informal playtime every Saturday, noon to 5 p.m. (except during the summer), in theHeimbolt Family Children's Learning Center at the Scandinavia House. Kids will find lots of toys to play with (coincidentally, Lego and Brio), Scandinavian costumes, storybooks in the Scandinavian languages (and English), and even a stage. Children, parents, and caregivers from all backgrounds are welcome. The Scandinavia House is located at 58 Park Avenue (between 37th and 38th Streets). For more information call (212) 879-9779 or check the website www .scandinaviahouse.org.

Barnes & Noble
www.barnesandnoble.com

At every Barnes & Noble superstore, you'll find lots of free readings every week for kids and adults. At these locations you'll find story times where B&N staff, authors, costumed characters, and other guest readers gather children around to hear a book or a story. Of course, the kind folks at Barnes & Noble wouldn't mind if you decided to buy the book, but that's up to you. Call stores or check their website to confirm dates and times.

Books of Wonder
16 W. 18th St. (between Fifth and Sixth Avenues)
(212) 989-3270
www.booksofwonder.com
Every Sun at noon.

This is a literary wonderland for kids and one of the few remaining independent bookstores in the city devoted solely to children's books. They host an overflowing schedule of readings and events (almost all free) that varies from week to week. You can join them every Sun for story time: Staff members read their favorite classic and contemporary children's stories.

CityParks Kids

Various parks throughout the five boroughs
(212) 360-8290
www.cityparksfoundation.org or www.nycparks.org
May through Aug.

Forget about the hassle of getting on a train or in a car to entertain the kids—CityParks Kids brings the fun to you. Throughout the summer, this program schedules a series of performances (storytellers, children's theater, puppet shows) in large and small public parks throughout the five boroughs. Call or check their website for locations and schedules.

Hans Christian Andersen statue

Central Park
Enter at 72nd Street and Fifth Avenue
www.hcastorycenter.org
Sat, 11 a.m.–noon, June through Sept (rain or shine).

This is storytelling at its purest: No reading, just master storytellers recounting tales from around the world (and, of course, featuring many by Mr. H. C. Andersen himself). Once the weather turns cooler, the storytelling moves to the comfortable confines of the Scandinavia House (58 Park Ave. between 37th and 38th Streets) on the second Sat of each month at 11 a.m. (from Oct through May). For more information on the Scandinavia House schedule, call (212) 879-9779 or check the website www.scandinaviahouse.org. The stories are appropriate for children age five and older.

Logos Bookstore

1575 York Ave. (between 83rd and 84th Streets)
(212) 517-7292
http://logosbookstorenyc.com
Mon at 3 p.m.

Join the wonderfully energetic staff storyteller Devorah Hankin every Monday afternoon at 3 p.m. for story time. Devorah picks out a few of her favorite new and classic children's stories and shares them with the little ones for a delightful afternoon.

New York Public Library
www.nypl.org/branch/events

Almost every branch of the NYPL has a children's section with regularly scheduled readings for kids at least once a week. Many—such as the Donnell Library (20 W. 53rd St., between Fifth and Sixth Avenues; 212-621-0618)— have lots of special classes and workshops in everything from poetry to cat's cradles. For more details pick up a copy of the monthly *Events for Children and Young Adults* catalogs at any branch or check out the library's website. (For branch locations see Appendix C.)

NYU Program in Educational Theatre
Provincetown Playhouse
133 MacDougal St. (between West 3rd Street and Washington Square South)
(212) 998-5868
http://steinhardt.nyu.edu/music/edtheatre
Sun at 3 p.m.

A popular series of professional storytellers from around the country and around the world. The program also presents a couple of free theater productions for children and young adults each year in the Black Box Theater. Call for schedule and details.

The Scholastic Store
557 Broadway (between Prince and Spring Streets)
(212) 343-6166
www.scholastic.com/sohostore

Drop by this colorful, energetic store almost anytime, and you'll find something going on for you to enjoy. Every month the people who brought you Clifford the Big Red Dog and Harry Potter put together a full schedule of special events and hands-on activities, including author signings, celebrity appearances, craft workshops, and, of course, regular story times (Tues and Thurs at 11 a.m.). Check the website or drop by the store for the schedule of events.

EDUCATION:
CENTS-LESS SMARTS

"We haven't the money, so we've got to think."

—LORD RUTHERFORD

From Ivy League colleges to technical schools, from GED to PhD., from continuing education to just-for-fun classes, if you can think of it (and even if you can't), you can learn it in New York. Many classes offered are completely free of charge and with no catch, while others can be had for nothing (or next to nothing) if you're willing to volunteer your time instead of paying. When volunteering, you're put to work in administrative offices, studios, or classrooms, and your work hours are exchanged for classroom hours. You will find the math for these exchanges spelled out in each listing, but always check with the school to confirm these details. The economics of these work-study programs can change over time.

ARTS

Chambers Pottery
153 Chambers St., second floor (between Church Street and West Broadway)
(212) 619-7302
www.chamberspottery.com

The Catch: Work-study in exchange for free classes. The math: 3 hours of work = 1 hour of free class time.

This small Tribeca pottery studio offers classes for children and adults. A limited amount of space is available for work-study students.

Dieu Donne Papermill
433 Broome St. (between Broadway and Crosby Street)
(212) 226-0573
www.dieudonne.org

The Catch: Internship/work-study program. The math: 8 hours of work = 1 hour of studio time, plus after 6 to 8 weeks of work you can take a class for free.

This is the place to go in New York to learn everything about the art of hand papermaking. This studio, gallery, and mill in SoHo is a very small operation, so interns often get the chance to work in the studio assisting masters of the art, as well as performing all the usual glamorous intern duties (cleaning, filing, running errands, etc.). You will need to commit to working one full day a week (11 a.m. to 6 p.m.), and they would like you to stay for at least six months.

Downtown Community Television Center (DCTV)
87 Lafayette St. (between White and Walker Streets)
(212) 966-4510
www.dctvny.org

The Catch: Interns work sixteen hours a week in exchange for free classes and equipment and facilities rental.

Learn the creative and technical skills you need to produce your own television programs. DCTV offers interns the use of top-of-the-line equipment and studios and classes in every aspect of television production, in exchange for time spent working in their offices or on their cable TV productions.

Downtown Third Thursday
Various historic locations around downtown
(212) 835-2789
www.downtownny.com/thirdthursdays

The Catch: Free admission, but reservations are required.

You are cordially invited into some of the most exclusive and eye-popping locations throughout downtown to hear some of the most informed authors and historians tell you what they know. This delightful lecture series runs the third Thurs of every month from Jan to May. The public gains access to some hidden architectural gems, both classic and modern, and gets to hear talks by some of New York's smartest folks on the issues, history, and architecture of the downtown area. Reservations are required, but all events are free.

Film/Video Arts
462 Broadway, Suite 520 (at Grand Street)
(646) 257-2246

The Catch: Interns work sixteen hours a week in exchange for free classes and equipment and facilities rental.

Michael Moore, the producer and director of the documentaries *Roger and Me, Bowling for Columbine, Fahrenheit 9/11, Sicko,* and *The Awful Truth* on

Bravo—and an F/VA alumnus—says this about F/VA: "Film/Video Arts puts this art form in the hands of people who really aren't supposed to be doing it because it is really such an expensive process. What Film/Video Arts has done is to say, 'Money should not be in the way of getting these resources in the hands of people whose stories we should hear.'" F/VA provides equipment, state-of-the-art facilities, and a full schedule of classes for film and video production to all for low rates, but for interns it's all free.

Greenwich House Pottery

16 Jones St. (between Bleecker and West 4th Streets)
(212) 242-4106
www.greenwichhousepottery.com

The Catch: Work-study assistants work in the office, gallery, library, studio, or classes in exchange for free or reduced-rate pottery classes.

A full schedule of pottery classes for children, teens, and adults. Greenwich House also has a very fluid and somewhat negotiable work-study program. Students can work in a variety of positions for one to eight hours a week to be a part of the program. Depending on what skills you have and the job you take on, you can get anywhere from $125 off tuition to full tuition plus free firing time and twenty-four-hour access to the studio.

Institute for Fine Arts at NYU

The James B. Duke House
1 E. 78th St. (at Fifth Avenue)
www.nyu.edu/gsas/dept/fineart

Though they don't like to advertise it, every Fri at 4 p.m. during the school year the institute invites the public to the elegant and monumental halls of the Duke mansion to attend the Silberberg Lectures in the Fine Arts. This is a series of lectures by leading scholars from institutions around the country. The lectures are aimed at the institute's grad students, so this is pretty serious stuff. For more information and a schedule of lecturers, check out their website.

The Jazz Museum in Harlem

Harlem School for the Arts
104 E. 126th St., Suite 2D (between Park and Lexington Avenues)
(212) 348-8300
www.jazzmuseuminharlem.org

Outside of its birthplace of New Orleans, no place has nurtured and had as much of an impact on jazz music's development as Harlem. This museum (which is more of a concept than an actual brick-and-mortar museum) takes on the mission of educating and enlightening audiences about jazz's storied past, vital present, and evolving future, especially as it relates to Harlem. They offer a full schedule of free courses and lectures throughout the year. Jazz For Curious Listeners is a hands-on exploration of various aspects of jazz history, techniques, and its personalities. These courses, held on Tuesday evenings (two to three sessions per course), are led by museum director Loren Schoenberg and guest lecturers. Harlem Speaks is a bimonthly lecture series with leading jazz musicians and others devoted to "keeping the flame of jazz alive in Harlem." They also present many free concerts throughout the year. Check their website for a schedule and details. Seating for classes is limited, and registration is required.

Manhattan Neighborhood Network (MNN)
537 W. 59th St. (between Tenth and Eleventh Avenues)
(212) 757-2670
www.mnn.org

The Catch: You must be a resident of Manhattan and agree to produce a program for public access TV.

These organizations administer public access for cable TV services in Manhattan and Queens. The federally mandated obligation of cable TV is that they must provide a channel for all residents to exercise their First Amendment right of freedom of expression. They provide training on production equipment (video production, studio production, editing, audio, basic lighting, digital video and editing, and so on) as well as equipment for programs aired on public access TV. Classes and equipment are also provided in each of the other four boroughs, but there's a small fee charged for classes and materials that runs between $50 and $100 per class. (Contact Queens Public Television [QPTV], 718-886-8160, www.qptv.org; Brooklyn Community Access Television [BCAT], 718-935-1122, www.bricartsmedia.org; Staten Island Community Television, 718-727-1414, www.sictv.org; or BronxNet, 718-960-1180, www.bronxnet.org.)

Urban Glass

647 Fulton St. (entrance on Rockwell, between Dekalb and Fulton Streets)
Brooklyn
(718) 625-3685
www.urbanglass.org

The Catch: Studio and office volunteers are "paid" at a rate of $7.50 an hour. This amount is applied to the cost of any class.

This is New York's only glass-art studio open to the general public. They offer classes in glassblowing, neon, lamp working, casting, and anything else that has to do with glass. The classes can be very expensive ($600 for beginning glassblowing), so it can take a while to gain enough hours to work off the class. The good news is that many of your volunteer hours can be spent in the studio. So you can get a lot of useful hands-on experience while you work (and you may even pick up a few great bits of discarded glass art while tooling around). The bad news is that it gets awfully hot in the studio; dress appropriately.

FOOD & WINE

The Natural Gourmet Institute for Food and Health

48 W. 21st St., second floor (between Fifth and Sixth Avenues)
(212) 645-5170
www.naturalgourmetschool.com

The Catch: Work as a kitchen assistant or in their office to audit classes.

Slice and dice, scrub the pots, and—*Bam!*—you can become the next Emeril (but healthier—the school offers classes in "Health Supportive Cooking"). They have a full schedule of classes to satisfy everyone from the novice cook to the most experienced chef. All classes are vegetarian and have a holistic healing bent. The classes range from basic cooking how-tos like "Knife Skills," "Snack Attack: Healthier 'Junk' Food," and "Choosing Safe Foods" to healthful vegetarian and ethnic specialties like "Dazzling Vegan Desserts," "The Miracle of Miso," and "Authentic Indian Buffet." Kitchen assistants begin working at 5 p.m., an hour before the classes begin, preparing ingredients and the kitchen; participate in and nibble their way through the classes; and clean up the kitchen after the class is over.

New School Food Studies Program

66 W. 12th St. (between Fifth and Sixth Avenues)
(212) 229-5615
www.newschool.edu/ce/foodstudies

The Catch: Work as a kitchen assistant to audit classes or as a work-study office assistant in exchange for classes. Office assistant math: 3 hours of work = 1 hour of class.

The kitchen assistant program is similar to the one at the Natural Gourmet Institute, except the classes are not limited to vegetarian subjects and can be much more indulgent. The schedule includes classes in basic techniques ("How to Boil Water," "Introduction to French Cooking," and "Creative Hors d'Oeuvres"), light and vegetarian cooking ("Low-Fat Sauces," "Light Italian Cooking," and "Cooking for the Way We Eat Today"), holiday cooking and baking ("The Hanukkah Feast," "For Pumpkin Lovers Only," and "Czech Christmas Cookies"), desserts ("Introduction to Cake Decorating," "Strudel Workshop," and "New Chocolate Desserts"). Kitchen assistants do not participate in the classes they work; they only observe. Work-study students are able to take part in classes. Everyone gets to feast on the results of the class work.

Williams-Sonoma

10 Columbus Circle (between 58th and 60th Streets)
(212) 823-9750
www.williams-sonoma.com

The New York flagship location of this high-end purveyor of everything kitchen hosts daily cooking demonstrations every day at 2 p.m. While it's not a hands-on cooking class, you will definitely pick up some useful tips and skills from their highly trained full-time kitchen staff that you can put to use in your own low-end kitchenette. The demonstrations include such subjects as "Knife Skills," "Cupcake & Cookie Decorations," "Braising," "Bread Baking," and many seasonal themes. Stop by the store to pick up a copy of their monthly schedule of demonstrations. If you can't make it for the demos, stop by anytime to try the tempting samples the kitchen is always churning out.

The Wine Workshop

160 W. 72nd St. (between Columbus Avenue and Broadway)
(212) 875-0222
www.ackerwines.com/workshop

As part of Acker Merral Wine Store, "America's oldest and finest wine shop" (if they don't say so themselves), the Workshop offers a full schedule of classes on wines. Prices range from $85 to $1,000 a class, but you can get in on these for nothing as a pourer. Pourers may not always get the chance to actually taste the pricey wines they are pouring for the paying students; this depends on the number of people in the class. If there is room, pourers are welcome to drink up. Of course, volunteer pourers must be prepared to show up early to help set up, pitch in during the class, and stay after to help clean up. Call the workshop to add your name to the list, and they will call you when they have an opening in a class. You can also stop by the store any Saturday afternoon (2 to 5 p.m.) to sample some of their fine wines (they will do all the pouring then).

MIND

Apple Store

767 Fifth Ave. (between 58th and 59th Streets)
(212) 336-1440
www.apple.com/retail/fifthavenue

If you are an Apple computer person, these stores will be heaven for you. The stores are more like community clubs with a jam-packed schedule of free workshops and performances. Every day they have classes on everything from digital photography and music to business applications and podcasting and more. In the evenings, the stores have a regular schedule of in-store performances every month by well-known musicians. Additional locations are at 103 Prince St. (212-226-3126, www.apple.com/retail/soho); 401 W. 14th St. (212-444-3400, www.apple.com/retail/west14thstreet); and 1981 Broadway (212-209-3400, www.apple.com/retail/upperwestside).

Brooklyn Public Library's Business Library

280 Cadman Plaza West (between Tillary and Pierrepont Streets)
(718) 623-7000
www.biz.brooklynpubliclibrary.org

An abundance of classes and workshops are offered throughout the year targeted toward entrepreneurs, small-business owners, students, small investors, and anyone interested in Brooklyn business. Some highlights include an entrepreneur series, a business fair in May and June, and the "Made in Brooklyn" breakfast series (Yes! Including a free continental breakfast) highlighting specific industries in Brooklyn, from music and film to key lime pies and Caribbean beef patties. They also play host to the SCORE program, in which small-business start-ups get personalized mentoring from established and retired business owners. Free Wi-Fi access is available as well.

The Cooper Union for the Advancement of Science and Art

Cooper Square (8th Street between Bowery and Third Avenues)
(212) 353-4120
www.cooper.edu

The Catch: Brains, brains, talent, and brains, plus a $65 application fee.

Every one of the 900 students at this top college of art, architecture, and engineering attends completely tuition-free. They do have to cover their own room, board, books, and student fees (totaling about $1,500 a year), but the $30,000 tuition bill is on the house. It shouldn't surprise you that the competition to get into this premier school is pretty stiff. Each year about 2,600 men and women from around the world apply for Cooper Union, and only about 300 are accepted. Gentlemen, start your slide rules.

Eglise Français Du St. Esprit

109 E. 60th St. (between Park and Lexington Avenues)
(212) 838-5680
www.stespritnyc.net

Free beginning and intermediate French classes are taught every Sun from 10 to 11 a.m. These are very small and intimate classes (they have room for no more than ten students per class). They run from Sept through Dec and Jan through June.

Libraries with Class!

At branches of the New York Public Library (www.nypl.org), Brooklyn Public Library (www.brooklynpubliclibrary.org), and Queens Public Library (www.queenslibrary.org), you will find literally thousands of free classes, lectures, and workshops in everything imaginable offered throughout the year. Here is just a sampling of classes. For details and schedules stop into any branch or check the websites.

The Art of Breathing and
   Relaxation
The Art of Public Speaking
Ballroom Dancing
Basic and Intermediate Internet
Bead Making Workshop
Become a Stamp Collector
The Big Apple on the Big Screen
Bridge Club
Cantonese Program for Parents
Career Exploration Inventory
Checking and Credit 101
   Workshop
Citizenship Preparation Workshop
   in Mandarin
Computers for Seniors
Conserving Home Energy
Create a Quilt
Create Your Own Photo Album
Crocheting Class
Dance with a Mexican Touch
Doing Business in Taiwan
Drum Clinic
E-mail Basics

ESOL Class
Estate Planning
401(k) Rollover
GED Class
The History of Greenwich Village
How to Read the NYC Subway
   Map
Illustrated Bookmaking
Introduction to Computers
Jewelry Making
Knitting Classes for Beginners
Learning about the Rights of
   Immigrants
Makeup Tips and Techniques
Origami
Picture Book Hour
Poetry Writing Workshop
Polish Your Résumé!
Success in Math
Tai Chi for Seniors
Telescope Moon Watching
Toddler Time
Watercolor Class
Work for the U.S. Postal Service

English Classes for Speakers of Other Languages
New York Public Library
Various branches in Manhattan, the Bronx, and Staten Island
(212) 340-0918
www.nypl.org

Beginner and intermediate English classes are offered three times a year (fall, winter, and spring). Space is limited, and registration is required. Check the website for branch locations and class schedules.

Henry George School of Social Science
121 E. 30th St. (between Park and Lexington Avenues)
(212) 889-8020
www.henrygeorgeschool.org

Free adult education classes that deal with the hidden factors at work in the economy. Classes include "Progress and Poverty" and "Applied Economics and Economic Science." The classes meet once a week for ten weeks; preregistration is required. They also offer free film forums and upper-level courses such as "Current Events," "The Genesis of Modern Economics," and "Money and Banking." All courses and forums are offered in Spanish as well.

Housing Education Program
NYC Department of Housing Preservation and Development
100 Gold St., Room 6C
(212) 863-8830
www.nyc.gov/hpd

The Catch: You must be a New York City resident or property owner.

This city-run program offers a comprehensive set of courses to help homeowners learn how to keep their properties in good fiscal and physical health. Classes include "Basic and Advanced Building Management," "Building Finances," "Tenant Relations," "Building Maintenance," and others. Courses are generally offered three to five times a year, but many fill up quickly; early registration is recommended.

Small Business Development Center (SBDC)

Pace University, 163 William St., sixteenth floor
(between Ann and Beekman Streets);
(212) 618-6655
Baruch College, 55 Lexington Ave. (at 24th Street); (646) 312-4790
www.nyssbdc.org

Ready to start your own business but haven't got a clue what to do? Well, you are going to want to get to know the folks at these development centers. Basically, this is your uncle in the business who is going to help you do it right. These centers (two of eighteen throughout the state) are sponsored by the federal government, New York State, and the local universities. They are there to help you through every step of the start-up process and will

---

Get a Job, Get a Degree

New York is home to many top-ranked universities and countless other colleges and technical schools throughout the five boroughs. Like any business, these schools need a large support staff to keep the doors open and the students happy—and that's where you come in. From office assistants and administrative staff to maintenance and mailroom clerks, almost all of these jobs include the fringe benefit of free or seriously reduced tuition for classes at these and affiliated schools. So instead of paying $30,000 a year for that graduate degree, why not have them pay you for your time? Forget about paying $10,000 to become a computer systems analyst; you can take advantage of the system to get it for nothing. Salaries at the schools vary, but you probably won't be making the kind of money you can retire on. Still, this extra benefit can make it a very profitable position. Here are some places to start your search:

Columbia University, 475 Riverside Dr., Room 1901 (between 119th and 120th Streets); (212) 870-2425; www.columbia.edu/cu/jobs.

New York University, 7 E. 12th St., first floor (at Fifth Avenue); (212) 998-1250; www.nyu.edu/employees/hr-at-your-service.html.

www.higheredjobs.com

---

continue to offer assistance for as long as you're in business, with one-on-one coaching and workshops in everything from business plan development and financial planning to marketing strategies and management. There is never a charge for any of their counseling services, and most classes and workshops are free as well.

BODY

Bikram Yoga NYC
797 Eighth Ave., fourth floor (between West 48th and West 49th Streets)
(212) 245-2525
www.bikramyoganyc.com
Fri at 11:30 a.m., pay-what-you-wish class.

The Catch: Work the front desk for five hours a week for unlimited free classes.

Bikram has become the hottest craze in yoga, in more ways than one. This popular yoga studio literally turns the heat up to more than one hundred degrees for its ninety-minute classes, guaranteeing you will be dripping and exhausted from this vigorous workout. This can be an addictive and expensive habit, with each class running $23. Of course, there is a way to stretch your dollars here. Every Fri at 11:30 a.m., they offer a pay-what-you-wish class where anyone can show up and pay as little as they want for the class. All proceeds from that weekly class go to benefit the AIDS organization Equity Fights AIDS. And if one class a week doesn't satisfy your need for sweat, you can sign up to work one five-hour shift a week at the desk for unlimited free classes. Students are required to take classes for a few months before they can take part in the work-study program. They have three other studios around the city where you can do your work-study, but you have to fill out an application and interview at this location.

Dias y Flores
520–522 E. 13th St. (between Avenues A and B)
(212) 260-9344
http://diasyfloresgarden.wordpress.com

This community garden offers free yoga, tai chi, and drawing classes during the summer months. All supplies for the drawing classes are provided free, but bring your own yoga mats and towel for the others. Class offerings vary from summer to summer; call for schedules and details. The website is also a great resource for free happenings in community gardens all around the city.

High Vibe Health & Healing
138 E. Third St. (between First Avenue and Avenue A)
(212) 777-6645
www.highvibe.com

This "living food" and health supplements store offers free classes on such subjects as fasting, family nutrition, essential oil treatments, and gallbladder and liver detox. They also hold raw food preparation workshops, but they charge for those.

Lululemon Athletica
1928 Broadway (at 64th Street)
(212) 712-1767
www.lululemon.com

Once a week this top-of-the-line yoga apparel store pushes the clothing racks aside and turns the shop into a yoga studio. They offer a free yoga class every Sun from 8 to 9 p.m. The classes change from week to week but are always led by instructors from some of New York's chichi-est gyms and yoga studios, including Clay, Reebok Sports Club, Bikram Yoga NYC, Exhale Spa, and others.

The Ohashi Institute
147 W. 25th St., sixth floor (between Sixth and Seventh Avenues)
(800) 810-4190
www.ohashiatsu.org

The Catch: Work-study students may work in the office, on the cleaning crew, or on special projects in exchange for credit toward classes. The math: 1 hour of work = $10 credit toward class for the first year, $12 thereafter.

Ohashi offers a six-level curriculum on its own style of shiatsu massage (Ohashiatsu) that can be taken by both professionals and laypeople. Ohashiatsu is a stretching, relaxing, and energizing acupressure type of massage that works with the Eastern healing philosophies of chi (energy) and the meridians (energy channels) of the body.

SPIRIT

The Asian Classics Institute/
Three Jewels Community Center
61 Fourth Ave. (between 9th and 10th Streets)
(212) 475-7752 or (212) 475-6650
www.world-view.org

The institute offers general-interest and teacher-training courses in Tibetan Buddhism, meditation, and Tibetan language, all free of charge. The general-interest courses are drop-in classes open to all, and the formal study teacher-training courses are open to those "willing to make a serious commitment to their studies." These courses have attendance requirements, homework assignments, and tests. The Three Jewels Community Center offers free meditation classes, free coffee and tea, free Internet access, and a free lending library.

Falun Dafa
Central Park (59th Street and Central Park West) and many other sites throughout the city
(212) 978-9511 or (877) FALUN-99
www.falun-ny.net

The Catch: None (as long as you aren't in China)

From the folks who brought you tai chi comes a new, very old traditional Chinese exercise, Falun Dafa (or Falun Gong). It's a practice that aims to improve mental and physical well-being through a series of easy-to-learn exercises, meditation, and development of "one's Heart/Mind Nature." And from the folks who brought you Tiananmen Square comes a whole new wave of oppression. Falun Dafa is the group that gained a lot of attention by being banned in China, and it has seen brutal suppression of its practitioners by the Chinese government. So there must be something to it. They offer free introductory classes as well as weekly group practices.

Manhattan Jewish Experience (MJE)

131 W. 86th St. (between Columbus and Amsterdam Avenues)
(212) 787-9533
www.jewishexperience.org

If you're like me and all you remember about Hebrew school as a kid was falling asleep, then here's your chance to try it again. The big difference is that this time you'll stay awake and maybe even enjoy it. MJE offers a full schedule of basic courses for free, including the Monday Night Lounge, which includes a sushi dinner and interesting discussions of how current issues (sexuality, free will, business and medical ethics) relate to the ancient religion, followed by music and dessert. They also offer free basic Learn to Read Hebrew classes (and intermediate and advanced courses for $5 a class). Classes are fun, unintimidating, interactive, and geared for all Jews, particularly those with little or no background in Judaism. These classes are not meant to recruit Jews into a particular sect, but to help you gain a deeper understanding of the age-old traditions and how they fit into modern life. Plus, it's not a bad place to meet a nice Jewish girl or guy and make your mother happy. They also have a full program of intermediate and advanced courses and lectures for which they do charge a small fee ($5 per class). Hey, they even set out some free soft drinks and noshes. MJE has two other locations: 5 E. 62nd St. between Fifth and Madison Avenues, and 133 E. 29th St. between Sixth and Seventh Avenues.

The Open Center

83 Spring St. (between Broadway and Lafayette Street)
(212) 219-2527, ext. 117
www.opencenter.org

The Catch: Volunteer four hours a week for unlimited free classes (depending on availability).

They offer a huge array of classes and workshops in holistic learning and living. There are classes in everything from feng shui, reflexology, belly dancing, and salsa aerobics to Taoism, Kabbalah, tantric sex, and herbalism. You can also find ongoing yoga and meditation classes here, as well as a number of certification programs. They treat their volunteers with great respect and support. If you're interested in alternative learning, this is the place for you.

Shambhala Center of New York

118 W. 22nd St., sixth floor (between Sixth and Seventh Avenues)
(212) 675-6544
www.ny.shambhala.org

The Catch: Three free classes each week (donations requested, but not required). Work-study is also available for other classes. The math: 1 hour work = $10 class credit.

The Shambhala Center offers a full schedule of classes and lectures on all forms of meditation, yoga, and Buddhist and Eastern practices. Each week they hold two "Learn to Meditate" classes (Wed at 6 p.m. and Sun at noon) and an "Open Dharma Gathering" (Tues at 7 p.m.), which includes a guided meditation and lectures by noted teachers. Both of these classes are on a donation basis. You can also take part in their work-study program to take any of their classes for free. Each hour of work nets you $10 credit toward classes.

HEALTH & MEDICAL:
LIVE FREE OR DIE

"Always laugh when you can. It is cheap medicine."

—LORD BYRON

New York surely ranks among the most expensive places to stay healthy. From ordinary checkups to health insurance, getting sick here will cost you. The good news is, New York is also one of the major centers for medical schools and clinical studies, which provide many opportunities for free and low-cost care, often with cutting-edge treatments (excuse the pun). New York is also a center for bleeding-heart liberals, so in this town big government still plays some role in providing services to those in need of low-cost health care through the extensive Health & Hospitals Corporation system and at some community clinics.

TO **YOUR** HEALTH: **FREE** CLINICS

In a day and age when medical costs are sky-high and the cost of health insurance is just as stratospheric, it would seem to be just a fantasy that such a thing as a free clinic still exists—right? Well, stop dreaming and start dialing to get yourself an appointment, because it really does, and not just one but two are right here in New York City. These two clinics, one in Manhattan and one in the Bronx, provide free medical care, health education, and social work services to anyone who is uninsured and older than age nineteen. Both clinics are open only on Saturday mornings and are staffed by the medical students and physicians from NYU Medical School in Manhattan and the Albert Einstein College of Medicine in the Bronx.

ECHO Free Clinic
Walton Family Health Center
1894 Walton Ave. (at East 177th Street)
Bronx
(718) 583-3060 or (800) 836-1316
www.einstein.yu.edu/echo/features.aspx

To make an appointment, call between 9 a.m. and 4:45 p.m. Mon through Fri. Appointments are usually about two months from the day you call. The clinic does take a limited number of walk-ins, but you should be prepared to wait a while.

NYC Free Clinic

The Institute for Urban Family Health
16 E. 16th St., third floor (between Fifth and Madison Avenues)
(212) 206-5200
http://nycfreeclinic.med.nyu.edu

To make an appointment here, you need to call and leave a message with the very specific information the clinic requests on their voice mail. No walk-ins are accepted.

WHATEVER **AILS** YOU:
CLINICAL STUDIES

Medical centers throughout New York run clinical trials for almost any condition imaginable, from cancer to acne, from athlete's foot to weight loss. People are always needed to participate in these studies, and all medication and care are provided free of charge—in fact, you can even get paid for participating in many of these studies.

Columbia-Presbyterian Medical Center

Department of Dermatology
161 Fort Washington Ave., Room 750 (between 165th
and 168th Streets)
(212) 305-6953
www.columbiaclinicaltrials.org

Columbia-Presbyterian is constantly organizing new trials for medication and treatment of various skin conditions, including acne, toe fungus, wounds, and more. Treatment and medication are free, and compensation is provided.

New York Headache Center

30 E. 76th St., second floor (at Madison Avenue)
(212) 794-3550
www.nyheadache.com

The New York Headache Center conducts clinical trials on different medication and treatments for migraines and other types of headaches. All research-related examinations and treatments are free, and financial compensation is often provided.

Guinea Pigs: Student Clinics

Calling all brave souls with sore feet, aching muscles, off-balance polarity, and clogged chi: Students at alternative health schools throughout the city are waiting to rub, prick, and stretch you back to health. All over New York there are schools for everything from acupuncture and herbal medicine to polarity therapy and shiatsu. Many of these schools have clinics attached to them where they offer low-cost (and sometimes free) appointments to the public, on whom the students try out their new skills. It may seem a bit scary to let a newbie acupuncturist loose on you with his needles, but rest assured that these are all advanced students, and they're always watched over by professionals. Here is a list of schools and the services they offer:

Ayurveda's Beauty Care Spa & Bioticare Holistic Center, 99 University Place, fifth floor (between 11th and 12th Streets); (212) 529-3300; www.ayurvedasbeautycare.com; free Ayurveda nutritional counseling is offered at various times throughout the year. They also plan to start offering free or low-cost facials and other skin-care services from students soon. Check their website or call for schedule and details.

The Open Center, 83 Spring St. (between Broadway and Lafayette Street); (212) 219-2527, ext 116; www.theopencenter.org; free reiki, reflexology, and polarity-therapy sessions. Call to put your name on the list of available clients, and a student will call you when they need a warm body to attend a class or to practice on.

Pacific College of Oriental Medicine & Acupuncture, 915 Broadway (between 20th and 21st Streets); (212) 982-4600; www.pacificcollege.edu; low-cost acupuncture and herbal medicine.

The Swedish Institute, 226 W. 26th St. (between Seventh and Eighth Avenues); (212) 924-5900; www.swedishinstitute.edu; massage, $150 for six one-hour sessions or $250 for twelve one-hour sessions; acupuncture, $325 for a consultation plus twelve sessions.

Tri-State College of Acupuncture, 80 Eighth Ave. (at 14th Street); (212) 242-2254 for acupuncture, (212) 242-4307 for herbal medicine; www.tsca.edu; $30 for acupuncture appointments; $20 for herbal medicine appointments (plus the cost of herbs, about $15).

HHC **TO** THE **RESCUE**

New York City Health & Hospitals Corporation (HHC) was created to provide comprehensive medical care to all people "regardless of their ability" to pay. The corporation consists of eleven acute-care hospitals, six diagnostic and treatment centers, four long-term-care facilities, and more than eighty community health clinics. HHC also operates MetroPlus Health Plan, a health maintenance organization (HMO) for Medicaid recipients. You can expect waits to be a bit longer for all appointments and at emergency rooms at these facilities than at private hospitals, but sit tight and they'll get to you. For more information call (212) 788-3321 or check the website www.nyc .gov/html/hhc/html/home/home.shtml.

Manhattan
Bellevue Hospital Center, 462 First Ave. (at 27th Street); (212) 562-4141.

Coler-Goldwater Memorial Hospital, 1 Main St., Roosevelt Island (Coler Campus: 212-848-6000); 900 Main St., Roosevelt Island (Goldwater Campus: 212-318-8000)

Gouverneur Nursing Facility and Diagnostic & Treatment Center, 227 Madison St. (between Jefferson and Clinton Streets); (212) 238-7000.

Harlem Hospital Center, 506 Lenox Ave. (at 135th Street); (212) 939-1000.

Metropolitan Hospital Center, 1901 First Ave. (97th Street, between First and Second Avenues); (212) 423-6262.

Renaissance Diagnostic & Treatment Center, 215 W. 125th St. (between Seventh and Eighth Avenues); (212) 932-6500.

The Bronx
Jacobi Medical Center, 1400 Pelham Parkway South (at Eastchester Road); (718) 918-5000.

Lincoln Medical and Mental Health Center, 234 E. 149th St. (between Park and Morris Avenues, near the Grand Concourse); (718) 579-5000.

Pick a Study, Any Study

To find a study for a particular condition, check out these websites:

National Databases

Center Watch, a friendly consolidated listing by category; www.center watch.com.

National Cancer Institute, a searchable database for clinical trials throughout the country for all forms of cancer; www.cancer.gov.

AIDS Clinical Trial Information Service, (800) 874-2572; www.aids info.nih.gov.

National Institutes of Health, a national database of conditions and studies for clinical trials in everything from acidosis to Zellweger syndrome; www.clinicaltrials.gov.

National Center for Complementary and Alternative Medicine, which has studies throughout the country funded by the National Institute for Health using every kind of alternative therapy, from acupressure to yoga; http://nccam.nih.gov.

New York Medical Centers

Beth Israel Medical Center, www.wehealny.org/studies.

NYU Langone Medical Center, www.med.nyu.edu/clinicaltrials.

NYU AIDS Clinical Trials Unit, (212) 263-6565; www.hivinfosource .org.

Morrisania Diagnostic & Treatment Center, 1225 Gerard Ave. (between East 167th and East 168th Streets); (718) 960-2777.

North Central Bronx Hospital, 3424 Kossuth Ave. (210th Street, between Gunhill and Jerome Avenues); (718) 519-5000.

Segundo Ruiz Belvis Diagnostic & Treatment Center, 545 E. 142nd St. (between Brock and St. Anns Avenues); (718) 579-4000.

Brooklyn

Coney Island Hospital, 2601 Ocean Parkway (between Avenue Z and Shore Parkway); (718) 616-3000.

Cumberland Diagnostic & Treatment Center, 100 N. Portland Ave. (between Park and Myrtle Avenues); (718) 260-7500.

Dr. Susan Smith McKinney Nursing and Rehabilitation Center, 594 Albany Ave. (at Rutland Road); (718) 245-7000.

East New York Diagnostic & Treatment Center, 2094 Pitkin Ave. (between Pennsylvania and New Jersey Avenues); (718) 240-0400.

Kings County Hospital Center, 451 Clarkson Ave. (between Albany and New York Avenues); (718) 245-3131.

Woodhull Medical and Mental Health Center, 760 Broadway (at Flushing Avenue); (718) 963-8000.

Queens

Elmhurst Hospital Center, 79–01 Broadway (at 79th Street); (718) 334-4000.

Queens Hospital Center, 82–70 164th St. (at the Grand Central Parkway); (718) 883-3000.

Staten Island

Sea View Hospital Rehabilitation Center and Home, 460 Brielle Ave. (Bradley and Rockland Avenues); (718) 317-3000.

DEPRESSION/**MENTAL** HEALTH **STUDIES** & CLINICAL **TRIALS**

A number of hospitals and research centers throughout New York conduct ongoing clinical studies of depression and medications for mental illnesses such as Prozac, Zoloft, Wellbutrin, and others. If you qualify for a study, they can provide you with up to one year of free medication and medical care. All studies are supervised and monitored by doctors and psychiatrists adhering to strict clinical testing protocols, some of which could involve the use of a placebo.

Mount Sinai Medical Center, Compulsive, Impulsive and Anxiety Disorders Clinic, 99th Street and Madison Avenue; (212) 241-3116; www.mssm.edu.

Neuropsych Research Associates, 1236 Park Ave. (at 96th Street); (212) 722-6604; www.npavt.org.

New York Psychiatric Institute, Depression Evaluation Service, 1051 Riverside Dr., Suite 3300; (212) 543-5734; www.depression-nyc.org.

St. Luke's/Roosevelt Hospital, Mood Disorders Research Program, 910 Ninth Ave. (at 58th Street); (212) 523-7666; www.wehealny.org.

STD **CLINICS**

There are eleven city-run STD (sexually transmitted disease) clinics located throughout the five boroughs that provide free testing and treatment for all common STDs. They also provide anonymous and confidential HIV testing and counseling. Of course, you can also get free condoms at all locations. These clinics all operate on a take-a-number-and-wait-on-line basis, so you can never predict how long the wait will be. Most clinics are open Mon through Fri from 8:30 a.m. to 4 p.m. and some offer Saturday hours, but always call to check hours and services before heading down to one of these clinics. For more information call the hotline at (212) 427-5120 or check the website www.nyc.gov/health.

Manhattan

Central Harlem STD Clinic, 2238 Fifth Ave. (at 137th Street); (212) 690-1760.

Chelsea STD Clinic, 303 Ninth Ave. (at 28th Street); (212) 239-1718 or (212) 239-0843.

Safety First: Free Condoms

A Cheap Bastard can be a sexy bastard, but there's no reason you can't also be a safe bastard. Here is a list of places to pick up your free condoms.

NYC Condom, locations throughout the five boroughs; www.nyc.gov /html/doh/html/condoms/condoms.shtml. New York City is no stranger to tall, erect structures—think the Empire State Building, the Chrysler Building—but now the city has taken its knack for extreme phallic symbols to the next level by branding its very own condom. The NYC Condom is distributed for free in hundreds of locations throughout the city. Check out the website for the location near you.

Gay Men's Health Crisis (GMHC), 119 W. 24th St. (between Sixth and Seventh Avenues). GMHC provides a huge number of free services for people with AIDS and everything you need for AIDS prevention, including condoms-a-plenty. Check out the front desks on the fourth and seventh floors. For more information on other services they provide, call (212) 807-6655 or (800) AIDS-NYC, or check the website www.gmhc.org.

The Lesbian, Gay, Bisexual & Transgender Community Center, 208 W. 13th St. (between Seventh and Eighth Avenues). The renovated center is home to a full schedule of weekly meetings, support groups, workshops, and social activities, many of which are free. You'll also find the free Pat Parker/Vito Russo Library, and there are always free condoms available at the front desk. For more information on the schedule and activities, call (212) 620-7310, or check the website www.gaycenter.org.

East Harlem STD Clinic, 158 E. 115th St. (off Lexington Avenue); (212) 360-5962.

Riverside STD Clinic, 160 W. 100th St. (between Columbus and Amsterdam Avenues); (212) 865-7757.

The Bronx
Morrisania STD Clinic, 1309 Fulton Ave. (at East 169th Street, off Third Avenue); (718) 579-7714.

Brooklyn
Bushwick Clinic, 335 Central Ave. (between Linden and Grove Streets); (718) 573-4820 or (718) 573-4823.

Fort Greene STD Clinic, 295 Flatbush Ave. Extension, fifth floor (at Willoughby Street); (718) 643-4133.

Queens
Corona STD Clinic, 34–33 Junction Blvd. (between Roosevelt and Northern Avenues); (718) 476-7815.

Jamaica STD Clinic, 90–37 Parsons Blvd., first floor (off Jamaica Avenue); (718) 262-5572.

Rockaway STD Clinic, 67–19 Rockaway Blvd. (at Beach 67th Street); (718) 945-7150.

Staten Island
Richmond STD Clinic, 51 Stuyvesant Place (at Wall Street); (718) 420-4994 or (718) 420-4995.

FITNESS, FUN & GAMES:
CHEAP THRILLS

"I cannot afford to waste my time making money."

—JEAN LOUIS AGASSIZ

Free time is a precious commodity in New York, whether you're visiting or you live here. And no place offers more extravagant ways to drop a load of cash when you're able to break away from the hustle and bustle of life in the big city. But wait! There are also tons of things to do and places to go to wind down without breaking the bank. Here are some suggestions for great destinations, recreational activities, and other ways to take it easy for free in New York City. From kayaking along the Hudson to in-line skating lessons in Central Park and a refreshing dip in any of the many public pools throughout the city, New York City really gives you a chance to enjoy your free time. The schedules change from time to time, so be sure to call and confirm all information before showing up.

PARK **IT** HERE! **PARKS** OFFERING **A** VARIETY **OF** ACTIVITIES

Battery Park City Parks
Hudson River (from Chambers to Vesey Streets)
(212) 267-9700
www.bpcparks.org

This delightful park offers a real windfall of free fun-and-games activities that include volleyball, chess, backgammon, concerts, and in-line skating lessons. You can also borrow a wide variety of recreational supplies like Frisbees, basketballs, jump ropes, board games, and more from the Park House at Rockefeller Park (at Chambers Street; bring a photo ID). They even have a couple of free pool tables available near the Park House. Other programs they run throughout the season include a drumming circle, fishing, bird watching, family dances, lots of children's programs, walking tours, concerts, and on and on. Check out the website for more information, or get a copy of their most recent calendar; they add new activities every season.

Bryant Park
Sixth Avenue (between 40th and 42nd Streets)
(212) 768-4242
www.bryantpark.org

This oasis at the dead center of the frenetic midtown bustle is awash with free activities and entertainment throughout the year. During the warmer months its beautiful lawn is the perfect destination for a quick lunchtime snooze or after-work picnic, as long as it is not crammed with throngs attending one of their many high-profile and star-studded free events. Such events include the early morning *Good Morning America* Concerts, the HBO Monday-night film series, Broadway and dance performances, and many others. They also offer free Pétanque lessons (pronounced *pay-Tonk*), which is basically the French version of boccie with smaller balls (fill in your own joke here). Stop by the free reading room to borrow a book, newspaper, or magazine while lounging around. And in the wintertime they roll up the lawn and bring out the Pond—a state-of-the-art ice-skating rink where the skating is all free (though you will have to pay a steep $7.50 if you need to rent skates).

Central Park
59th Street to 110th Street (between Fifth Avenue and Central Park West)
(212) 310-6600
www.centralparknyc.org

Whole books have been written about this oasis of natural splendor amid the concrete jungle, and there are many entries in this one about specific destinations for free goings-on. Here's a quick rundown of some of the park's free delights: walking tours; in-line skating lessons; tango, salsa, and swing dance; nature exhibits; the Conservatory Gardens; fishing and birding; borrowed sports equipment from the North Meadow Recreation Center; art galleries; theater; concerts; and much more. To get information about anything going on in the park, check the website or stop by one of the park's three visitor centers: Belvedere Castle (mid-park at 79th Street; 212-772-0210), the Dairy (mid-park at 65th Street; 212-794-6564), and the Charles A. Dana Discovery Center (inside the park at 110th Street and Lenox Avenue; 212-860-1370).

Governors Island
New York Harbor
(212) 440-2202
www.govisland.com

After over 200 years as a military facility, this island in the center of New York Harbor has now been turned into a public park and national monument with a fantastic selection of free offerings during the summer. The gratis goodies start off with free ferry rides to and from the island from downtown Manhattan and also include guided tours of the island, concerts, exhibitions, lectures, many family-friendly activities, and breathtaking views of New York and the Statue of Liberty. Check out the website or call for the ferry schedule and event lineups.

Hudson River Park
Harris Street to 59th Street (at the Hudson River)
(212) 627-2020
www.hudsonriverpark.org

Making the link between Battery Park City Park up to Riverside Park, the Hudson River Park is the greatest addition to New York's recreation landscape since 700 swampy acres in the center of Manhattan were made into a humble little park. Once an industrial wasteland, the West Side waterfront is now a major destination for bicyclists and skaters, who can now traverse the entire length of Manhattan. During the summer months it is one of the major epicenters of free fun in New York City. Some of the many free offerings include movies, swing dancing, arts and crafts activities for the kids, Ping-Pong, catch-and-release fishing, open-air professional boxing matches, and concerts. Free kayaking is available at Pier 40 (at Houston Street) and at Pier 96 at 56th Street, and you can roll around the ramps of the state-of-the-art skate park (at Franklin Street), visit a water-park playground on Pier 51 (at Jane Street), and enjoy lots of lush lawns for relaxing and tossing a Frisbee around. The park is still in the building stage and every year brings new activities, facilities, and free fun to the West Side.

Riverside Park
Hudson River between 62nd and 155th Streets
(212) 870-3070 or 311
www.riversideparkfund.org or www.nyc.gov/parks

Riverside Park picks up where the Hudson River Park leaves off to complete the glorious waterfront park that runs practically the entire length of Manhattan. The park's bike and running trails connect, giving you the chance to ride from the South Ferry to the George Washington Bridge, and in between there are endless opportunities for free fun every step of the way. Riverside Park has a full schedule of free events every summer in Riverside Park South (between 62nd and 72nd Streets) that includes films, music and dance performances, and children's events, as well as weekly yoga and Pilates classes. The downtown boathouse has an outpost uptown at 72nd Street for you to enjoy some free kayaking. The remainder of the park is awash in other amenities like public tennis courts, ball fields, a bird sanctuary, a public skate park, gardens, monuments, spectacular views of the Hudson River, and loads of free events throughout the year.

RECREATION **CENTERS**

New York City Department of Parks and Recreation runs forty-two recreation centers throughout the five boroughs, and for the price of $75 a year (yes, a year!) you have access to every single one of them. Now, to be totally honest, some of these are not exactly state-of-the-art facilities, but they do have much of the same equipment you'd find at the high-price gyms around town (Nautilus machines, Lifecycles, free weights, dumbbells, etc.). Some also offer a full schedule of classes (aerobics, yoga, tai chi, boxing, and more), and some even have indoor and outdoor pools (you won't find that at many of the more expensive clubs around town!). Many of the centers also have extensive programs for children and seniors, and all have free after-school programs for kids ages eight through thirteen. The computer resource facilities at many of the centers offer classes and instruction on the Internet and computer programs.

For information check the website **www.nycgovparks.org** and click on "Things to Do," or call 311 (see Appendix D for recreation center locations).

The Catch: Some of the adult classes charge a small fee in addition to the membership.

SKATING, **BIKING** & **RUNNING**

Bike New York
Recycle-A-Bicycle Training Center
5th Street and Forty-sixth Avenue
Long Island City, Queens
(212) 932-BIKE (2553)
www.bikenewyork.org

The Catch: A $20 refundable deposit is required to register for a class.

Whether you are new to navigating New York traffic on your bike or getting back on that bike after years away, you will benefit from taking Bike New York's Savvy Cyclist class. The free one-day class provides the essential knowledge and skills you need to know how to adjust, repair, and ride your bike like an experienced pro. The class is offered on Sat once a month from Mar through Nov. While the class is totally free, they do require a $20 refundable deposit to hold your place in the class. Bike New York also offers other free classes for adults and kids, including classes on commuting with your bike and teaching children how to ride a bike.

Bryant Park Skating Rink
Sixth Avenue (between 40th and 42nd Streets)
(212) 768-4242
www.bryantpark.org

The Catch: Skating is free, but they charge for skate rentals.

Bryant Park is not just a great place for freebies in the summer anymore. From late Oct through Jan, Bryant Park is converted into a winter wonderland with a full-size state-of-the-art ice-skating rink open to the public for free all week long. On the weekends the lines do get long and the ice can be crowded, but the setting is truly a glorious one. If you have your own ice skates, bring them along, or else you will have to pay about $7 to rent skates. Check out the website for the schedule and special events including performances and fun theme nights.

Empire Skate Club of New York

(212) 774-1774
www.empireskate.org

This is a membership organization that welcomes all skaters to join in a number of group skates every week. The Tuesday Night Skate (meets at Blades West, 156 W. 72nd St., between Columbus and Amsterdam Avenues, at 8 p.m.) is for high-intermediate and advanced skaters. The Thursday Evening Roll (convenes at the Columbus Circle entrance to Central Park at 59th St. at 6:45 p.m.) is for all levels. The Sunday Morning Skate (also meets at the Columbus Circle entrance to Central Park at 59th Street, at 11 a.m.) is open to all levels. All skates are canceled in the case of rain or wet streets; call to confirm.

Niketown Running Club

6 E. 57th St. (between Fifth and Madison Avenues)
(212) 891-6453
http://help-us.nike.com/app/answers/detail/article/events
Tues and Thurs at 6:30 p.m. and Sat at 9 a.m.

This is one of those freebies that seems just too good to be true, but trust me, it is for real. Three times a week Niketown hosts a group run for any and all runners of all levels and abilities, and it is absolutely free. Tuesday and Thursday nights at 6:30 and Saturday mornings at 9, runners gather at the store on 57th Street and head into the park for organized runs. The session starts off with a group stretch, and then runners can choose between three different courses that range between 3 and 6 miles. Along the way, the running-savvy Nike staff coach you through the runs and cheer you on as you cross the finish line. You can then head back to the store to top the experience off with another quick group stretch, and then gorge yourself on the free bagels, fruit, pastries, and bottled water. And if you are heading there from work, you can even check your belongings . . . for free! Obviously, they would not mind if you eventually bought a pair of their pricey running shoes, so they always have plenty on hand for you to try on and even sample during your run.

Sky Rink at Chelsea Piers

Pier 61 (23rd Street and the Hudson River)
(212) 336-6100
www.chelseapiers.com

The Catch: *Skating is free, but they charge for skate rentals.*

If you are looking to cool yourself off during the heat of the summer, strap on your ice skates and head down to the Sky Rink at Chelsea Piers on Sunday afternoon from noon to 4 p.m., late May to late Aug. They offer four hours of free general skating, but you will have to choke up about $7 for the skate rentals if you don't have your own pair.

Time's Up

(212) 802-8222
http://times-up.org

An environmental activist organization puts together bike and skate rides throughout the year with a point: Get rid of the cars! Critical Mass is an "organized coincidence" that aims to exercise the rights of skaters and

Ladies, Start Your Skates!

You may have thought Roller Derby was a thing of the past (if you bothered to think about it at all), but the sport is making a subculture comeback with a feminist twist and punk-rock attitude. The **Gotham Girls Roller Derby** is the home of this all-girl sport/spectacle. The league is made up of four teams, Manhattan Mayhem, Brooklyn Bombshells, Queens of Pain, and Bronx Gridlock, with team members who have aliases like Bitchie Slambora, Surly Temple, Stevie Kicks, and Barbara Ambush. And you can play a part in the slam-bash by volunteering to help lay the skating floor and unloading equipment at one of their raucous bouts. Of course, you will get to stick around and enjoy the games for free as well as the live music and after party. They generally have about fifteen volunteers help out each match, and they need you to commit to showing up a few hours before the skating begins and hang out for about forty-five minutes after. To volunteer, e-mail info@gothamgirlsrollerderby.com, or for more information check out their website, www.gothamgirlsrollerderby.com

Get In-Line: Central Park Skate Patrol

Not too steady on those in-line skates? Don't let that stop you from getting out there and hitting the road, but make your first stop (or crash!) at the Free Braking and Safety Clinic in Central Park, taught by certified volunteers. Stationed at the East and West Side 72nd Street entrances to the park every Saturday and Sunday from 12:30 to 5:30 p.m. (mid-Apr to mid-Oct), these kind and patient volunteers will hold your hand while you master the art of staying in an upright position with blades on your feet. Be sure to pick up a copy of their free *Central Park Pocket Guide for Skaters,* which offers a great map and lots of useful information for the beginning skater. They also offer advanced group classes and lessons (but they charge for those). For more information call (212) 439-1234 or check out the website www.skatepatrol.org.

cyclists as road users. Meet at Union Square (14th Street and University Place) at 7 p.m. on the last Fri of every month, year-round. The Moonlight Ride/Roll through Central Park happens on the first Fri of every month at 10 p.m. The group meets at the Columbus Circle entrance to Central Park at 59th Street. The Prospect Park Moonlight Ride/Roll is the second Sat of every month at 9 p.m. and starts at Grand Army Plaza (Flatbush Avenue and Eastern Parkway). Both are relaxing and easygoing tours through these parks. They also run many other rides throughout the five boroughs; check their website for details.

Wednesday Evening Skate club
North end of Union Square (17th Street, between Broadway and Park Avenue)
www.weskateny.org

This very popular Wednesday night skate tours different sections of the city each week and meets between 7:30 and 8 p.m. The group rides for about two hours. Open to all levels.

BOATING

The Downtown Boathouse

Pier 40 (Hudson River at Houston Street); Sat and Sun, 9 a.m.–6 p.m.,
and holidays.
Pier 96 (56th Street and the Hudson River); Sat and Sun, 9 a.m.–6 p.m.,
and holidays; open weekdays (June 15 to Sept 15) 5–7 p.m.;
Wed classes, 6–8 p.m.
Riverside Park (at 72nd Street); Sat and Sun, 10 a.m.–5 p.m.
info@downtownboathouse.org
www.downtownboathouse.org
May through Oct.

These three locations offer free kayaking on a first-come, first-served basis.
They provide the boats, safety equipment, and brief instructions, and you
provide the muscle. You can take a leisurely ride in the local embayment,
and once you have some experience, you can join them on their free three-
hour rides to the Statue of Liberty or the Intrepid Museum. The long rides
leave from Pier 40 at 9 a.m. every Sat and Sun; get there earlier to put your
name in the lottery for a slot. They also hold introductory kayaking classes
every Wednesday evening from 6 to 8 p.m. at Pier 96. The boathouse is
entirely volunteer-run. Volunteer and get yourself some advanced lessons
and extra access to the boats.

Floating the Apple

Pier 40 (Hudson River at Houston Street); Tues and Thurs, 6 p.m. to dusk.
Pier 84 (Hudson River at 44th Street); call for schedule.
(212) 564-5412
www.floatingtheapple.org

Join the crew and hit the high seas . . . well, the choppy Hudson . . . for an
exhilarating afternoon of rowing. This volunteer organization builds their
own vintage-style Whitehall gigs and puts land-loving New Yorkers on the
water. No experience necessary. These friendly folks will deftly guide you
through the whole experience, and you will soon feel like you were born
with an oar in your hand.

The Gowanus Dredgers Canoe Club

2nd Street near Bond Street
Red Hook, Brooklyn
(718) 243-0849
www.waterfrontmuseum.org/dredgers
Weekday evenings and weekends by appointment, spring through fall.

Question: What do Venice and Brooklyn have in common? Answer: Great Italian food, pigeons, and canals. Yes, canals—but you can take a ride through Brooklyn's canals for free! (though the "O Solo Mio" may not be quite as good). E-mail a member of the club through the website, and they will be happy to take you on a canoe trip down this undiscovered trail. They also offer introductory canoe classes many Wednesday evenings and Sunday afternoons and the occasional walking or bicycle tour. Check their website for schedule and details.

For more free kayaking and canoeing in Brooklyn, check out the Red Hook Boaters (www.redhookboaters.org), and in Queens try the Long Island City Community Boathouse (www.licboathouse.org).

EVERYBODY **IN!** PUBLIC **POOLS**

In addition to the pools at the recreation centers (see Appendix D), there are a number of city-run outdoor pools to cool yourself off in during those steamy summer months. These pools are all free and are open from July 4th through Labor Day. Daily hours are generally 11 a.m. to 7 p.m. You can get more information by clicking on "Things to Do" at **www.nycgovparks.org** or by calling the pools directly.

Manhattan

Asser Levy (Midtown East), Asser Levy Place and East 23rd Street; (212) 447-2020.

Dry Dock (East Village), East 10th Street between Avenues C and D; (212) 677-4481.

Hamilton Fish (Lower East Side), Pitt and Houston Streets; (212) 387-7687.

Highbridge (Washington Heights), Amsterdam Avenue and West 173rd Street; (212) 927-2400.

Jackie Robinson (Harlem), Bradhurst Avenue and West 146th Street; (212) 234-9606.

John Jay (Upper East Side), East 77th Street east of York Avenue; (212) 794-6566.

Lasker (Central Park), 110th Street and Lenox Avenue; (212) 534-7639 (Olympic-size pool).

Marcus Garvey (Central Harlem), 124th Street and Fifth Avenue; (212) 410-2818.

Sheltering Arms, West 129th Street and Amsterdam Avenue; (212) 662-6191.

Thomas Jefferson, East 112th Street and Amsterdam Avenue; (212) 860-1372 (Olympic-size pool).

Tony Dapolito (West Village), Clarkson Street and Seventh Avenue South; (212) 242-5228.

Wagner (East Harlem), East 124th Street between First and Second Avenues; (212) 534-4238.

The Bronx

Claremont, 170th Street and Clay Avenue; (718) 901-4792.

Crotona, 173rd Street and Fulton Avenue; (718) 822-4440.

Haffen, Ely and Burke Avenues; (718) 379-2908.

Mapes, East 180th Street (between Mapes and Prospect Avenues); (718) 364-8876.

Mullaly, East 164th Street between Jerome and River Avenues; (718) 538-7083.

Van Cortlandt, West 242nd Street and Broadway; (718) 548-2415.

Brooklyn

Betsy Head, Boyland, Livonia, and Dumont Avenues; (718) 965-6581.

Bushwick Houses, Flushing Avenue and Humboldt Street; (718) 452-2116.

Commodore Barry, Flushing and Park Avenues (between Navy and North Elliot Streets); (718) 243-2593.

Douglas and Degraw, Third Avenue and Nevins Street; (718) 625-3268.

Howard, Glenmore and Mother Gaston Boulevard (at East New York Avenue); (718) 385-1023.

Kosciusko (between Marcy and DeKalb Avenues); (718) 622-5271 (Olympic-size pool).

Red Hook, Bay and Henry Streets; (718) 722-3211.

Sunset Park, Seventh Avenue (between 41st and 44th Streets); (718) 965-6578 (Olympic-size pool).

Queens

Astoria, 19th Street and 23rd Drive; (718) 626-8620 (Olympic-size pool).

Fisher, 99th Street and Thirty-second Avenue; (718) 779-8356.

Fort Totten, 338 Story Avenue (between Murray Avenue and Shore Road); (718) 224-4031.

Liberty, 173rd Street and 106th Avenue; (718) 657-4995.

Staten Island

Faber, Faber Street and Richmond Terrace; (718) 816-5259.

Lyons, Pier 6 and Victory Boulevard; (718) 816-9571.

Tottenville, Hylan Boulevard and Joline Avenue; (718) 356-8242.

West Brighton, Henderson Avenue (between Broadway and Chappel Street); (718) 816-5019.

Everything and Anything

Be sure to get yourself one of the invaluable New York City Department of Parks and Recreation special-events calendars for the year. It lists the vast numbers of activities going on in parks throughout the five boroughs from April through October. Many of these are one-day events that you don't want to miss—the Urban Park Rangers' Falcon Olympics, Haunted Halloween Walks, ethnic celebrations from every corner of the world in every corner of the city, opera, symphony, and philharmonic performances, sports tournaments, and much more. Call 311 or (212) New-York to get a copy, or check their website, www .nycgovparks.org, for an up-to-date schedule. And fear not: The schedule is free, and all the activities are gratis as well.

BEACHES

While no one would confuse New York City with Maui, it does have its fair share of sandy beaches within city limits. The city parks department maintains 14 miles of public beaches, all of which are open from Memorial Day through Labor Day. And you know New York has a much better subway system than Maui. In fact, all city beaches are accessible by public transportation, though some more easily than others. For more information go to **www.nycparks.com** and click on "Things to Do"; then click "Activities/Facilities."

Brighton Beach and Coney Island
Brighton 1st Street to West 37th Street
Brooklyn
(718) 946-1350
www.nycgovparks.org

These two beaches are really one long stretch of shoreline that's a very popular destination because of its legendary reputation and easy accessibility. It's located at the end of the F, D, N, B, and Q subway lines. The throngs also show up because the area offers so much more than just sand and sun. A trip to Coney Island isn't complete without a walk through the new Luna Park and a ride on the oh-so-rickety and oh-so-thrilling roller coaster, the Cyclone (718-373-5862; www.lunaparknyc.com). Don't miss the stalls of antiques/junk/whatever being hawked along Surf Avenue. Farther down the boardwalk is Brighton Beach. Known as "Odessa by the Sea," Brighton has become the home of New York's thriving Russian immigrant community, and a walk along Brighton Avenue certainly makes you feel like you've been transported to the heart of Mother Russia. There are also some amazing deals to be found on fresh fruits, vegetables, and *rugelach* along the avenue.

Jacob Riis Park
Fort Tilden, Gateway National Park
Rockaway, Queens
(718) 318-4300
www.nps.gov/gate

Run by the National Park Service, this small strip of sand located just a short hop from Brooklyn is a very popular destination, particularly on the weekends. When the public beach is overrun, venture onto the private beaches of Rockaway, just a short walk along the dunes. From Brooklyn take the Q35 bus, and from Queens take the Q35 or the Q22 bus.

Manhattan Beach
Oriental Boulevard (from Ocean Avenue to Mackenzie Street)
Brooklyn
(718) 946-1373
www.nycgovparks.org

Located just a bit farther down the shore from Brighton Beach, this more secluded beach isn't quite as populated as the big guys next door and also offers areas for you to fire up the barbecue and picnic. The buses B1 and B49 will take you to the beach.

Orchard Beach
Pelham Bay Park
The Bronx
(718) 885-2275
www.nycgovparks.org

Looking out on Long Island Sound, this is the beach of choice for Bronx residents. The waters are generally calm, and the promenade is quite lively, especially on weekends. They offer free Latin music concerts on the beach

Open the Gate:
Gateway National Recreation Area
Administered by the National Park Service, Gateway is made up of 26,000 acres of parkland that runs through Brooklyn, Queens, and Staten Island, and into northern New Jersey. There's a huge array of activities for kids and adults, from nature walks, concerts, and campfire sing-alongs to sailing lessons, gardening classes, and yoga on the beach. All activities run by the NPS are free and open to all. For a guide to their programs, locations, and activities, call (718) 338-3338 or check their website, www.nps.gov/gate.

every Sunday in the summer. Take the number 12 bus from the Pelham Bay subway station (6 train).

Rockaway Beach
Beach 9th Street in Far Rockaway to Beach 149th Street
Neponsit, Queens
(718) 318-4000
www.nycgovparks.org

Popular with Brooklyn and Queens residents, this long stretch of beach (7 miles) runs almost the entire length of Rockaway. Take the A train toward Far Rockaway; there are many beach stops along the way. If you are looking to hang ten, head to New York's best surfing beaches from Beach 87th to 92nd Streets (take the A train to Beach 90th Street) or Beach 67th to 69th Streets (take the A train to Beach 67th Street).

South and Midland Beaches
Fort Wadsworth to Miller Field
Staten Island
(718) 987-0709
www.nycgovparks.org

Staten Island's has its own secret beaches for sunbathing, swimming, and other activities—and they're hardly ever crowded. South Beach's boardwalk stretches for nearly two miles and is the site for free concerts and fireworks. At the north end of the boardwalk is Ocean Breeze Fishing Pier, one of the largest in the city. Along with plenty of sand and surf, South Beach also has bocce courts, benches, a playground, and picnic areas. Nearby Midland Beach has concession stands, boardwalk vendors, live music, and Sea Turtle Fountain, a fountain with sprinklers that is always popular with little tykes.

LIBRARIES:
FREE ACCESS

*"No entertainment is so cheap as reading,
nor any pleasure so lasting."*

—LADY MARY WORTLEY MONTAGUE

Libraries are the ultimate resource for anyone who wants it all but doesn't want to spend anything to get it. After all, the libraries were established by Mr. "A Penny Saved Is a Penny Earned" himself, Benjamin Franklin. New York has three public library systems: the New York Public Library (in Manhattan, the Bronx, and Staten Island), the Brooklyn Public Library, and the Queens Borough Public Library. The three systems have a network of research libraries and local branches with more than 200 locations throughout the five boroughs (see Appendix C for a complete list of branch locations). At each of these branches, you'll find not only bookshelves full of reading material but also a wide selection of videos and CDs of every kind of music conceivable.

You also have access to computers and the Internet as well as computer classes. In fact, you can find free classes in everything from origami and quilting to job placement and starting a small business. Many branches also have a regular schedule of music, films, theater, and readings. There are many private libraries in New York, too; some charge a membership fee to borrow materials, but all can be a great source for in-house research.

RESEARCH **CENTERS**

The New York Public Library for the Performing Arts
40 Lincoln Center Plaza (65th Street and Amsterdam Avenue)
(212) 870-1630
www.nypl.org/research/lpa/lpa.html

Returned to its home at Lincoln Center after a three-year renovation, this is home to one of the world's most extensive collections of materials in the performing arts. Not limited to books, the library is particularly well known for its huge collections of historic recordings, videotapes, CDs, records, autograph manuscripts, correspondence, sheet music, stage designs, press clippings, programs, posters, and photographs. You can borrow a great deal of the materials in the library, though the archival collections are only available for reference. Being the performing arts library, you would expect they might have a performance or two every now and then—and they certainly don't disappoint. You'll find a full schedule of presentations by prominent actors, composers, musicians, writers, choreographers, and dancers throughout the week.

The New York Public Library Humanities and Social Sciences Library
Fifth Avenue and 42nd Street
(212) 930-0830
www.nypl.org/research/chss

This landmark Beaux Arts building is home to more than one million books, 135 miles of hidden bookshelves, and two friendly lions named Patience and Fortitude. You cannot take any books out of this library, but you are welcome to spend endless hours in their stunning reading rooms—and you will want to. The building underwent a multimillion-dollar renovation, and the grandeur of these rooms, particularly the Rose Reading Room, guarantees you'll be thinking exceptionally intelligent thoughts. Don't miss the one-hour tours of the historic facility every Mon through Sat at 11 a.m. and 2 p.m. Tours of changing exhibitions in Gottesman Hall begin at 12:30 and 2:30 p.m. They also offer an array of classes at the South Court Training Center.

Schomburg Center for Research in Black Culture

515 Malcolm X Blvd. (at 135th Street)
(212) 491-2200
www.nypl.org/locations/schomburg

This is a national research library devoted to collecting, preserving, and providing access to resources documenting the experiences of peoples of African descent throughout the world. Their collection is entirely noncirculation, but they make many of the historic materials available to the public through an extensive schedule of exhibitions, publications, and educational, scholarly, and cultural programs. They do charge for some performances, but many are free. Be sure to grab a free MP3 audio tour when viewing any of their exhibitions.

Science, Industry, and Business Library

188 Madison Ave. (at 34th Street)
(212) 592-7000
www.nypl.org/research/sibl

The nation's largest public information center devoted solely to science and business, the research center houses both a circulating library and an extensive noncirculating collection (1.5 million volumes). The library's Electronic Information Center connects users to the hundreds of internal and external

"Get Ya Free Money Heeere!"!"

Okay, it's not as simple as that, but there is plenty of it out there in the form of grants and scholarships from private and public organizations, and the **Foundation Center** can help you find it (free of charge, of course). The library will help you sift through the more than 47,000 private and corporate giving programs to find the ones that are the best targets for your project. They have free training sessions on funding research, proposal writing, proposal budgeting, and even the occasional networking breakfast (with free pastries and coffee!). The Foundation Center (79 Fifth Ave., second floor, at 16th Street) is open Mon, Tues, Thurs, and Fri, 10 a.m. to 5 p.m.; and Wed until 8 p.m. For more information call (212) 620-4230 or check the website www.fdncenter.org.

electronic information resources, including Internet databases, CD-ROMs, electronic journals, and online services. The Electronic Training Center offers ongoing classes in computer programs, the Internet, research, and business and industry issues. Combined, the two centers have more than a hundred computer workstations ready for public use. Take the free one-hour tour Tues or Thurs at 2 p.m. to learn more about the facilities. For tour information call (212) 592-7000.

PRIVATE **LIBRARIES**

French Institute/Alliance Française
22 E. 60th St. (between Park and Madison Avenues)
(212) 355-6100
www.fiaf.org
Hours: Mon through Thurs, 11:30 a.m.–8 p.m.; Sat, 9:30 a.m.–1:30 p.m.

The Catch: Nonmembers do not have borrowing privileges. Membership is *$95 a year.*

This is the largest collection of all-French materials in the United States. You're welcome to spend all day in the spacious library reading any of the 30,000 French books, perusing the hundreds of French magazines, watching any of the 1,000 French videos, or listening to the many French CDs and French books on tape. In other words, if it's French, it's here.

Goethe Institute
1014 Fifth Ave. (between 82nd and 83rd Streets)
(212) 439-8700
www.goethe.de/uk/ney
Hours: Tues and Thurs, noon–7 p.m.; Wed, Fri, and Sat, noon–5 p.m.

The Catch: Nonmembers do not have borrowing privileges. Membership is *$10 a year.*

This is the German version of the French Institute. The big difference here is that they have half as many books, videos, CDs, newspapers, and magazines (and, of course, they're in German, not French.)

Instituto Cervantes Library

211–215 E. 49th St. (between Second and Third Avenues)
(212) 308-7720, ext. 104
www.cervantes.org
Hours: Tues and Wed, 11:30 a.m.–7:30 p.m.; Thurs and Fri, noon–7 p.m.;
Sat, 10 a.m.–1:30 p.m.

The Catch: Nonmembers do not have borrowing privileges. Membership is
$50 a year.

Okay, this time take the French Institute, double the size of the collection,
translate everything into Spanish, and you have the Instituto Cervantes Library.

The New York Academy of Medicine Library

1216 Fifth Ave. (at 103rd Street)
(212) 822-7300
www.nyam.org
Hours: Mon, Tues, Thurs, and Fri, 9 a.m.–5 p.m.; Wed, 9 a.m.–7 p.m.

This noncirculating research library houses the second-largest medical collection in the United States, following the National Library of Medicine in
Bethesda, Maryland. Its extensive facilities include more than one million
volumes, more than 1,400 current journal subscriptions, and a variety of
electronic resources. They also offer a full curriculum of free classes in various research methods and techniques to make your use of their library (and
all libraries!) much more effective.

Pat Parker/Vito Russo Center Library

The Lesbian, Gay, Bisexual & Transgender Community Center
208 W. 13th St. (between Seventh and Eighth Avenues)
(212) 620-7310
www.gaycenter.org
Hours: Mon through Thurs, 6–9 p.m.; Sat, 1–4 p.m.

The Catch: Nonmembers do not have full borrowing privileges. Membership
is $75.

The collection at this library is geared toward everything to do with gay,
lesbian, bisexual, transgender, and AIDS studies. The library has a collection
of about 12,000 books and more than 500 videos (documentaries and features). When you borrow videos, they ask you to leave a refundable deposit
for the one-week loan.

NEWSPAPERS:
THE FREE PRESS

"Opinions are the cheapest commodities on Earth."

—FRANK BACIC

Times, shmimes. You don't need to throw away $2 a day ($5 on Sunday!) to get your fill of information in New York City. Whatever your interest or point of view, there's a free newspaper out there for you. Granted, the news you get from some of the free presses in the city might have a bit of a skewed worldview. But if you're looking for community news, local entertainment listings, and happenings around town, there are plenty of papers to pick up that you don't need to drop a quarter, a dime, a nickel, or even a penny to get. You'll find most of these papers in those ubiquitous newspaper boxes on almost any major street corner in Manhattan. Some can be found throughout the boroughs but are easiest to come by in Manhattan.

AM New York
(212) 239-5555
www.amny.com

Headline: Pint-size Publication Packs a Punch. One of the most welcome additions to the freescape of New York City, this easily digestible daily newspaper gives you all the news that fits in twenty pages. The perfect companion for your subway ride to work, the tabloid touches on local, national, and international topics and has sections (okay, pages) devoted to travel, food, sports, classifieds, and local events. My favorite feature is their *4 for Free* section, which lists four free events going on around New York every day.

Extra! Extra!

I have to confess that there are times when even I read one of the big daily newspapers, either to get better informed or, in the case of the *Post*, just for laughs. Still, that's no excuse to spend money. If you have access to the Web, you have free access to the newspapers—at least for now (at the time of writing, the New York Times will begin charging for Web access in January). Every one of the major dailies publishes practically its entire contents, along with even more information, on the Web every day. For the *New York Times*, check out www.nytimes.com. The *New York Daily News* is at www.nydailynews .com, and the *New York Post*'s website is www.nypost.com. If you feel the need to get some ink on your hands, you can always find a copy at any local library.

Pick up your free copy any weekday at street-corner boxes throughout the five boroughs.

Downtown Express
(212) 242-6162
www.downtownexpress.com

Downtown Express is a biweekly newspaper covering all the goings-on in Tribeca, Battery Park City, the South Street Seaport, and the Wall Street area in lower Manhattan. This slim publication manages to cover the huge amount of local news, arts, sports, and other happenings below Canal Street. The listings section includes local theater, music, and particularly good coverage of art galleries in the area. The paper is widely distributed in street-corner boxes and stores below Canal Street.

Go NYC
(888) 466-9244
www.gomag.com

This glossy monthly mini-magazine is the place to GO for all things lesbian in NYC. You can find copies in bars and stores all around downtown and selected locations in Brooklyn and Queens. Check their website to find a copy near you.

Jewish Sentinel
(212) 244-4949

As you might imagine, this is the source for all things Jewish around New York—from articles on Israel and the Jewish perspective on New York to a selected listing of cultural events, gatherings, galleries, and performances that might be of interest to the Jewish community. You can pick up a copy at street-corner boxes placed randomly around Manhattan; call for specific locations.

New York Blade News
(212) 352-3535
www.nyblade.com

New York's weekly gay community newspaper covers local and national issues, personalities, and events affecting gay men and lesbians in the city.

It's also a good source for arts listings and community events. The paper is distributed widely on street corners and stores throughout Manhattan and at selected locations throughout the boroughs; call or check the website for specific locations.

New York Press
(212) 244-2282
www.nypress.com

New York's alternative alternative newspaper, the *Press* is chock-full of opinionated and often very funny articles on the politics, characters, events, and arts of the city. Its film, music, and events listings are among the best in the city. You'll find copies on almost any street corner in Manhattan and parts of Brooklyn (downtown, Park Slope, and Cobble Hill). Like the *Voice,* the *Press* is easier to find early in the week; you may have a hard time obtaining one once the weekend rolls around.

Next Magazine
(212) 627-0165
www.nextmagazine.com

Next is a gay magazine that occasionally touches on such subjects as politics and current events but is best relied on for its bar and club listings, reviews, gossip, and nothing-left-to-the-imagination advertising. You can find copies at every gay bar and store in the city, as well as at some street-corner boxes in Chelsea.

NY Metro Parents
(212) 315-0800
www.nymetroparents.com

These monthly magazines, one for each borough (*Brooklyn Parent, Queens Parent,* etc.), are dedicated entirely to parenting in New York City. Each month's issue has intelligent and informative articles, an extensive calendar of events, and lots and lots of advertising. Be aware that the magazine is targeted toward parents with no shortage of cash, so there's no focus on doing things on the cheap. There is, however, some very useful information for all to be found within their pages and on the website. You can find copies in street-corner boxes and stores throughout Manhattan, in Brooklyn Heights, Carroll Gardens, and Park Slope in Brooklyn, and throughout Queens. Check the website or call for specific locations.

The Onion
(212) 627-1972
www.theonion.com

This on-target satirical news weekly takes on national issues, news figures, and "local" events all over the country. While their view on the news can be hysterically funny, their arts section, "The A.V. Club," is surprisingly serious and extensive. The section doesn't include timetables or movie locations, but they do include in-depth reviews and features on almost every film in the theaters at any given time, from Hollywood blockbusters to independents and documentaries. You'll also find good articles on videos and local music picks. You can grab a copy from their boxes located all over Manhattan (most plentifully below 23rd Street and in the Columbia University area) and in Park Slope and Williamsburg in Brooklyn.

Resident
(212) 993-9410
www.resident.com

This weekly magazine focuses on the culture and politics of the city. You'll find regular articles on health, fashion, travel, and restaurants, as well as weekly theater, film, and music picks. The *Resident* is distributed widely in street-corner boxes in Manhattan.

The Village Voice
(212) 475-3300
www.villagevoice.com

The original and still the largest alternative news weekly. Since 1955 the *Voice* has been the place to go to get the other view on anything: politics, art, theater, film, literature, sex, and even a unique take on horoscopes. The paper is sure to annoy you with some of its articles and engage you with others, but you will almost always find them provocative. Even if you never agree with what they have to say, the *Voice* is always worth picking up for the extensive music, film, theater, dance, and art listings, and the sprawling classifieds, which include their no-holds-barred personals. Grab a copy out of one of the red boxes on most street corners around the five boroughs or free at newsstands and stores around the city. Get your copy early in the week; by the time the weekend rolls around, the boxes are usually empty. You can always find a pile of papers outside their downtown office on Bowery between 5th and 6th Streets. Check the website to find a place to pick up a copy near you.

West Side Spirit
(212) 268-8600
http://westsidespirit.com

This weekly paper covers (you guessed it) the West Side. The paper reports on local politics, crime, and events of the areas, and it includes a good citywide listing of arts and community events, with a strong focus on free activities. You can find a copy in corner boxes and stores between 59th and 110th Streets.

FURNITURE &
HOUSEHOLD GOODS:
ONE MAN'S TRASH . . .

*"There are many things that we would throw
away, if we were not afraid that others might
pick them up."*

—OSCAR WILDE

All around the city you'll spot them every other day of the week. Some people call them piles of trash, but the trained eye clearly recognizes them as mountains of treasures. Furnishing New York apartments by "recycling" is not only good for the environment, it's great for the bank account. It's a long-held tradition and a way of life for students, artists, collectors, and anyone with an open mind and a creative eye. You will be shocked at the high caliber of items some people consider garbage, but it makes sense. Consider the fact that New Yorkers on average earn a great deal of money but are forced to live in some of the smallest apartments this side of a shoe box. The result is, folks end up throwing away some mighty fine used stuff to make room for some newer, finer stuff.

Freecycle:
A Little Give & Take

Here is the scenario: Someone across town has just upgraded to a brand-new couch and wants to get rid of that oh-so-cozy but slightly shoddy pullout that has seen him through the leaner times. You are new to town and just finished shelling out every dime you have to secure that pricey New York studio, but now you have to furnish it. It is a match made in heaven, but how do we make the connection? Freecycle! This Web-based recycling group is in existence to empty out your spare closet and fill your neighbor's, or vice versa. All you have to do is go to their website, www.freecycle.org, and connect to the New York branch (this is an international movement verging on two million members worldwide). Once you become a member, for free of course, your inbox will literally be flooded with e-mail offers for stuff (useful and not so useful) every day. A typical day's offerings can run the gamut from the worthwhile (including furniture, books, appliances, clothes) to the kooky (advice, leftovers, broken glass bottles) to the incredibly specific (two yards of yellow felt, size 9.5 women's sensible brown shoes, seventy-five small packets of soy sauce). You are even able to post "Wanted" messages for practically anything you might need. The New York list has a membership of more than 35,000 members (and growing), so, anything you want you can get, anything you want to get rid of someone else wants, and many things you did not know you needed are up for grabs.

FAVORITE **FINDS**

Almost anything you need or want can be found on the street. I can't tell you how many times I have said "I need" this or that, only to come across that exact "this or that" a few days later on the street. You are limited only by your willingness to forage and schlep. Obviously, the smaller the item you're in the market for, the more effort you'll have to put into your search. If you're interested in larger furnishings, however, the sky's the limit. Here are some of my favorite items I've picked up from the street over the years:

Antique trunks
Antique wooden milk crate
Artwork
Bookcases
Chest of drawers
Coffee table
Couch
Decorative window flower box
Desk
Desk chairs
Director's chairs
Doctor's office scale
End tables
Exercise mat
File cabinets
Footstool
Halogen torch lamp

Ironing board
Leather easy chair
Luggage
Microwave oven
Mirrors
Oriental rugs
Ottoman
Plates, bowls, silverware
Power Mac computer, monitor,
    and printer
Spice rack
Storage boxes
Telephone
Toaster oven
Vacuum cleaner
Wicker basket
Window screens

CURBSIDE **SHOPPING** TIPS

Here are some helpful rules to live by when you are on the prowl:

1. Shop in the best neighborhoods: The better off the neighbors, the better the garbage.

2. Know when the shops are open for business: Consult the accompanying map to see what days the Department of Sanitation will be around to

The Big Salvation (Army)!

Not that I'm endorsing the idea of spending cash, but there are times when you can't wait to stumble across that perfect headboard, desk, or butcher-block countertop, and money must be spent. The best option is always to shop at any of New York's many thrift stores. While whole books have been written on this subject alone, there are some standout shops to head for when you're in the market for furniture, appliances, or knickknacks of any kind. Most local thrift stores offer a smattering of sofas, chairs, and china, but their space is limited, so the selection is as well. Still, in each borough you'll find a main **Salvation Army Thrift Store** (usually connected to a warehouse) with huge assortments of goods. While these stores may not be around the corner, the prices and selection make them worth the trip. For some other shopping ideas, see the chapter "Shopping: A Tale of Two Streets," and for a good list of thrift stores throughout the city, check the website www.use.salvationarmy.org/gnyd. Here are the super Salvation Army stores in each borough:

Manhattan:

536 W. 46th St. (between Tenth and Eleventh Avenues); (212) 757-2311.

Brooklyn:

436 Atlantic Ave. (between Bond and Nevins Streets); (718) 834-1562.
22 Quincy St. (between Classon and Downing Streets); (718) 622-5686.

The Bronx:

4109 Park Ave. (at 175th Street); (718) 583-3500.

Queens:

34–02 Steinway St. (between Thirty-fourth and Thirty-fifth Avenues); (718) 472-2414.

Staten Island:

2053 Clove Rd. (at Mosel Avenue); (718) 442-3080.

take away the merchandise. It's best to do your hunting the night before scheduled pickups. You'll generally start to notice piles appearing in the late afternoon and early evening.

3. When in doubt, don't leave it out: If you're considering an item, take it. Undoubtedly it will not be there if you decide to come back for it. But if you take it and it doesn't work or fit your need, you can always re-donate it. Nothing ventured, nothing gained.

4. Don't be a hog: If you find something that turns out not to fit your need, set it back out on the street right away. The temptation is to hold on to this great find and hope you can find a use for it someday. The problem is, you'll

Freegans: Dumpster Dining

The Freegans, truly the masters of the fine art of Dumpster diving, are a group that is on a mission to put an end to our society's rampant materialism by recycling and making use of all the handy materials already produced . . . and chucked out. Every week they lead "trash tours" in various neighborhoods throughout the city where they come up with a huge smorgasbord of discards, and they are always happy to share their techniques and bounty. Nothing is off limits to these folks—furniture, cleaning supplies, household items, office supplies, and food—yes, food! In fact, they specialize in finding gratis goodies. This may sound a bit gross to you, but rest assured we are not talking about half-eaten sandwiches and rotten apples here; this is all packaged and sanitary stuff. Their plan is to "shop" in the trash of some of the finer markets (Food Emporium, Gourmet Garage, Zabar's, etc.) and pick out the items that the retailers feel they can't put on their shelves any longer but are perfectly delicious treats for the savvy scavenger. The Freegans also take part in a wealth of other activities every week, including free build-a-bicycle and bicycle-repair workshops and furniture hunts and repair classes. Even if you are not interested in taking part in their tours and hunts, you should definitely sign up for their e-mails. These people are in on the ground floor of every free event and activity in New York, and they send out great listings to all who sign on. Check them out at www.freegans.net.

end up cluttering up your small studio apartment with stuff you can't use, and the longer you hold on to it, the harder it will be to part with it. Just like ripping off that Band-Aid, do it quick and it will be less painful. And no doubt, someone else will pick it up and be very grateful to you.

5. A little work goes a long way: Repaint it, refinish it, change the knobs, or reupholster the cushion and presto! It's good as new!

6. Clean it. (Hey, you never know. Bedbugs love the furniture in this city, so be sure to clean it good.)

7. Enjoy it.

Happy Hunting!

SHOPPING:
A TALE OF TWO STREETS

"I always say shopping is cheaper than a psychiatrist."

—TAMMY FAYE MESSNER

If you must spend money—and as a rule I do not endorse the practice—there are a couple of streets you should know about to keep this awful habit in check. Of course, there are thousands of stores throughout the city where you can find "a deal." There are also tons of books that tell you where to find these stores, but I'm just going to include a few of the best. On 17th and 32nd Streets, you'll find clusters of some of my favorite shops in New York City—the places where I shop almost to the exclusion of any other stores in town. What makes them so great? You guessed it: great stuff, really cheap.

On West 32nd Street you will find a couple of stores that can supply you with all the essentials of life (food, dishes, books, clothes, furnishings, office supplies, cosmetics, electronics, toys . . .) and many of the absurdities of life ("As Seen on TV" items, last year's fad items, "has-been" pop star paraphernalia, and more) at ridiculously low prices. West 17th Street is the place to head to check out three of the best thrift stores around. These secondhand shops are not necessarily the cheapest in the five boroughs, but you can snag some amazingly high-quality finds at very respectable prices at these shops.

32ND STREET: BARGAIN PARADISE

Jack's 99¢ Stores
110 W. 32nd St. (between Sixth and Seventh Avenues)
(212) 268-9962

You may have come across other 99-cent stores in your travels, but Jack's is hands-down the best there is. This huge store is overflowing with bargains, from the frozen foods section to every household item or office supply you could ever need. While some of the goods are made by companies you may not recognize, a surprisingly large amount of the merchandise is brand name. The wares change on a daily basis, so you could walk the aisles every day and be almost guaranteed of finding something you can't live without (for 99 cents, that is). Located upstairs is Jack's World, where they have another great selection of bargains on higher-ticket items (appliances, furniture, clothes, housewares, toys and games), but here they don't keep to the 99-cent limit. There is a second Jack's 99¢ location at 16 E. 40th Street (between Fifth and Madison Avenues) and another Jack's World at 45 West 45th Street (between Fifth and Sixth Avenues).

32nd Street Gifts
150 W. 32nd St. (between Sixth and Seventh Avenues)
(212) 594-4922

If you're looking for souvenirs, trinkets, balloons, and women's wear, 32nd Street Gifts is a must stop along the strip. Inside its fairly organized, and you can find bargains galore. You won't find many popular brand names, but you're sure to find something interesting, cheap, and maybe even cool among the treasure-filled shelves.

17TH **STREET:** FIRST **IN** SECONDHAND

Angel Street
118 W. 17th St. (between Sixth and Seventh Avenues)
(212) 229-0546

Continue along 17th Street a bit farther and you'll come across Angel Street. Much like Housing Works, it gets great high-quality donations but with more of an emphasis on furnishings and accessories than clothes (though the clothes they do sell, they sell very cheaply). You'll also find enticing daily specials at this boutique-like shop. All proceeds from Angel Street benefit individuals and families affected by substance abuse, HIV, AIDS, and mental illness.

Housing Works Thrift Shops
143 W. 17th St. (between Sixth and Seventh Avenues)
(212) 366-0820
www.shophousingworks.com

Think of Housing Works Thrift Shops as the Bergdorf Goodman of second-hand. The designer clothing, furniture, housewares, art, antiques, books, CDs, and records are certainly a cut above what you would find in your neighborhood Salvation Army or Goodwill. The prices are also a bit higher, but not much. They often run daily specials, making the place a steal. There are six other locations around the city (202 E. 77th St., between Second and Third Avenues; 306 Columbus Ave., between 74th and 75th Streets; 157 E. 23rd St., between Third and Lexington Avenues; 245 W. 10th St., between Hudson and Bleecker Streets; 1730 Second Ave., on the corner of 90th Street; and in Brooklyn at 122 Montague St., near the corner of Henry Street). Housing Works is New York's largest provider of housing and supportive services to homeless, formerly homeless, and at-risk men, women, and children living with HIV and AIDS.

17 @ 17 Thrift Store
17 W. 17th St. (between Fifth and Sixth Avenues)
(212) 727-7516

Walk farther down the street. Okay, you do actually have to cross an avenue, but since you're in the neighborhood, it's worth stopping in. This store is almost always so overflowing with furniture, clothes, and tchotchkes that you can count on them having a 50 to 75 percent off sale going on. All proceeds benefit the Women's Campaign of the UJA-Federation of New York, helping Jewish people in need around the world.

PETS:
CANINE, FELINE,
BOTTOM LINE

"And the turtles, of course . . . all the turtles are free.
As turtles and, maybe, all creatures should be."

—DR. SEUSS

Whether your preference is cats or dogs (or hamsters, rabbits, or even the occasional turtle), there are plenty of little companions to be had for the asking. By opting for an adopted pet, you will not only be saving a cage full of cash and giving a home to a needy (and loving) buddy, but you will also be doing your part to put an end to the animal mills that churn out unhealthy dogs and cats for pet stores. Most of the shelters around the city do require some "donation" to offset their expenses, but here are some ways to increase the size of your household without decreasing the size of your bank account. Also here are some suggestions on where to go to keep your Pekinese in the pink without spending much green.

Surfing for Pets

Here are a few good websites to check out for free pet adoptions. There is also no charge to list pets on these sites for adoption.

www.animalalliancenyc.org, New York City's official animal information site, provides information and links to practically everywhere you can possibly adopt a pet in the five boroughs as well as information on licensing; low-cost spay, neuter, and pet-care options; events; and discounts for services.

http://newyork.craigslist.org, the classified section of the Internet, has a listing for every pet need from pet portraits to adopting or buying every kind of pet you can think of. New listings are added every day and throughout the day. Craigslist includes my favorite section, "Free," where you will find listings for furniture, tickets, appliances, books, antiques, classes, and so much more.

www.petfinder.org is a national and local clearinghouse for shelters and rescue organizations that list thousands of animals by breed and location. Many of these shelters do suggest donations ranging from $30 to $100.

LOW-COST **PET** CARE **&** ADOPTIONS

Animal Care & Control of New York City

Bronx: 464 E. Fordham Rd. (between Washington and Third Avenues)
Brooklyn: 2336 Linden Blvd. (between Essex Street and Shepherd Avenue)
Manhattan: 326 E. 110th St. (between First and Second Avenues)
Queens: 92–29 Queens Blvd. (between Eliot and 62nd Avenue)
Staten Island: 3139 Veterans Rd. West (near Arthur Kill Road)
(212) 788-4000
www.nycacc.org

The Catch: Charges between $25 and $150 for adoptions.

These shelters in each borough are overflowing with dogs, cats, rabbits, and occasionally some other surprises for you to take home and make a part of your family. Start your search for Fluffy on their website, where they post pictures and information on all the pets they have up for adoption. They do charge a fee for adoptions that includes all immunizations, spay or neutering, and microchips. All cats are $25 and most dogs are $100 or less, but they charge $150 for purebred dogs.

ASPCA

Bergh Memorial Animal Hospital & Clinic
424 E. 92nd St. (between York and First Avenues)
(212) 876-7700
www.aspca.org

The Catch: Charges $75 for an appointment with a doctor and $110 for an emergency visit.

The granddaddy of all humane organizations, the ASPCA's clinic and hospital provide low-cost health care for your little loved ones. They provide the full range of medical care for pets, including spaying and neutering ($40 to $65), vaccines, and an on-site pharmacy. They also offer adoptions of all sorts of pets starting at a $75 donation. The adoption package includes microchip ID, spaying or neutering, follow-up exams, medical support, vaccines, literature, private behavior counseling, and starter equipment.

Bide-A-Wee

410 E. 38th St., second floor (between First Avenue and FDR Drive)
(212) 532-5884 (clinic)
(212) 532-4455 (adoptions)
www.bideawee.org

The Catch: *Charges $60 for exams, $90 for emergency visits, and $70 to $80 for adoptions.*

This full-service veterinary clinic provides everything to keep your feline feeling fine. Appointments are available about a week in advance. They also have a large shelter and offer adoptions for a $70 to $80 fee, which includes spay or neutering, all vaccinations, and two weeks of free clinic services.

PET **POSTINGS**

Another way to find a free companion is to check out the bulletin boards and windows of local pet stores and veterinarians for notices from your neighbors who need to give up their pets. Whether it's because they're moving and can't take the Tonkinese to Tupelo, or their Labrador just had a litter, or the new hubby is allergic to the husky, often owners and their pets must be parted. Here are some places where you're sure to find postings:

East Side

Calling All Pets, 1590 York Ave. (at 84th Street); (212) 249-7387.
Calling All Pets, 301 E. 76th St. (at Second Avenue); (212) 734-7051.
The Country Vet, 430 E. 75th St. (between First and York Avenues); (212) 535-3250.
Litter and Leashes, 343 E. 66th St. (at First Avenue); (212) 734-8400.
The Natural Pet, 238 Third Ave. (between 19th and 20th Streets); (212) 228-4848.
Petco, 560 Second Ave. (at 31st Street); (212) 779-4550.
Petco, 860 Broadway (at East 17th Street); (212) 358-0692.

West Side

Animal General, 558 Columbus Ave. (at 87th Street); (212) 501-9600.
Barking Zoo, 172 Ninth Ave. (between 20th and 21st Streets); (212) 255-0658.

Clinton Veterinary Center, 357 W. 52nd St. (between Eighth and Ninth Avenues); (212) 333-5548.

The Pet Health Store, 440 Amsterdam Ave. (at 81st Street); (212) 595-4200.

Pet Stop, 564 Columbus Ave. (between 87th and 88th Streets); (212) 580-2400.

Spoiled Brats, 340 W. 49th St. (between Eighth and Ninth Avenues); (212) 459-1615.

Westside Animal Hospital, 733 Ninth Ave. (between 49th and 50th Streets); (212) 247-8600.

Downtown West

Parrots and Pups, 45 Christopher St. (east at Seventh Avenue); (212) 352-8777.

Pet Bar, 132 Thompson St. (between Prince and Houston Streets); (212) 253-9250.

Downtown East

Animal Cracker, 103 E. 2nd St. (between Avenue A and First Avenue); (212) 614-6786.

Whiskers, 235 E. 9th St. (between Second and Third Avenues); (212) 979-2532.

WALKING TOURS:
THE FREEDOM TRAIL

" Afoot and lighthearted I take to the open road, Healthy, free, the world before me, The long brown path before me, leading wherever I choose."

—WALT WHITMAN

Whether you're a visitor to New York or a native, there is always so much to discover about every corner of the city. The best way to get to know New York is to walk the streets with someone who knows it well. There are free guided tours of every fashion: leisurely strolls; historical, architectural, and nature tours; one-on-one explorations and groups. Most of the tours happen at regularly scheduled times every week, and some can be scheduled at your convenience.

Austrian Cultural Forum
11 E. 52nd St. (between Fifth and Madison Avenues)
(212) 319-5300
www.acfny.org
Mon through Fri at noon and 3 p.m.

A unique addition to the New York skyline, this building is a pure example of making the most out of a little. Stop in for a free tour of this narrow twenty-four-story glass-and-concrete skyscraper that looks like a huge totem pole designed for a science fiction movie. They also host a full schedule of other free events, including readings, concerts, art exhibitions, film screenings, and panel discussions.

Battery Park City Walking Tours
Battery Park City Parks Conservancy
2 South End Ave. (at West Thames Street)
(212) 267-9700
www.bpcparks.org
Various dates May through Oct.

They offer a variety of walking tours, including nature walks, garden tours, river walks, art tours, and historic tours. Some tours are offered weekly, others on occasion. Check the website or call for schedules.

Big Apple Greeters
1 Centre St., Room 2035 (at Chambers Street)
(212) 669-8159
www.bigapplegreeter.org
Any day, any place, year-round.

This is your dream-come-true tour of New York. You choose the time and day, you choose the place, and you don't pay anything—in fact, they'll even give you a one-day unlimited-use MetroCard for the subway. You think I'm kidding, don't you? Well, I'm not. Friendly and knowledgeable New Yorkers volunteer their time for this amazing organization to show you around any neighborhood in the city. They usually live in the area they show, so they can give you firsthand accounts of the area's history, off-the-beaten-trail spots, and great tips for finding some tasty (and cheap!) food and drink. Walks can run from two hours to all day. They don't accept tips, but if you offer to buy them lunch, they probably won't argue with you. Call at least two weeks in advance.

Brooklyn Brewery

79 N. 11th St. (between Wythe Avenue and Berry Street)
Williamsburg, Brooklyn
(718) 486-7422
www.brooklynbrewery.com
Sat, noon–6 p.m. (last tour at 4).

Brooklyn's mom-and-pop brewery walks you through the process of mixing up a batch of beer in intricate detail, right down to the molecular physics. And somehow it seems so very interesting once you've been plied full of generous samples of their fine (and fresh!) brew. Also, on Friday night they have free music and cheap beer.

Central Park

Central Park Conservancy
(212) 310-6600
www.centralparknyc.org
Various days and times throughout the week, year-round.

Explore the wilds of New York City with the many tours led by volunteers for the Central Park Conservancy. With a wealth of knowledge about the flora, fauna, history, trivia, secret passageways, and hidden trails of Central Park, these tours are always worthwhile for natives and visitors alike. Call for schedule information.

Columbia University

213 Low Library (116th Street and Broadway)
(212) 854-4900
www.columbia.edu
Mon through Fri, 11 a.m. and 2 p.m., year-round.

This one-hour tour of New York's very own Ivy League school uncovers the history, architecture, and personalities behind these prestigious walls.

8th Street Walking Tour
The Village Alliance
(212) 777-2173
www.villagealliance.org
Every other Sat at 11:30 a.m., late May through Sept.

The ninety-minute tour called "Discover Places, Tidbits & Gossip That Even New York's Cognoscenti Don't Know" delivers just what it promises as it traipses through the East and West Villages. The tour meets at the northwest corner of Second Avenue and St. Marks Place (8th Street). Call or check the website for the schedule.

The Federal Reserve Bank
33 Liberty St. (between Nassau and William Streets)
(212) 720-6130
www.newyorkfed.org
Mon through Fri at 9:30 a.m., 10:30 a.m., 11:30 a.m., 1:30 p.m., 2:30 p.m.; make a reservation one month ahead.

You've heard the sayings "Follow the money" and "Show me the money," right? Well, here's your chance to do both. This sixty-minute tour of the richest bank in the world takes you through their gold vaults, tells you all about the Fed's cash-processing procedures, and even gives you some free money at the end of the tour! Okay, so it happens to be shredded. You can't have everything.

Grand Central Terminal
42nd Street and Vanderbilt Ave.
(212) 439-1049
http://mas.org
Wed at 12:30 p.m., year-round.

The Catch: While there's no charge for the tour, they do ask for a donation of any amount, though you aren't obligated to give one.

For more than twenty-five years, the Municipal Art Society has been showing folks around this Beaux Arts landmark. The tour includes the history of the terminal as well as a look at the major restorations completed in 1998. The tour runs a little more than an hour and meets at the main information booth on the main level of Grand Central.

The Grand Tour: Grand Central Station Area
42nd Street and Vanderbilt Avenue
(212) 883-2420
www.grandcentralpartnership.org
Every Fri at 12:30 p.m., year-round.

This free ninety-minute walking tour organized by the Grand Central Partnership leaves from the Philip Morris Building across the street from Grand Central. This walk points out some of the architectural splendors of East 42nd Street, including Grand Central Station, the Chrysler Building, the Chanin Building, and many others, as well as passing along some of the area's rich history and curious events.

John J. Harvey Fireboat
Pier 63 (Hudson River and 23rd Street)
www.fireboat.org
Various days and times, year-round.

Since she was put into service in 1931, the *John J. Harvey* fireboat has greeted every passenger cruise ship that has made its way into New York Harbor with a spectacular water display. But this boat wasn't made just for show. To this day, although she was officially retired from service by the New York City Fire Department in 1994, she remains one of the most powerful and fastest fireboats ever to take to the water. The ship is now under private ownership and does not rest on her impressive laurels. She's now pressed into action for tours up and down the Hudson and around New York Harbor. The schedule of events is erratic, but they go on throughout the year (more from spring through fall and less in the winter). Some tours have themes and knowledgeable guides, like their "History of Garbage" tour and a tour of historic fires the *Harvey* worked on. Other tours are just pleasant days on the water. All are free, because the boat doesn't meet the strict standards set by the U.S. Coast Guard for the carriage of passengers for hire. If you come onboard, it's as private guests of the boat, and you may be asked to sign a release to this effect. Trips are limited to the first fifty passengers. And yes, they do "fire up" the powerful hoses at some point on every trip, and yes, you will get wet. For schedule information check out the website or sign up for their mailing list though the website.

Lincoln Square

Columbus Circle fountain (59th Street and Broadway)
(212) 581-3774
www.lincolnbid.org
Sat at 11 a.m., June through Nov.

This ninety-minute tour (that can actually run as long as three hours) explores the historic Lincoln Square district, which has become a world center for arts and entertainment—and is also full of historic treasures, architectural jewels, peaceful green areas, and surprising enclaves of public art. The tour meets at the Columbus Circle fountain.

New York City Hall

(212) 788-2170 or 311
www.nyc.gov/artcommission
Tues at 10 a.m. and Fri at 2 p.m. (reservations required);
Wed at noon (no reservations required).

Stroll through this early-nineteenth-century Federal-style building that's home to the mayor's office and city council chambers and is chock-full of historic American portraits and artifacts. You can make reservations for tours on Tues at 10 a.m. and Fri at 2 p.m. by calling or through their website. The tours are limited to twenty people, so it is a good idea to make a reservation a least a week in advance, but you can try up to two days before. Or you can just show up for the Wednesday tour at noon, which is open to the first twenty people who sign up that morning at the Heritage Tourism Center, located at the southern end of City Hall Park. All tours are free, of course.

Hostelling International New York

891 Amsterdam Ave. (between 103rd and 104th Streets)
(212) 932-2300
www.hinewyork.org
Mon at 10:30 a.m., Central Park (every other week);
Monday afternoons, Twilight In Brooklyn (every other week).

Meet up at the International Youth Hostel every Monday for a morning jaunt to Central Park or at twilight for a tour of Brooklyn Heights. Even if you are not staying at the hostel you can tag along. Stroll through Central Park and take in the highlights of the city's green oasis or explore downtown Brooklyn and its spectacular views of Manhattan, as well as a walk over the historic Brooklyn Bridge. These tours take place on alternating Mondays.

The hostel also hosts a full schedule of other tours throughout the week, but they do charge a small fee for most of the others. The one tour that might actually be worth shelling out the bucks for is Jerry's Grand Tour ($10). This is a sixteen-hour marathon that covers up to 22 miles and every New York sight you might ever want to see. The Grand Tour takes place every Sat at 8:30 a.m. You do need to call or stop by the hostel to sign up for all tours at the information desk. Check out their website for more details and a schedule of other tours and events, including the free stand-up comedy every Wednesday night at 8:30. And if you are looking for a bed in New York, the hostel is the way to go. It is clean, friendly, fun, and, most importantly, cheap. With beds running only $30 to $38 a night, this is just about the best deal you're going to find in the city.

New York Public Library (NYPL)
Humanities and Social Science Library, 476 Fifth Ave.
(entrance at 42nd Street)
(212) 930-0501
www.nypl.org
Mon through Sat at 11 a.m. and 2 p.m., Sun at 2 p.m., year-round.

The lions welcome you to a one-hour walk through the stunningly renovated main branch of the public library. They also offer guided tours through their major art exhibits daily at 12:30 and 2:30 p.m.

Orchard Street Walking Tour
Katz's Deli
205 E. Houston St. (at Ludlow Street)
(212) 226-9010
www.lowereastsideny.com
Sun at 11 a.m., Apr through Dec.

From pushcarts to pulsing beats, this tour explores a neighborhood that started out as a hub for immigrants from Russia and Eastern Europe and is now turning into the newest chic area on the isle of Manhattan. Tours run about ninety minutes.

Pennsylvania Station Tours
34th Street Partnership tourist information kiosk
32nd Street and Seventh Avenue
(212) 719-3434 or (212) 868-0521
www.34thstreet.org
The fourth Mon of every month at 12:30 p.m., year-round.

Tour the grandeur that once was New York's Penn Station. The tour resurrects this behemoth by using vintage photographs and surviving remnants to tell the story of New York's lost railroad station. This ninety-minute walk tells the tale from Penn Station's turn-of-the-twentieth-century beginnings to the forces that brought about its destruction in the early 1960s.

Prospect Park Audubon Center
Lincoln Road and Ocean Avenue
Brooklyn
(718) 287-3400
www.prospectpark.org/audubon
Sat at noon: Bird-Watching Tour.
Sat and Sun at 3 p.m.: Discovery Tour.

The restored boathouse is home to this state-of-the-art wildlife preserve and education center. Their busy schedule abounds with free events, activities, and tours through the wilds of Brooklyn's only forest with a gorge and waterfall (okay, even without the gorge and waterfall, it would still be Brooklyn's only forest). Take the Discovery Tour offered every Sat and Sun at 3 p.m., the Bird-Watching Tour every Sat at noon, or stop in for any other of the tons of ongoing activities for kids and adults throughout the week.

Steinway & Sons
1 Steinway Place (Nineteenth Avenue and 38th Street)
Long Island City, Queens
(718) 721-2600
www.steinway.com
Mon and Tues at 9:30 a.m., Sept through June.

Take a walk back in time through the Steinway factory, where they still craft each of their world-famous pianos by hand using the same techniques created and patented by Henry Engelhard Steinway (and his sons) starting in 1853. From bending and shaping one long piece of wood into the entire outer rim of the piano to hand-sanding, sawing, rubbing, regulating, voicing, and stringing the instruments, the tour is an in-depth two-and-a-half-hour master class in the art of piano making from those who do it best. Tours are held on Monday and Tuesday mornings Sept through June, and reservations are required.

Take a Walk, New York!
(212) 228-3126
www.walkny.org
Various locations throughout the five boroughs, year-round.

Your government thinks you're getting too fat. So they want you to hit the streets and start exercising. This federally funded local group organizes guided walks all around the city that aim to stimulate you intellectually and visually so they can sucker you into walking, walking, walking. This is a great chance to explore sections of the city you've never visited before (or may not have even known existed). The walks are always easily accessible by public transportation, led by knowledgeable guides, and free.

Thirteen/WNET
450 W. 33rd St. (between Ninth and Tenth Avenues)
(212) 560-2711
www.thirteen.org
Tues at 11 a.m.; reservations required.

Channel 13 offers a fascinating one-hour peek inside the country's largest public television station.

Times Square Walking Tour
Times Square Visitors Center
1560 Broadway (between 46th and 47th Streets)
(212) 869-1890
www.timessquarenyc.org
Fri at noon.

What was once a center for horse trading has now become the center of the commercial theater world. This two- to three-hour tour fills you in on all the history, intrigue, and ever-changing architecture of Broadway and its surrounding areas. The visitor center also offers free Internet access, loads of information, and clean bathrooms!

Trinity Church
Broadway and Wall Street
(212) 602-0800
www.trinitywallstreet.org
Daily at 2 p.m., year-round.

A short fifteen- to twenty-minute tour that covers the long history of one of New York's oldest churches (established 1697). Concerts are also offered every Thurs at 1 p.m.

Union Square Walking Tour

16th Street between Union Square East and West (Park Avenue and Broadway)
(212) 460-1200
www.unionsquarenyc.org
Sat at 2 p.m., year-round.

Take a ninety-minute, opinionated, totally interactive tour of Union Square's past, present, and future. Meet at the Lincoln statue mid-park at 16th Street.

Urban Park Rangers

Parks throughout the five boroughs
(866) NYC-Hawk (692-4295)
www.nyc.gov/parks
Various times, days, and locations, year-round.

Yogi Bear has nothing on New York. Yes, we have our own pack of park rangers, and they're a useful bunch of folks to know. They run an extensive and ever-changing array of walks, hikes, nature explorations, canoe trips, and even camping trips. Call to get a schedule or check out the website.

Wall Street Walking Tour

Museum of the American Indian
1 Bowling Green (at the end of Broadway, across from Battery Park)
(212) 606-4064
www.downtownny.com
Thurs and Sat at noon, year-round.

Explore this area that takes in everything from founding fathers of the United States to the financial capital of the world. This free ninety-minute tour weaves together the history, events, architecture, and people of downtown with stops at the U.S. Custom House, Trinity Church, New York Stock Exchange, and many other sites along the way. No two walks are ever the same, so join in often.

TRAVEL:
FREE-WHEELIN'

*"We're gonna see America. We take no map.
We'll follow the sun. Stay in cheap motels and
steal what we need along the way."*

—AL BUNDY

Just because you're low on cash is no reason to sit at home. Whether it's getting around the city or getting out of town, there are some great options. Of course, the best way to get to see New York is the cheapest—by foot (biking and in-line skating are great choices as well). More than any other place in America, New York is a walking city—logically laid out, compact, lots to see, and plenty of people to bump into along the way (figuratively and literally). While New York is undoubtedly a big city, as you walk the streets, you realize that it's also very much a small town. There may be eight million people, but you'll be amazed at how many friends and acquaintances you'll run into on the streets and how many familiar faces in the crowds you'll see over and over again. When walking is out of the question, though, the subway is the answer. The unlimited-use MetroCard ($8.25 for one day, $27 for one week, $89 for one month) makes getting from here to there a bargain. The MetroCard is good for all subways and buses (see below). Here are some other suggestions for getting around and out of New York.

GETTING **AROUND** NEW **YORK**

MTA New York City Transit
(718) 330-1234
www.mta.info

Okay, I know I'm not offering you any special deals here. Yes, you do have to pay to get on the trains. This isn't Germany; there ain't no such thing as an

---

Get the 411

1-800-FREE-411 is just that, free directory assistance. Forget about paying your phone or cell phone company a buck or two every time you need a number. Simply call this number from your home or cell phone and get any number in the country for free. What's the catch? Well, you will have to sit through a short ad, which is how they make their money, but the call and the info are totally free. Visit their website at www.free411.com.

honor system on these trains. You pay your fare and you ride your train. You will be ticketed if you hop the turnstiles. Don't try it. But the unlimited-use MetroCards make it easy and cheap to get to anywhere in the five boroughs by subway and/or bus.

Staten Island Ferry
Whitehall Terminal (at Whitehall and South Streets)
311 or (718) 727-2505
www.nyc.gov/dot

This not-to-be-missed trip runs about every twenty minutes most times, but once an hour late at night. It's absolutely free, and with the spectacular views of lower Manhattan and the Statue of Liberty, how can you pass it up? Particularly dramatic views at sunset, but any time of day it's an awe-inspiring voyage.

GETTING **OUT** OF **NEW** YORK

Auto Driveaway Company (ADC)
2786 Rte. 23 North, Suite B
Stockholm, New Jersey
(973) 208-8700
www.autodriveaway.com

The Catch: There's a $15 registration fee and a $350 refundable deposit. The registration fee is good for one year and at all locations.

Forget about flying, Greyhound, or Amtrak; here's your chance to see America the way it was meant to be seen, behind the wheel of your very own gas-guzzling, pedal-to-the-metal, "where the hell is the next rest stop" automobile. With sixty-four locations throughout the United States and Canada, these folks can provide you with the free use of a late-model car to practically any major city you want to visit. If your plans are somewhat flexible, this is a great way to drive yourself around the states. The deal is: ADC acts as a kind of matchmaker between people or companies that need vehicles moved from place to place and drivers who want to get from here to there. Call them up to see what's available, pay your registration and deposit, and hit the road. Cars go on a first-come, first-served basis to drivers age twenty-three or older with two photo IDs. They give you time to do plenty of sightseeing along the way by allotting you extra time to get to where you're going (four days to Florida, for instance, and ten days to the West Coast). When you deliver your car, you get back your deposit and call the nearest ADC office to see when you can get a car back or off to your next destination. The looser your travel plans, the better this system will work for you. The cars come with a free first tank of gas; otherwise, all gas and lodging costs along the way are your responsibility.

Club Getaway
Kent, Connecticut
(800) 643-8292 or (877) 746-7529
www.clubgetaway.com

The Catch: You must have the ability to teach something fun or provide some useful service to campers in exchange for free weekends.

This summer camp for adults is a "Club Med in Connecticut" and is always on the lookout for volunteers to commit to spending some weekends with their swinging singles. If you can offer some useful service to the paying campers—teaching yoga, arts and crafts, or in-line skating, say, or even cooking up a killer pie—they will give you room, board, and free run of the extensive grounds and facilities in exchange for the time you spend working with the campers. Even if you don't necessarily think you have some great expertise, they're pretty open to any idea; it's definitely worth a shot. The camp has been rated "one of the top ten hottest destinations for singles" by the Travel Channel and has everything you need to do almost any sport under the sun.

Rowe Camp & Conference Center

Rowe, Massachusetts
(413) 339-4954
www.rowecenter.org

The Catch: Chop wood and carry water in exchange for a peaceful week in the mountains.

For one week every spring and fall, the Rowe Center holds "Work Weeks" where folks from far and wide, both young and old, come to help spiff up the grounds and have a great time. This community-oriented camp offers lots of fun activities and free room and board for all those helping out these weeks. Throughout the year they also offer various conferences on a wide variety of artistic and spiritual subjects, and you can work off the cost of these programs through other work-study programs. Check the website for more details and schedule.

Vipassana Meditation Center

386 Colrain-Shelburn Rd.
Shelburn Falls, Massachusetts
(413) 625-2160
www.dhamma.org

The Catch: Donations of any amount are accepted, but not required, at the end of the ten-day retreat.

Vipassana offers its ten-day meditation "Boot Camp" free of charge (including all accommodations, meals, and instructions)—the only hitch is you

---

The Virtual Thumb

There are a number of websites where you can find yourself a free ride out of town or a companion to ride with you wherever you're going. These ride-share listings are a great way to travel to or from New York, save a load of cash, and maybe even make a good friend along the way. You are usually expected to split the cost of gas, but not always. Check out these sites for details:

www.erideshare.com

http://newyork.craigslist.org

www.shareyourride.net

---

can't say a word about the service. In fact, you can't say a word about anything; this is a completely silent retreat. No meditation experience is required to take part, and their focus in not religion-based at all. They are all about the technique and practice of meditation as a "universal remedy for universal ills." Fill out an application at their website and make a reservation one to two months in advance.

THE **TRAIN** TO **THE** PLANE

Getting to New York's three major airports can be an expensive affair. It can cost you $60 by cab, $20 by shuttle van, or $13 by bus service, but it can be done for next to nothing if you have some time and patience.

Kennedy Airport

This is the easiest and most user-friendly airport to get to by public transportation, with four cheap options for getting there (two dirt cheap and two not-quite-as cheap). The pricier and slightly more convenient plan is to pick up the AirTrain at either the Howard Beach Station (A train) or at the Sutphin Boulevard Station (E, J, or Z trains). The AirTrain is officially part of the MTA system, but your MetroCard will not get you on board. To take the ten-minute monorail ride to the terminals, you will have to cough up an additional $5. But if you are a purist like me, you will hop on one of the two city buses that will get you to the terminals for just the swipe of your unlimited MetroCard or a $2.25 subway fare (free transfer from the subway!). Grab the Q10 bus from the Kew Gardens/Union Turnpike subway station (E or F trains) or Q3 at Jamaica Center/Parsons/Archer subway station (E, J, or Z trains). The travel time from Manhattan for any of these routes is about sixty to ninety minutes. The big difference is the AirTrain is a bit plusher and luggage friendly, while the buses are, well, buses.

Next Year in Jerusalem

How about an all-expenses-paid ten-day trip to Israel? Well, if you're between eighteen and twenty-six years old, Jewish, and have never been to the Holy Land before, **Birthright Israel** wants to take you for free.

Sound inviting? To date they have sent more than 90,000 people from all around the country (including many groups from New York City), and they're looking for more every year. The aim is to build a strong link between young American Jews and Israel. While they try to keep the proselytizing to a minimum, there are many discussions of all things Jewish while you visit historic sites like Masada, the Wailing Wall, and the Dead Sea. Of course, they wouldn't mind you spending your own cash to come back to Israel in the future, or even deciding to settle in Israel, but there's no pressure to do either.

Birthright Israel puts together more than thirty groups to make the trip each winter and spring. These trips take into account the full spectrum of ideological, religious, educational, and cultural backgrounds of the Jewish community. There are groups for those who are nonobservant, Reform, Conservative, and Orthodox. Some trips have a traditional hotel and sightseeing agenda, while others are for those with special interests like biking, sports, or history. In recent years they have also begun to coordinate their activities with the Israeli government to ensure the safety and security of those on the trips. For more information stop by the Birthright Israel offices at 521 Fifth Ave., twenty-seventh floor (at 43rd Street); call (888) 99-ISRAEL (994-7723); or check the website www.birthrightisrael.com.

La Guardia Airport

Getting here can be an adventure, but it can be done for the cost of a subway ride as well. From 106th Street and Broadway or 125th Street and Lenox Avenue, hop on the M60 bus. The bus winds its way around Upper Manhattan and Queens and takes you directly to the airport. Travel time is forty-five to ninety minutes (depending on traffic). Another option is to take the E or the F train to the 74th Street and Roosevelt Avenue stop, then catch the

Q33 bus. Neither of these are specifically meant to be airport shuttles. That means they make many stops along the way before getting to the terminals, and they do not have any special luggage racks. You won't be making friends with your fellow passengers if you block the aisle with your steamer trunk. For information on all MTA buses and subways, call (718) 330-1234 or check the website www.mta.info.

Newark Liberty Airport

Making it to Newark Liberty Airport from Manhattan can be pretty cheap and easy, as long as you know the schedules ahead of time. If you head off without a plan, it could take you a while or wind up costing you a few more bucks than you planned on. The easiest option is to hop on the New Jersey Transit bus number 107 ($6.50) at Port Authority in midtown (41st Street and Eighth Avenue) and take it straight to the airport. The good news is this bus will get you to the airport in about thirty minutes and for only $6.50; the bad news is it has a very limited schedule. If that doesn't work for you, take the Path Train to Newark Penn Station ($1.50) and get the New Jersey Transit bus number 62 ($1.35) to the airport. The bus runs about every ten to twenty minutes and is about a twenty-minute ride. The more convenient but much pricier option is to take the AirTrain from Penn Station in Manhattan directly to the airport ($14), or you can save a few bucks by taking the Path Train to Newark Penn Station and grabbing the AirTrain there ($7.75). For detailed schedules and more information, call (800) 772-2222 or check the website www.panynj.gov.

GARDENS & GARDENING:
DIRT CHEAP

"Your first job is to prepare the soil. The best tool for this is your neighbor's motorized garden tiller. If your neighbor does not own a garden tiller, suggest that he buy one."

—DAVE BARRY

Gardens may not be the first thing you think of when you think of New York, but there's a surprising amount of greenery to be found within this urban jungle—and I'm not just talking about fire-escape gardens. From quaint community gardens to grand botanical gardens, some of the most stunning horticulture anywhere in the world is within the city limits. Not only can you partake in the sights and smells of the gardens, but you can also produce some lovely flowers and vegetables yourself. Cultivate your own free plot of land in one of New York's many community gardens, get free bulbs and cuttings, or develop your own green thumb through free gardening classes around town.

PUBLIC GARDENS

The Brooklyn Botanic Garden (BBG)
1000 Washington Ave. (at Flatbush Avenue)
(718) 623-7200 (info) or (718) 623-7333 (events hotline)
www.bbg.org

The Catch: Free Hours: Tues and Sat from 10 a.m. to noon; seniors are also free all day Fri.

Hailed by the *New York Times* as "the premier horticultural attraction in the region," the BBG's endless gardens and greenhouses will bring your senses to life. They also provide free gardening and composting classes and workshops throughout the year (see below for details).

The Central Park Conservatory Gardens
105th Street and Fifth Avenue
(212) 360-2766 or (212) 310-6600
www.centralparknyc.org

Always free, this is the only formal garden in Manhattan open to the public. It covers a relatively small area (when compared to the other botanical gardens in New York) but provides a welcome escape from the clamor of city life. They offer free tours of the gardens from spring through fall on Sat at 11 a.m. Also be on the lookout for their annual plant giveaways—tulips in May and mums in Nov.

The New York Botanical Garden

200th Street and Kazimirov Boulevard
The Bronx
(718) 817-8700
www.nybg.org

The Catch: Free Hours: Wed and Sat from 10 a.m. to noon. Additional fees apply to certain exhibits within the garden.

Who could want anything more than 250 acres of flora from every corner of the world, including forty-eight gardens and plant collections and fifty acres of forestland? This is one of the oldest and largest gardens in the world and should not be missed. They offer free admission to the grounds on Wednesday and Saturday mornings, but you will still have to pay additional fees to gain entry into some venues within the gardens. They also run an extensive adult education curriculum, which you can get free or at reduced tuition by taking part in their work-study program.

The Queens Botanical Garden (QBG)

Flushing Meadows Park, 43–50 Main St. (at Dahlia Avenue)
(718) 886-3800
www.queensbotanical.org

You can always get in free at this twenty-acre garden (closed on Mon). The QBG also presents a free concert series during the summer and many free classes throughout the year.

Snug Harbor Botanical Gardens

1000 Richmond Terrace
(718) 448-2500
http://statenislandusa.com/pages/botanical_garden.html

The Catch: Free admission to the garden grounds, but they do charge admission to the Chinese and Secret Gardens.

This is a small garden when compared to the big guys in the Bronx and Brooklyn, but it makes a lovely place to take a respite. Admission to the garden grounds is free every day, but you will need to pay your way into the enticing and well-regarded Chinese Scholar's Garden.

Wave Hill Public Garden and Cultural Center

675 W. 252nd St. (enter at 249th Street and Independence Avenue)
The Bronx
(718) 549-3200
www.wavehill.org

The Catch: Free Hours: Tues and Sat from 9 a.m. to noon; no admission charges during Dec, Jan, and Feb.

This former private estate, now a city-owned garden, offers some outstanding views of the Hudson River and New Jersey (yes, it is possible), and some gorgeously maintained gardens.

GARDENING **EDUCATION**

Brooklyn GreenBridge & Urban Composting Project

Brooklyn Botanic Garden
1000 Washington Ave. (at Flatbush Avenue)
(718) 623-7250 or (718) 623-7209
Compost Help Line: (718) 623-7290
www.bbg.org/greenbridge

The Catch: Classes and workshops are free, but you must register at least one week in advance.

Classes and workshops offered throughout the year on such topics as "Composting in the City," "Perennial Flowers Basics," "Gardening with Native Plants," and "Battle the Asian Long Horn Beetle!" The classes are targeted toward community gardeners, but all are welcome.

New York Botanical Garden Adult Education

200th Street and Kazimirov Boulevard
The Bronx
(718) 817-8610
www.nybg.org/adulted

The Catch: Work-study is available: Perform administrative duties in exchange for free or discounted classes. The math: 2 hours of work = 1 free classroom hour.

Choose from more than 700 courses in botanical art and illustration, botany, crafts, floral design, gardening, commercial horticulture, landscape design, and horticultural therapy. Take a short how-to class, explore a topic in depth, or pursue a new career in one of their seven certificate programs.

COMMUNITY **GARDENS**

Community gardens are generally free to join. They provide you with a plot of land to plant in and all the supplies and materials you need, from seeds and soil to how-tos and hothouses. Some long-established, centrally located gardens have long waiting lists, while newer, off-the-beaten-trail gardens have many spots available. These gardens are not only a good place to grow rutabagas but also great gathering spots for the communities they are in. Many of the gardens have full schedules of free classes, performances, and activities for all.

Green Guerillas

151 W. 30th St., tenth floor (between Sixth and Seventh Avenues)
(212) 402-1121
www.greenguerillas.org

This all-volunteer organization converts vacant, rubble-filled city land into community gardens. They also cultivate green spaces and plant trees on treeless blocks. Green Guerillas is a good starting point to find a community garden in your neighborhood to participate in.

GreenThumb

49 Chambers St., Room 1020 (between Broadway and
Center Street)
(212) 788-8070
www.greenthumbnyc.org

This organization has more than 600 member community gardens in practically every neighborhood in the five boroughs. The website also has a great events calendar where you will find all kinds of free goings-on in the gardens: classes (tai chi, writing, yoga, drawing), concerts, barbecues, community gatherings, film screenings, and more. Check the website or call for the community garden near you.

ART GALLERIES:
SHOW ME THE MONET

"I hate flowers. I paint them because they're cheaper than models and they don't move."

—GEORGIA O'KEEFFE

New York is home to hundreds, perhaps thousands, of art galleries, and every one of them is free for you to wander through. In this city where space is at a premium, many of these are small single-room galleries with limited exhibition space, yet there are others that rival some of the major museums around town in the caliber of artists they show and their vast spaces. In some cases, in fact, the line between commercial gallery and museum is hard to define. Ultimately, though, the prime difference between the two remains simple and clear: money. You will never pay an admission charge at a commercial gallery, because everything you see hanging on the walls, lying on the floor, and dangling from the ceiling is for sale. Does the Gap charge you to browse? As New York is the center of the art world, the artists you'll find at these galleries may be the same ones you'd see at any major contemporary or modern art museum around the world. The styles of works you will find in these galleries run the full spectrum from fine art to the kind of contemporary installations that keep right-wing Republicans in business.

While there are galleries scattered all over the city, you'll find a large concentration of them clustered in just a few neighborhoods: Chelsea, SoHo, and Williamsburg, Brooklyn. Each of these areas caters to a different clientele and mind-set, but all have a huge variety of styles, techniques, and talents within their own worlds. The galleries I'm including in this listing are those where you're sure to find some of the most intriguing, world-class, cutting-edge, or otherwise eye-opening works in these neighborhoods and around the city. Don't take this list as the comprehensive survey of galleries in the five boroughs but as a jumping-off point. Galleries generally change shows every four to six weeks. The best way to take them in is to wander these neighborhoods with an open mind (but you can keep the purse closed).

CHELSEA

Chelsea has become the most popular area in Manhattan for galleries. Most of those located here are considered blue-chip galleries that work with lists of established, well-known, high-profile artists. In other words, the galleries can charge thousands of dollars for any given work. There are about 150 galleries crammed into a 10-block area, and most are open Tues through Sat, 10 a.m. to 6 p.m. Below are some of the big-shot galleries you don't want to miss, but the best way to discover a favorite spot is to walk the streets and check out everything that looks inviting. Most of the galleries are located between 21st and 26th Streets, and between Tenth and Eleventh Avenues.

Barbara Gladstone Gallery
515 W. 24th St. (between Tenth and Eleventh Avenues)
(212) 206-9300
www.gladstonegallery.com

Barbara Gladstone Gallery presents high-minded shows with a focus on conceptual sculpture.

Cheim & Read
547 W. 25th St. (between Tenth and Eleventh Avenues)
(212) 242-7727
www.cheimread.com

This large gallery presents the works of such artists as Diane Arbus, Louise Bourgeois, Robert Mapplethorpe, and Andy Warhol.

Gagosian Gallery
555 W. 24th St. (between Tenth and Eleventh Avenues)
(212) 741-1111
522 W. 21st St. (between Tenth and Eleventh Avenues)
(212) 741-1717
www.gagosian.com

Where Else to (van) Gogh

Stop into any gallery along the way and pick up a copy of *ChelseArt* and *Art Now's Gallery Guide.* ChelseArt is both a concise map and up-to-date listing of all the goings-on in the Chelsea area. The Gallery Guide is a monthly publication of happenings at every major gallery in Manhattan and selected listings in the other boroughs and beyond. You can get both of these free at any gallery. You may notice the $3 price tag on the Gallery Guide, but don't pay any attention; everyone gives it away for free. You can also view the guide online at www .artinfo.com. Click on "Gallery Guide" for the New York listings.

Shows are always headline grabbing here, and the huge space allows them to present works on a grand scale.

Galerie Lelong

528 W. 26th St. (between Tenth and Eleventh Avenues)
(212) 315-0470
www.galerie-lelong.com

The gallery's long history includes a dedication to abstract and minimalist paintings, contemporary sculpture, and contemporary Latin American artists.

Luhring Augustine Gallery

531 W. 24th St. (between Tenth and Eleventh Avenues)
(212) 206-9100
www.luhringaugustine.com

For more than twenty-five years, the Luhring Augustine Gallery has been presenting cutting-edge, big-budget shows.

A Feast for the Eyes (with an Open Bar!)

You are cordially invited to rub shoulders with the trendsetters of the New York art scene, be the first to see what's happening at the happening galleries, and grab yourself a glass (or three) of fine wine or a few bottles of beer. Whenever you stop in to view a gallery, be sure to put your name on their mailing list, and you will start receiving invitations to their upcoming shows, including information about the opening reception. Every gallery holds an opening reception a couple of days before the show opens to the public, where anyone has a chance to meet the artist(s), mix and mingle, drink, and sometimes even eat. These events are almost always open to anyone in the know, and now that means you. Other ways to find out about openings are to check out **the Douglas Kelley Show List** (http://dks.thing.net) or pick up a free copy of the Gallery Guide at any gallery.

Matthew Marks Gallery

523 W. 24th St. (between Tenth and Eleventh Avenues)
(212) 243-0200
www.matthewmarks.com

One of the first galleries to settle in Chelsea, its space is always home to an unpredictable but intriguing array of works.

Metro Pictures

519 W. 24th St. (between Tenth and Eleventh Avenues)
(212) 206-7100
www.metropicturesgallery.com

This gallery primarily presents photography shows by such artists as Cindy Sherman and Robert Longo.

The Pace Gallery

545 W. 22nd St. (between Tenth and Eleventh Avenues)
(212) 929-7000
http://thepacegallery.com

The Pace Gallery has mounted exhibits by such artists as Chuck Close, Isamu Noguchi, Pablo Picasso, Robert Rauschenberg, Mark Rothko, and Julian Schnabel.

303 Gallery

525 W. 22nd St. (between Tenth and Eleventh Avenues)
(212) 255-1121
www.303gallery.com

The 303 represents a battery of young artists working in a variety of forms, including photography, film, painting, sculpture, and whatever else moves them.

SOHO

SoHo is the original art gallery neighborhood of New York, and while gentrification and skyrocketing real estate prices have forced many galleries to relocate, it still remains well populated by galleries presenting vital work. The galleries are often smaller than those in Chelsea, but they display works that are generally more cutting edge and riskier. The spaces are sometime storefronts and clearly marked, but they're often up a few flights and out of the way. Most galleries are open Tues through Sat, 11 a.m. to 6 p.m. You will find most of the galleries located between West Broadway and Mercer, from Grand to Houston. There's a good map and extensive area listings in the *Gallery Guide,* available free at any gallery. Here are some of the highlights.

Artists Space
38 Green St. (between Grand and Broome Streets)
(212) 226-3970
www.artistsspace.org

This nonprofit gallery is often the first stop in a professional career for artists. Since 1972 this large gallery has played host to the first works of many artists who've gone on to international recognition working in almost any style and medium.

Deitch Projects
18 Wooster St. (between Canal and Grand Streets)
76 Grand St. (between Wooster and Greene Streets)
(212) 343-7300
www.deitch.com

These two galleries play host to wildly diverse solo and group shows of contemporary artists.

DIA Center for the Arts
393 W. Broadway (between Spring and Broome Streets)
141 Wooster St. (between Prince and Houston Streets)
www.diacenter.org

Without giving too much away about these two long-term installations, they are worth viewing if only to ponder the question, "What would Starbucks give to get this real estate?" These two works, the *Earth Room* and the *Broken Kilometer,* have been on display in these spaces since 1977 and 1979, respectively. Open Wed through Sat noon to 6 p.m., but closed from 3 to 3:30 p.m.

The Drawing Center

35 Wooster St. (between Grand and Broome Streets)
(212) 219-2166
www.drawingcenter.org

A cross between a museum and a gallery, this is the only institution in the United States dedicated exclusively to the exhibition, study, and promotion of the medium of drawing.

Ronald Feldman Fine Arts

31 Mercer St. (at Grand Street)
(212) 226-3232
www.feldmangallery.com

One of the oldest and best-respected galleries in SoHo, they have a strong focus on performance, installation, political, and conceptual works from both emerging and long-established artists. Among the collection is the largest selection of Andy Warhol prints of any gallery.

Rosenberg + Kaufman Fine Art

115 Wooster St. (between Prince and Spring Streets)
(212) 431-4838
www.artnet.com (search for "Rosenberg + Kaufman")

Up four flights you'll find this small gallery that's well worth the haul. Working with emerging and midcareer artists, the studio specializes in what it calls contemporary contemplative art. They seek out art that reveals itself slowly to the viewer, operating under the motto, "The more you look, the more you see."

WILLIAMSBURG, BROOKLYN

The Williamsburg art galleries are the newest and freshest additions to the New York art world. Since the late 1990s a set of young, brash, daring, less serious, more innovative galleries has begun to sprout up in some unusual settings in this formerly industrial/working-class, now artsy-hip neighborhood. Spread throughout the area, there are about forty spaces located in lofts, storefronts, and even a backyard toolshed. The spaces are a mix of larger studios and some closet-size galleries that are not always clearly marked, and can be off the beaten trail, but a hearty stroll around the neighborhood should give you a chance to see most of the sights. There is a good continually updated map of all the area galleries at the website **www.williamsburggalleryassociation.com.** Most galleries are open Friday through Monday or just on weekends. Here are some of the area galleries where you can always count on seeing something interesting.

Capla Kesting Fine Art
121 Roebling St. (at North 5th Street)
(917) 650-3760
www.caplakesting.com

Capla Kesting presents the works of neighborhood and international artists working in all forms. The shows are always full of humor, and they are daring and thought-provoking. During the summer don't miss their free film festival every Tuesday evening and the free-flowing Kelso beer at their openings throughout the year.

Holland Tunnel
61 S. 3rd St. (between Berry and Wythe Avenues)
(718) 384-5738
http://hollandtunnel.nfshost.com
Hours: Sat and Sun, 1–5 p.m.

You might call it intimate, petite, confined, even claustrophobic, but whatever you call it, there's no getting around the fact that this gallery started out in life as a toolshed from Home Depot. This space has gained quite a reputation partly because of the space itself, but also because of its daring programming. At times, this two-by-four of a gallery has hosted as many as one hundred artists in a single show.

Momenta Art
359 Bedford Ave. (between South 4th and South 5th Streets)
(718) 218-8058
www.momentaart.org
Hours: Thurs through Mon, noon–6 p.m.

Momenta is a not-for-profit gallery dedicated to giving opportunities to emerging artists. Many exhibitions are the first solo shows by these artists.

Beer Here!

If your style is more Budweiser than Beaujolais, Williamsburg art may be right up your alley. At these decidedly less pretentious Brooklyn galleries, beer is the official drink of choice for the opening receptions. So chugalug your way down to these opening nights for some free beer and intriguing art. For information on openings check out the calendar at **www.williamsburggalleryassociation.com** or put your name on each gallery's mailing list to receive invitations.

Pierogi 2000
177 N. 9th St. (between Bedford and Driggs Avenues)
(718) 599-2144
www.pierogi2000.com
Hours: Fri through Mon, noon–6 p.m.

One of the oldest, best-respected, and most spacious of the area galleries, Pierogi 2000 highlights the works of Brooklyn artists in a series of mostly solo shows.

OTHER **GALLERIES** & **SHOWS** AROUND **NEW** YORK

Broadway Windows
Broadway at East 10th St.
(212) 998-5751
http://steinhardt.nyu.edu/80wse
Hours: 24/7.

These are innocent-looking shop windows that serve as a gallery. They display a wide range of styles including paintings, sculpture, and site-specific work. Be careful when walking in this neighborhood: People are forever crashing into each other, because they can't take their eyes off these often surprising windows.

BWAC Pier Shows

141 Beard St.
Red Hook, Brooklyn
(718) 596-2507
www.bwac.org
Hours: Sat and Sun, noon–6 p.m., May through Sept only.

The Brooklyn art scene is brought to the public's eye at this series of annual events showcasing more than 200 emerging and established artists. Painting, sculpture, installation art, photography, and experimental forms are on display. It's a bit of a haul to get there, but the Civil War–era warehouse location, amazing view of the Statue of Liberty, passing barge traffic, and enough art to fill the Louvre all make it worth the effort. Call or check their website for a schedule of shows.

80 Washington Square East Galleries

New York University
80 Washington Sq. East
(212) 998-5747
http://steinhardt.nyu.edu/80wse
Hours: Tues, 10 a.m.–7 p.m.; Wed and Thurs, 10 a.m.–6 p.m.;
Fri and Sat, 10 a.m.–5 p.m.

This group, comprised of eight galleries, presents different solo shows or one group show. Don't miss the "Small Works" international competition every February.

Feature Inc.

131 Allen St. (between Rivington and Delancey Streets)
(212) 675-7772
www.featureinc.com

This contemporary art gallery displays a variety of cutting edge works in a number of different mediums. Exhibits include paintings, drawings, sculptures, and photography.

Kenkeleba Gallery

214 E. 2nd St. (between Avenues B and C)
(212) 674-3939
Hours: Wed through Sat, 11 a.m.–6 p.m.

This gallery specializes in works by African-American, third-world, and emerging artists, and experimental works.

Performance Space 122 gallery

150 First Ave. (entrance on 9th Street)
(212) 228-4249
www.ps122.org
Hours: Thurs and Fri, noon–6 p.m.;
Sat and Sun, noon–4 p.m.

This is the gallery wing of the birthplace of downtown performance art, where you'll find shows of paintings, photography, drawings, sculptures, videos, installations, multimedia, and many other things sure to upset Bill O'Reilly and his conservative friends. You can also volunteer-usher to see performances here for free. (See the chapter, "Theater: Free Speech" for details.)

The Rotunda Gallery

33 Clinton St. (at Pierrepont Street)
Brooklyn
(718) 875-4047
www.bricartsmedia.org/contemporary-art/exhibitions
Hours: Tues through Fri, noon–5 p.m.; Sat,
11 a.m.–4 p.m.

The Rotunda Gallery presents exhibits from Brooklyn-based artists working in all forms, from painting and sculpture to installations and performance art.

Socrates Sculpture Park

Broadway at Vernon Boulevard
Long Island City, Queens
(718) 956-1819
www.socratessculpturepark.org
Hours: Daily, 10 a.m.–sunset.

This four-and-a-half-acre stretch of land along the Queens side of the East River has been transformed into a delightful green space that highlights the works of up-and-coming artists. They also offer free tours and occasionally free films and music as well. Call or check the website for details and schedule.

West Side Arts Coalition

On the mall at Broadway and 96th Street
(212) 316-6024
www.wsacny.org
Hours: Sat and Sun, noon–6 p.m.; Wed, 6–8 p.m.

From cheesy kitsch to winsome watercolors, you never know what you'll find at this little gallery, which showcases the works of community artists in the middle of the road, literally (it's located on the median between the traffic running up and down Broadway). Stop by and take a look; it'll just take you a minute—again, literally.

White Columns

320 W. 13th St. (enter on Horatio Street, between Eighth Avenue and Hudson Street)
(212) 924-4212
www.whitecolumns.org
Hours: Tues through Sat, noon–6 p.m.

Specializing in large-scale installations by emerging and underrepresented artists, White Columns was the first to commission works by many artists who have gone on to international fame (and infamy), including William Wegman and Andres Serrano.

MUSEUMS:
FREE TO SEE

"I went to the museum where they had all the heads and arms from the statues that are in all the other museums."

—STEPHEN WRIGHT

The museums of New York City are world-class, abundant—and most of these collections can be seen free of charge. Whatever your taste or interest, whatever your age, background, or curiosities, there are museums to satisfy you. Many are completely free of charge at all times, while others have specific days and hours when they allow the public in for free or "pay what you want" (and you know what I want to pay!). Chances are, if the institution you would like to visit does not fit into one of those two categories, the admission charge is a "suggested donation." (Can you guess what I suggest you donate?)

ALWAYS **FREE**

American Folk Art Museum
Eva and Morris Feld Gallery
2 Lincoln Sq. (Columbus Avenue, between 65th and 66th Streets)
(212) 595-9533
www.folkartmuseum.org
Hours: Tues through Sat, noon–7:30 p.m.; Sun, noon–6:30 p.m.

While much of the Folk Art Museum has moved down to fancier digs on 53rd Street where they charge you to get in (except Friday evening), they still maintain these galleries at the original location of the museum, filled with enticing selections from their extensive permanent collection as well as temporary exhibitions. It's always a joy to take a walk through these halls and see what new treasures they have discovered. A sign at the front desk suggests a $3 donation, but no one seems to take any notice of that, and the staff doesn't stop you and ask for any cash. (See pages 256–257 for more information on the 53rd Street location.)

Audubon Terrace
Hispanic Society of America, (212) 926-2234;
www.hispanicsociety.org
Hours: Tues through Sat, 10 a.m.–4:30 p.m.; Sun, 1–4 p.m.

American Academy of Arts and Letters, (212) 368-5900;
Broadway, between 155th and 156th Streets
www.artsandletters.org

These regal buildings in Upper Manhattan are home to two small but impressive collections. The Hispanic Society is a collection of paintings, sculpture, archaeological finds, textiles, rare books, and manuscripts from Spain, Portugal, and Latin America dating as far back as the seventh century BC and is always free and open to the public. The Academy of Arts and Letters is a private organization of 250 preeminent American writers, composers, painters, sculptors, and architects. The building is home to many of the works of these artists and is free, but it's open to the public only for exhibitions during the spring and fall. Call for a schedule and details.

Carnegie Hall
The Rose Museum
154 W. 57th St., second floor (between Sixth and Seventh Avenues)
(212) 903-9629
www.carnegiehall.org
Hours: Daily, 11 a.m.–4:30 p.m., and during concert intermissions.

Explore the history of the architectural splendor and acoustical wonder that is Carnegie Hall. From Toscanini's baton to Benny Goodman's clarinet, this museum has hundreds of artifacts, photographs, and memorabilia.

Castle Clinton
Battery Park
(212) 344-7220
www.nps.gov/cacl
Hours: Daily, 8:30 a.m.–5 p.m.

Originally built in 1811 as the vanguard in the defense of New York Harbor, Castle Clinton has over its long history served as a fort, an opera house, and the New York Aquarium; it was finally saved from destruction and returned to its original fort design to serve as a national monument. A small museum and video display tell you about the long and varied history of the building, as does a well-marked self-guided tour. Be sure to check out the tours and programs led by the park rangers throughout the day.

Fashion Institute of Technology Museum
Shirley Goodman Resource Center
Seventh Avenue (between 27th and 28th Streets)
(212) 217-5800
www.fitnyc.edu/3662.asp
Hours: Tues through Fri, noon–8 p.m.; Sat, 10 a.m.–5 p.m.

Located in the fashion district, this school museum is home to the largest collection of costumes, textiles, and apparel dating from the eighteenth century in the world. You won't find all their finery on display at all times, though; exhibitions change throughout the year. Still, whatever they have on display is sure to thrill any fashion bug.

Federal Hall National Memorial
26 Wall St. (at Broad Street)
(212) 826-6888
www.nps.gov/feha
Hours: Mon through Fri, 9 a.m.-5 p.m.

The site of George Washington's first inauguration as president and the first home of the U.S. Congress, this building now houses a museum about its role in the early history of the city and country. Free guided tours at 10 a.m., noon, and 2 p.m.

The Fisher Landau Center For Art
38–27 30th St. (between Thirty-eighth and Thirty-ninth Avenues)
Long Island City, Queens
(718) 937-0727
www.flcart.org
Hours: Thurs through Mon, noon to 5 p.m.

A spacious museum dedicated to contemporary art from the 1960s until today. The collection of over 1,100 pieces contains the works of such artists as Jasper Johns, Donald Judd, Robert Rauschenberg, Kiki Smith, and Andy Warhol. They also occasionally offer free walking tours in conjunction with other nearby arts organizations. Check their website for schedules and exhibitions.

Forbes Magazine Galleries
62 Fifth Ave. (at 12th Street)
(212) 206-5548
www.forbesgalleries.com
Hours: Tues, Wed, Fri, and Sat, 10 a.m.–4 p.m.

The business magazine shows its lighter side in their galleries with a permanent collection that includes thousands of toy soldiers, hundreds of toy boats, the untold history of the game Monopoly, and hundreds of unusual trophies. Their other galleries house changing exhibits of jewelry and historical letters and documents, as well as classical and contemporary art.

General Grant's National Monument

Riverside Drive and 122nd Street
(212) 666-1640
www.nps.gov/gegr
Hours: Daily, 9 a.m.–5 p.m.

Here you'll finally get an answer to that age-old question: Who's buried in Grant's Tomb? You can also see some exhibits about U. S. Grant's life (childhood, the Civil War years, and the presidency) as well as some pretty stunning views of the Hudson River.

Hall of Fame for Great Americans

Hall of Fame Terrace
181st Street and University Avenue
The Bronx
(718) 289-5161
www.bcc.cuny.edu/halloffame
Hours: Daily, 10 a.m.–5 p.m.

If there was a hall of fame for halls of fame, this one would certainly be in it, because this is where the whole idea began. On this covered walkway you'll find bronze busts of great American political leaders, scientists, soldiers, and authors.

Louis Armstrong Archives

Queens College
65–30 Kissena Blvd. (at the Long Island Expressway)
(718) 997-3670
www.satchmo.net
Hours: Mon through Fri, 10 a.m.–5 p.m.

This museum features more than 5,000 photographs, home recordings, scrapbooks, music, and instruments from the home of one of the (if not the!) greatest trumpet players in the history of jazz. They also lead tours through the Armstrong house at 34–57 107th Street in Corona, Queens, but they charge for that. The archives are free and open to the public, but by appointment only.

Museum of American Illustrators

128 E. 63rd St. (between Park and Lexington Avenues)
(212) 838-2560
www.societyillustrators.org
Hours: Tues, 10 a.m.–8 p.m.; Wed through Fri,
10 a.m.–5 p.m.; Sat, noon–4 p.m.

This East Side town house is home to a private club for illustrators, but the public is always invited to explore their two gallery spaces. They put up anywhere from fifteen to twenty-two shows a year from their extensive permanent collection of historical book and magazine covers and illustrations. Some of the true prizes of the collection reside in the upstairs dining room, which is not officially open to the public. If you ask nicely, though, they'll be happy to let you up there to see the Norman Rockwell, Maxfield Parrish, and other treasures.

National Museum of the American Indian

1 Bowling Green Place (between State and Whitehall Streets)
(212) 514-3700
www.nmai.si.edu
Hours: Daily, 10 a.m.–5 p.m.; Thurs until 8 p.m.

A branch of the Smithsonian Institution, this museum is overflowing with dazzling artifacts, interactive displays, firsthand oral histories, music, and crafts of Native Americans. The changing exhibits explore the histories, beliefs, customs, and cultures of these once vast civilizations. The museum offers free workshops in such things as traditional basket weaving and beadwork (small materials fees are required), and free guided tours at 2 p.m. every day. If you miss the official guided tour, drop by the information desk on the second floor anytime—there's usually someone available to show you around free of charge. They also have a schedule of free films and live performances. Call or check the website for a schedule and details.

New York Unearthed

207 Front St. (at Fulton Street)
(212) 748-8628
www.southstseaport.org
By appointment only.

Explore 5,000 years of New York history in fifteen minutes at this free branch of the South Street Seaport Museum. The museum is free, but you must call to make an appointment.

Nicholas Roerich Museum
319 W. 107th St. (between Broadway and Riverside Drive)
(212) 864-7752
www.roerich.org
Hours: Tues through Sun, 2–5 p.m.

This museum houses more than 200 works by the artist Nicholas Roerich that deal mainly with Himalayan scenery and spiritual subject matter. Sundays they also almost always present a free classical concert or poetry reading. Call or check the website for details.

Queens County Farm Museum
73–50 Little Neck Parkway
Floral Park, Queens
(718) 347-FARM (3276)
www.queensfarm.org
Hours: Mon through Fri, 9 a.m.–5 p.m. (outside only); Sat and Sun,
10 a.m.–5 p.m.

Where the City Mouse meets the County Mouse. This forty-seven-acre working farm is the last remaining tract of undisturbed farmland in New York City and dates back to the seventeenth century. On the weekend take a free guided tour of the farmhouse and greenhouse, wander the farmyards, and—hey!—they even have hayrides (for $2).

Tibet House New York
22 W. 15th St. (between Fifth and Sixth Avenues)
(212) 807-0563
www.tibethouse.org
Hours: Mon through Fri, noon–6 p.m.

The galleries host exhibitions of artworks having to do with the culture, beliefs, history, and mythology of Tibetan Buddhism. They also hold open meditations every Tuesday evening with talks afterward. They ask for a $10 donation or "whatever you like."

Urban Center

Architectural League of New York; (212) 753-1722;
http://archleague.org
The Municipal Art Society; (212) 935-3960; www.mas.org
457 Madison Avenue (between 50th and 51st Streets)
Hours: Mon through Wed, Fri, and Sat, 11 a.m.– 5 p.m.

The galleries on the first two floors of the Urban Center play host to exhibitions from both of these organizations. The Municipal Art Society works usually highlight the city as a work of art, while the Architectural League's shows concentrate on the art of making the city.

Whitney Museum at Altria

120 Park Ave. (at 42nd Street)
(917) 663-2453
www.whitney.org
Hours: Mon through Wed and Fri, 11 a.m.–6 p.m.; Thurs until 7:30 p.m.

A branch of the Whitney Museum, this small gallery and atrium plays host to four or five shows a year with a focus on contemporary emerging artists. There isn't much gallery here, but it's a nice indoor public space for a brown-bag lunch. They also host a series of performances every spring.

SOMETIMES **FREE**

American Folk Art Museum

45 W. 53rd St. (between Fifth and Sixth Avenues)
(212) 265-1040
www.folkartmuseum.org
Hours: Tues through Sun, 10:30 a.m.–5:30 p.m.; Fri until 7:30 p.m.
When free: Fri, 5:30–7:30 p.m.

This glorious building is home to a huge collection of American folk art. The works on display from their permanent collection or from temporary exhibitions are created by artisans and artists from all walks of life throughout American history to the present time. These mostly self-taught artists have created pieces that are often whimsical and surprising, and could be anything from weather vanes to handwoven Shaker rugs. The Lincoln Center gallery is open Tues through Sun and is always free. (See page 250 for details on the museum's other location at 2 Lincoln Sq.)

Asia Society
725 Park Ave. (between 70th and 71st Streets)
(212) 288-6400
http://asiasociety.org
Hours: Tues through Sat, 11 a.m.–6 p.m.;
Fri until 9 p.m.; Sun, noon–5 p.m.
When free: Fri, 6–9 p.m.

Inside this terrifically modern museum are exhibits from every corner of Asia that encompass antiquities as old as humankind as well as the most startling new technologies and contemporary art commissions. They offer free guided tours and audio tours on Free Fridays as well.

Bartow-Pell Mansion Museum
895 Shore Rd. North
Pelham Bay Park, the Bronx
(718) 885-1461
www.bartowpellmansionmuseum.org
Hours: Wed, Sat, and Sun, noon–4 p.m.
When free: The first Fri of every month, 5:30–9 p.m.

Travel back to the early part of the nineteenth century, when living in the Bronx was considered living in the country. The estate predates the signing of the Declaration of Independence, and the mansion was built and furnished in the early 1800s. The museum has returned the home, carriage house, and gardens to their original splendor. You are welcome on the first Fri of every month from 5:30 to 9 p.m., when they open the doors for free and also offer free music, refreshments, and crafts.

Bronx Museum of the Arts
1040 Grand Concourse (at 165th Street)
The Bronx
(718) 681-6000
www.bronxmuseum.org
Hours: Wed, Thurs, Sat, and Sun, noon–to 6 p.m.; Fri, until 8 p.m.
When free: Fri.

The Bronx Museum of Arts primarily shows twentieth-century contemporary art by African, African- American, Latino, and Asian artists as well as artists who have lived in the Bronx.

Brooklyn Museum
200 Eastern Parkway (at Washington Avenue)
(718) 638-5000
www.brooklynmuseum.org
Hours: Wed through Fri, 10 a.m.–5 p.m.; Sat and Sun, 11 a.m.–6 p.m.
When free: The first Sat of every month, 5–11 p.m.

Don't miss the First Saturday event every month: free theater, free music, free movies, free dancing, free art, free guided tours. What a night! All other times they have a "suggested" donation of $8 for admission, but you can give as much (or as little!) as you would like.

Guggenheim Museum
1071 Fifth Ave. (at 89th Street)
(212) 423-3500
www.guggenheim.org
Hours: Sun through Wed, 10 a.m.–6 p.m.; Fri and Sat until 8 p.m.
When free: Fri, 5:45–7:45 p.m., is "Pay What You Wish."

The art museum that is a work of art itself. Designed by Frank Lloyd Wright, the building houses modern works that are sometimes controversial, sometimes commercial, but always worth seeing.

International Center of Photography (ICP)
1133 Avenue of the Americas (at 43rd Street)
(212) 857-0000
www.icp.org
Hours: Tues through Thurs, 10 a.m.–6 p.m.; Fri until 8 p.m.; Sat and Sun until 6 p.m.
When free: Fri, 5–8 p.m., is "Pay What You Wish."

The huge gallery spaces of the ICP mount shows that celebrate the art, craft, and images caught in the blink of an eye by the finest photographers from around the world and throughout the history of this ever-evolving art form.

Jewish Museum

1109 Fifth Ave. (at 92nd Street)
(212) 423-3200
www.jewishmuseum.org
Hours: Sat through Wed, 11 a.m.–5:45 p.m.; Thurs until 8 p.m.; closed Fri.
The shops have the same hours with the exception of being closed Sat and
open Fri, 11 a.m. to 3 p.m.
When free: Sat, 11 a.m.–5:45 p.m.

Ancient traditions and modern sensibilities clash, collide, and mesh in this
museum that follows the development and culture of the Jewish experience
from antiquity to the present day. The walls are full of rare artifacts, interactive displays, and intriguing works of art that span the centuries.

Museum of Arts and Design

40 W. 53rd St. (between Fifth and Sixth Avenues)
(212) 956-3535
www.madmuseum.org
Hours: Daily, 10 a.m.–6 p.m.; Thurs until 8 p.m.
When free: Thurs, 6–8 p.m., is "Pay What You Want."

This elegant three-story museum essentially serves as an excuse for a very
popular gift shop. The museum displays functional objects handcrafted by
contemporary American artists working in such areas as glass, baskets,
quilts, furniture, instruments, utensils, and even boats, kites, brooms, and
paper plates. And yes, many of the artists on display in the museum have
pricey items available at the gift shop.

Museum of Chinese in America (MoCA)

70 Mulberry St., second floor (at Bayard Street)
(212) 923-3700
www.mocanyc.org
Hours: Tues through Sun, noon–6 p.m.
When free: Fri.

MoCA is a small museum dedicated to preserving and chronicling the full
experience of Chinese immigrants and their descendants.

Museum of Jewish Heritage

36 Battery Place (in Battery Park City Park)
(646) 437-4200
www.mjhnyc.org
Hours: Sun through Thurs, 10 a.m.–5:45 p.m.; Wed until 8 p.m.; Fri and the
eve of Jewish holidays, 10 a.m.–3 p.m.
When free: Wed, 4–8 p.m.

The museum exists as a living memorial to the Holocaust and uses the two
quotes "Remember, Never Forget" and "There Is Hope for Your Future" to
define its mission. The lives, culture, beliefs, and traditions of those who
perished in the Holocaust are celebrated while the museum also looks for-
ward to the present-day Jewish communities around the world that are the
legacy of those Holocaust victims.

The Museum of Modern Art (MoMA)

11 W. 53rd St. (between Fifth and Sixth Avenues)
(212) 708-9480
www.moma.org
Hours: Mon, Wed, Thurs, Sat, and Sun, 10:30 a.m.–5:30 p.m.;
Fri, 10 a.m.–8 p.m.
When free: Fri, 4–8 p.m., is "Pay What You Wish."

From Monet to milk cartons, everything modern can be found here. Films,
gallery talks, and jazz in the sculpture garden as well as high-profile temporary exhibitions and the permanent collection are all available during the
"Pay What You Wish" Friday hours.

Museum of the Moving Image

Thirty-fifth Avenue at 36th Street
Astoria, Queens
(718) 784-4520
www.movingimage.us
Hours: Wed and Thurs, 11 a.m.–5 p.m.; Fri, 11 a.m.– 8 p.m.; Sat and Sun,
11 a.m.–6:30 p.m.
When free: Fri, 4–8 p.m.

With the nation's largest collection of film, television, and digital media
artifacts, the museum explores, catalogs, entertains, and educates visitors
on the complete history of everything having to do with the moving image.
Its many exhibits go behind the scenes and delve into every area from penny

arcades to the secrets of Yoda's puppetry. There is an additional charge for screenings during the free hours, but there are enough fascinating galleries and interactive exhibits to keep any film buff happy.

New York Hall of Science

47–01 111th St.
Flushing Meadows–Corona Park, Queens
(718) 699-0005
www.nysci.org
Hours: Tues through Thurs, 9:30 a.m.–2 p.m.; Fri, 9:30 a.m.– 5 p.m.;
Sat and Sun, 10 a.m.–6 p.m.
When free: Fri, 2–5 p.m.; Sun, 10–11 a.m.; except in July and Aug.

Kids of all ages love this place. A lot of hands-on science experiments, space stuff, and a big glowing brain—who could ask for anything more?

The Noguchi Museum

32–37 Vernon Blvd. (at 33rd Road)
Long Island City, Queens
(718) 204-7088
www.noguchi.org
Hours: Wed through Fri, 10 a.m.–5 p.m.; Sat and Sun, 11 a.m.–6 p.m.
When free: The first Fri of every month.

Housed in a former photo-engraving factory, the museum is devoted entirely to the sculpture and art of Isamu Noguchi. Noguchi sculptures and designs are on display in public and private spaces throughout the world, and the museum houses many of his most striking and noted works in its thirteen galleries and garden space.

The Studio Museum in Harlem

144 W. 125th St. (between Lenox and Seventh Avenues)
(212) 864-4500
www.studiomuseum.org
Hours: Wed through Fri and Sun, noon–6 p.m.; Sat, 10 a.m.–6 p.m.
When free: The first Sat of each month.

The Studio Museum of Harlem presents a variety of ever-changing contemporary exhibitions from established and emerging African artists. The Artist-in-Residence program has cultivated a number of up-and-coming artists including Chakaia Booker, Kerry James Marshall, and Kehinde Wiley. The small loft space also hosts a variety of programs for adults and children.

Whitney Museum of American Art
945 Madison Ave. (at 75th Street)
(212) 570-3600
www.whitney.org
Hours: Wed, Thurs, Sat, and Sun, 11 a.m.–6 p.m.; Fri, 1–9 p.m.
When free: Fri, 6–9 p.m., is "Pay What You Wish."

One of the most impressive collections of modern art in the world, the permanent collection follows the developments of modern work from Hopper to Pollock and from Rauschenberg to today's cutting-edge artists. A couple of floors of the museum are always reserved for changing shows, from historic solo works to daring group shows. Drop by any Fri for pay-what-you-wish night and also take in the free live music and guided and audio tours.

MUSEUMS **WITH** SUGGESTED DONATIONS

A large selection of major and smaller museums in New York operate under a "suggested donation" system. So, while they may "suggest" a $20 "donation," you are under no obligation to make that specific donation. There's no reason to feel bad about giving less than they ask or as little as you can afford. The fact of the matter is, most of these institutions are members of the Cultural Institutions Group (CIG) and receive a tremendous amount of money from the city of New York. One of the obligations that goes along with this cash from the city is that they have to let folks into their museums for whatever they are willing to pay. In essence, you've already paid your admission when you pay your taxes. You can get away with giving as little as a penny. My standard contribution is a quarter (see, I can be generous).

American Museum of Natural History, Central Park West (at 79th Street); (212) 769-5100; www.amnh.org.

Brooklyn Museum, 200 Eastern Parkway (at Washington Avenue); (718) 638-5000; www.brooklynmuseum.org.

The Cloisters, Fort Tryon Park, Washington Heights; (212) 923-3700; www.metmuseum.org.

El Museo del Barrio, 1230 Fifth Ave. (at 105th Street); (212) 831-7272; www.elmuseo.org.

Metropolitan Museum of Art, 1000 Fifth Ave. (at 82nd Street); (212) 535-7710; www.metmuseum.org.

Museum of Chinese in America, 70 Mulberry St., second floor (at Bayard Street); (212) 619-4785; www.mocanyc.org.

Museum of the City of New York, 1220 Fifth Ave. (at 103rd Street); (212) 534-1672; www.mcny.org.

New York City Police Museum, 100 Old Slip (between Water Street and FDR Drive); (212) 480-3100; www.nycpolicemuseum.org.

New York Fire Museum, 278 Spring St. (between Varick and Hudson Streets); (212) 691-1303; www.nycfiremuseum.org.

P.S. 1 Contemporary Art Center, 22–25 Jackson Ave. (at 46th Avenue), Queens; (718) 784-2084; www.ps1.org.

Queens Museum of Art, Flushing Meadows Park; (718) 592-9700; www.queensmuseum.org.

ZOOS:
BORN FREE

"All good things are wild, and free."

—HENRY DAVID THOREAU

It used to be that the best place to see the wildlife for free in New York was to walk around Times Square on any late night. But now that 42nd Street has gotten its face-lift, the closest you will come to seeing anything too wild on those streets are the fake furs and leather worn by visitors to the Disney Shop and Madame Tussaud's. So for some real roars, New York offers some fine collections of everything from African lions, Chilean flamingos, Indian elephants, and Australian lizards to grizzly bears, Goliath beetles, lowland gorillas, and Grevy's zebras. You will find zoos in each of the boroughs, but the only ones that have free hours are the Bronx and Staten Island Zoos. Free days for both zoos are on Wednesday.

The Bronx Zoo

Fordham Road and the Bronx River Parkway
(718) 367-1010
www.bronxzoo.com

The Catch: Free general admission all day on Wed, but you will have to pay to get into some exhibits (which can add up!).

The rain forest of the Congo or the African savanna may not be what you expect to see in the Bronx, but at this, the largest metropolitan zoo in the country, you'll find more than 6,000 animals and exhibits set in startlingly realistic natural habitats. As part of the Wildlife Conservation Society, the Bronx Zoo has played an integral part in saving such endangered species as the snow leopard, the American bison, lowland gorillas, Chinese alligators, Mauritius pink pigeons, and more than forty other species. And bring the family by on any Wednesday to save a fistful of cash. Wednesday is Donation Day, and everyone gets in for whatever they want to pay, even if that's nothing. Beware, many of the more enticing and exciting exhibits and rides do charge additional fees (even on Wednesday), so you might want to pony up some cash for their Pay-One-Price ticket upgrade ($16) if you plan on taking in all the wild sights.

Staten Island Zoo

614 Broadway (off Glenwood Avenue)
(718) 442-3100
www.statenislandzoo.org

The Catch: Free on Wed after 2 p.m.

Particularly well known for its collection of snakes and other reptiles, this small zoo also boasts an aquarium, children's zoo, rain forest, and African savannah habitats and free parking.

ROMANCE: **SWEET** NOTHINGS

Hey, even Cheap Bastards need love. And while it's true that intro-
ducing yourself as a Cheap Bastard may not be the most successful way to
get a date, being a Cheap Bastard shouldn't get in the way of having a great
time. In fact, you might even score extra points by coming up with some
original ideas for romantic liaisons around New York. Here are some great
ways to spend days and evenings with that special someone that won't cost
you a thing (except maybe your heart).

The Untraditional Traditional Date

Why not put a twist on the usual date by seeing a free movie? In the summer
you can pick any number of starlit nights to set out a blanket and cuddle
while you watch the stars of Hollywood twinkle on the screen. My personal
favorite romantic setting is the **Movies with a View,** at the foot of the
Brooklyn Bridge—not too crowded, the skyline of New York as a backdrop,
and fun films on the screen. During the cooler months move indoors with
the free screenings at RiFiFi or Casa Italiana at **NYU.** For more details and
other film ideas, see the chapter titled "Film: Cheap Shots."

The Sweep-Her-Off-Her-Feet Date

Swing down to the **MoonDance** at Hudson River Park any Sunday during
the summer for dancing under the stars to live music. Show up early for
a free lesson. During the cooler months, stick a rose in her mouth and
heat things up by going down to Chelsea Market to do the **Dance of Love**
any Saturday afternoon, when they offer a traditional Argentinean tango
milonga. For details and more dance ideas, see the chapter titled "Dance:
Free Expression."

The Sure-Way-to-Score Date

Spend a day of fun and games in Central Park by borrowing a free **Field Day
Kit** from the folks at the North Meadow Recreation Center. They throw in
all kinds of equipment for almost any sport you can think of. Your big sack
of fun includes a basketball, bats, Wiffle balls, football, Nerf ball, horseshoe

set, Frisbee, jump rope, and even hula hoops. If that doesn't get the two of you working up a sweat, nothing will. For more information see pages 285–286.

The This-Isn't-Quite-Venice-But-Hey-You-Aren't-Quite-Sophia-Loren Date
Your gondola awaits you at the **Downtown Boathouse** on Pier 40 or Pier 96. The bad news is, you have to do all the rowing and serenading yourself; the good news is, it's free. Borrow a kayak for you and your love to paddle up and down the Hudson any weekend from May through Oct. For details see page 179.

The Troubadour Date
If you don't have the voice to serenade your sweetheart by yourself, here's the next best thing. Catch one of the very intimate performances at the **Postcrypt Coffeehouse** on the campus of Columbia University any Friday or Saturday night during the school year. Any candlelit evening of acoustic music is the perfect setting for a romantic evening for two. And hey, there's even free popcorn. For details see pages 29–30.

The Make-'Em-Laugh Date
A surefire way to win someone's heart is to put a smile on their face, and there are many free funny nights every week around the city. During the week you'll find some top-notch comedy performances at the **Upright Citizens Brigade** on Wednesday and Sunday nights. For more details and other comedy destinations, see the chapter titled "Comedy: Cheap Jokes."

The Love-Birds Date
See if a walk among the birds and the bees inspires anything for you. Stop by **Belvedere Castle** in Central Park and borrow a free Birding Kit for a delightful stroll through the wilds of the park. Your kit comes equipped with your very own set of binoculars, a field guide, a sketch pad, and colored pencils. For more details see page 136.

The Pretentious Date
Show your date you can bandy around words like *cubist, conceptual, minimalistic,* and *postmodernist* with the best of them at any of the many art

gallery openings that go on every week. If that doesn't have any effect, maybe all the free wine or beer will. For more details see the chapter titled "Art Galleries: Show Me the Monet."

The Fun-in-the-Sun Date
Spend a day at any one of the local beaches. An old reliable free day. Sorry, they can't all be gems. See pages 183–185 for beaches.

The Show-'Em-You-Got-Class Date
Take in a museum on one of the many free, suggested donation, or pay-what-you-want nights. The best one is **First Saturday Night** at the **Brooklyn Museum**—free live music and dancing, free films, and, oh yeah, there's some art there, too. For more museum details see the chapter titled "Museums: Free to See."

The Not-Quite-The-Great-White-Way Date
Take my advice: If you want a second date, don't try this on a first date. If you've been dating for a while, though, and it's clear that you're both Cheap Bastards, then why not pick a Broadway or Off Broadway show for you to volunteer-usher at together? For a list of theaters to usher at, see the chapter titled "Theater: Free Speech." If you don't want to seem chintzy, get free tickets to a production or concert at Juilliard or NYU or any of the other free theaters listed on pages 19–24.

The You-Think-We've-Got-Problems? Date
Hitting one of those rough patches in the relationship? Well, there's nothing like reveling in someone else's misery to make you feel good about your own life. Take your date to see a taping of *The People's Court* or *Maury* and by comparison, your troubles will surely seem insignificant. For details and more TV taping ideas, see the chapter titled "Television Tapings: Public Access."

The Getting-To-Know-You Date
Why not take the time to get to know each other as you get to know a bit of New York? There are some great walking tours that will give you the time to walk and talk your way around the city. Check out **Take a Walk, New York!,**

Urban Park Rangers tours, or the delightful jaunts through Central Park given by the **Central Park Conservancy.** For more details see the chapter titled "Walking Tours: The Freedom Trail."

The Hey-This-Is-Going-Pretty-Swell-I-May-Just-Want-To-Kiss-You Special Add-On to Any Date

It may not be as romantic as the *Titanic,* but a ride on the Staten Island Ferry will leave you feeling like you're on top of the world. Particularly if you end that date with a romantic kiss on the boat while you ride by the dramatic New York skyline with the wind in your hair. For more details see page 226.

FINDING A CHEAP DATE . . . .

Um, I mean *finding a date, cheap.* It's a big city with lots of single folks out there trying to find each other, but hanging out in bars or going to "singles" parties and events can be costly, not to mention depressing. Here are a couple of alternative ways to make the connection by volunteering and just being your own cheap self.

HurryDate

(646) 435-8264
www.hurrydate.com

The Catch: Door Hosts help set up the event and welcome paying guests. They are not always guaranteed a chance to participate in the "dating" but can mingle and meet potential dates . . . and get paid for it!

Got a minute? Have a date . . . or a dozen. HurryDate puts together energetic evenings where throngs of New York singles meet each other in a rapid-fire succession of mini-dates. They hold events targeted for gay and straight daters of all ages. There are two parts to any HurryDate evening. The evening starts and ends with the usual mix-and-mingle that you'd expect in any singles soiree, but what makes this different is that you're guaranteed twelve to twenty on-the-spot dates. Each date consists of a four-minute conversation where you two can get to know the basics about each other and see if there is enough chemistry there to give the real thing a try. If you both check off "Yes" on your scorecards, HurryDate will hook you up through their website and let nature take its course. You can take part in the evening by being a Door Host, which basically means they will pay you about $40 to help organize the event and greet the paying daters. Door Hosts are able to participate in the face-to-face dating only when there is an odd number of participants and you fit into the age or category of the evening. In any case, you are always able to participate in the schmooze-fest part of the evening.

PARADES: **GRATIS** GATHERINGS

New Yorkers don't need much of an excuse to throw a parade, and nobody does a parade bigger or better than us. Whether celebrating a national holiday, one of New York's many ethnic groups, or just to whoop it up, if it is the weekend, there is almost always a parade heading down a major avenue near you. Here is a detailed list of most New York City parades throughout the year, including approximate dates and locations. For more information on specific dates and locations, I have included contact information wherever possible. For further information call 311, the New York City information line.

JANUARY

Three Kings Day Parade, Third Avenue from 106th to 116th Street; (212) 831-7272; www.elmuseo.org/en/event/33rd-annual-three-kings-day-parade; January 6.

Martin Luther King Jr. Parade, Fifth Avenue from 61st to 86th Street; third Mon in Jan.

Idiotarod, a wild and drunken shopping cart race from Fulton Ferry Pier at the foot of the Brooklyn Bridge, over the bridge and through downtown Manhattan to Tomkins Square Park; www.cartsofbrooklyn.com; last weekend in Jan.

FEBRUARY

Chinese Lunar New Year Celebration and Festival, Mott Street; www.explorechinatown.com.

MARCH

St. Patrick's Day Parade, Fifth Avenue from 44th to 86th Street; March 17; www.saintpatricksdayparade.com.

Brooklyn Irish American Parade, Park Slope, Brooklyn; Seventh Avenue and Prospect Park West from 15th to Union Street; www.saintpatricksday parade.com.

There are many other local St. Patrick's Day parades throughout the city on the weekends near Mar 17; visit www.saintpatricksdayparade.com for all the listings.

Ringling Brothers, Barnum & Bailey Circus's Elephant Walk, 34th Street from the Queens Midtown Tunnel to Madison Square Garden; (212) 465-6741; www.ringling.com; the parade of elephants and other circus animals usually takes place on the Tuesday night before the first performance at Madison; mid-Mar.

Greek Independence Day Parade, Fifth Avenue from 62nd to 79th Street; http://paradeonfifth.org.

Persian-Iranian Parade, Madison Avenue from 41st to 27th Street.

APRIL

Easter Parade, Fifth Avenue between 49th and 57th Street; (212) 484-1200; www.nycgo.com.

New York Tartan Day Parade, Sixth Avenue from 45th to 58th Street; (212) 980-0844; www.tartanweek.com.

Phagwah: Hindu New Year's Parade, Queens, Liberty Avenue from 133rd to 123rd Street to Smokey Oval Park.

Sikh Cultural Society Parade & Festival, Madison Avenue from 41st to 23rd Street.

MAY

Cuban Day Parade (La Gran Parada Cubana), Sixth Avenue from 34th to 59th Street; (212) 348-8270; first Sun in May.

Marijuana March, Broadway from Houston Street to Battery Park; (212) 677-7180; www.cures-not-wars.org; the first Sat of May.

Turkish American Day Parade, Madison Avenue and 56th Street to Second Avenue and 47th Street; www.tadf.org; a Sat in mid-May.

Haitian Flag Day Parade, Brooklyn; Eastern Parkway from Utica Avenue to Grand Army Plaza; third Sun in May.

Norwegian-American 17th of May Parade, Brooklyn; Fifth Avenue and 90th Street to Seventh Avenue and 67th Street; www.may17paradeny.com.

Salute to Israel Parade, Fifth Avenue from 52nd to 79th Street; (646) 472-5388; www.salutetoisrael.com.

JUNE

Philippine Independence Day Parade, Madison Avenue from 40th to 23rd Street; (212) 764-1330; www.pcgny.net.

Queens Pride Parade, Queens; Thirty-seventh Avenue from 89th to 75th Street; www.queenspride.com; first Sun in June.

Puerto Rican Day Parade, Fifth Avenue from 44th to 86th Street; (718) 401-0404; www.nationalpuertoricandayparade.org; second Sun in June.

Hare Krishna Day Parade, Fifth Avenue from 59th Street to Washington Square Park; (718) 855-6714; second Sat in June.

Brooklyn Pride Parade and Festival, Brooklyn; Seventh Avenue from 15th Street to Lincoln Place; (718) 670-3337.

Children's Evangelical Parade, Third Avenue from 96th Street to 122nd Street; third Sun in June.

Bronx Week Parade, the Bronx; Moshulu Parkway; last Sat in June.

International Cultures Parade, Sixth Avenue from 35th to 56th Street; www.10.org.

Mermaid Parade, Brooklyn; Coney Island boardwalk from Stillwell Avenue to West 15th Street; (718) 372-5159; www.coneyisland.com; last Sat in June.

Heritage of Pride Parade, Fifth Avenue from 52nd Street to Christopher Street; (212) 807-7433; www.hopinc.org; last Sun of June.

JULY

Macy's Fourth of July Fireworks, FDR Drive from 14th to 42nd Street; (212) 494-4495; www.macys.com; 9 p.m. on July 4th.

Travis Fourth of July Parade, Staten Island; Victory Boulevard and Cannon Street.

Chinatown Independence Day Parade and Festival, Canal Street to Mott Street and through Chinatown; www.explorechinatown.com; Sun closest to July 4th.

Captive Nations Parade, Fifth Avenue from 59th to 72nd Street; third Sun in June.

Gran Parada Dominicana del Bronx, the Bronx; Grand Concourse from East Tremont Avenue to 161st Street; (718) 993-4463; third Sun in July.

Colombia Day Parade, Queens; Northern Boulevard from 70th to 90th Street; third Sun in July.

AUGUST

Bronx Puerto Rican Day Parade, the Bronx; Grand Concourse from East Tremont Avenue to 161st Street; (718) 401-0404; first Sun in Aug.

Dominican Republican Day Parade, Sixth Avenue from 36th to 58th Street; (212) 795-0107; mid-Aug.

Brooklyn Puerto Rican Day Parade, Brooklyn; Graham Avenue from Broadway to Grand Street; (718) 401-0404; third Sunday in August.

India Independence Day Parade, Madison Avenue from 41st to 27th Street; third Sun of Aug.

Pakistan Independence Day Parade, Madison Avenue from 41st to 27th Street; last Sun of Aug.

SEPTEMBER

Labor Day Parade, Fifth Avenue from 44th to 72nd Street.

West Indian American Day Carnival Day Parade, Brooklyn; Eastern Parkway between Utica Avenue and Grand Army Plaza; (718) 467-1797; Labor Day weekend.

Mexican Day Parade, Madison Avenue from 41st to 23rd Street; second weekend of Sept.

The German-American Steuben Day Parade, Fifth Avenue from 61st to 86th Street; (201) 763-7285; www.germanparadenyc.org; third Sun of Sept.

African-American Day Parade, Adam Clayton Powell Boulevard from 111th to 142nd Street; (212) 862-8497; third Sun in Sept.

Muslim Day Parade, Madison Avenue from 41st to 26th Street; late Sept.

OCTOBER

Nigerian Independence Parade, Second Avenue from 54th to 43rd Street; www.oanweb.org; first Sat in Oct.

Pulaski Day Parade, Fifth Avenue from 26th to 52nd Street; www.pulaski parade.org; first Sun in Oct.

Korean Parade, Broadway from 41st to 23rd Street; (212) 255-6969; first Sun in Oct.

Columbus Day Parade, Fifth Avenue from 44th to 79th Street; (212) 249-9923; www.columbuscitizensfd.org; second Mon in Oct.

Hispanic Day Parade, Fifth Avenue from 44th to 86th Street; second Sun in Oct.

The Village Halloween Parade, Sixth Avenue from Houston to 21st Street; www.halloween-nyc.com; Oct 31.

NOVEMBER

New York City Marathon, throughout the five boroughs; www.ingnycmarathon.org; first Sun in Nov.

Veterans Day Parade, Fifth Avenue from 23rd to 57th Street; (212) 693-1476; Nov 11.

Macy's Thanksgiving Day Parade, Central Park West and Broadway from 79th to 34th Street; (212) 494-4495; www.macys.com; Thanksgiving Day.

DECEMBER

Times Square New Year's Eve, Broadway and Seventh Avenue from 42nd to 57th Street; (212) 768-1560; www.timessquarenyc.org; Dec 31.

PUBLIC **LIBRARY** BRANCH **LOCATIONS**

MANHATTAN

Mid-Manhattan Library, 455 Fifth Ave. (at 40th Street); (212) 340-0833; Telephone Reference, (212) 340-0849, ext. 3; www.nypl.org

East Side
58th Street, 127 E. 58th St.; (212) 759-7358
67th Street, 328 E. 67th St.; (212) 734-1717
96th Street, 112 E. 96th St.; (212) 289-0908
125th Street, 224 E. 125th St.; (212) 534-5050
Aguilar, 174 E. 110th St.; (212) 534-2930
Epiphany, 228 E. 23rd St.; (212) 679-2645
Macomb's Bridge, 2650 Adam Clayton Powell Jr. Blvd.; (212) 281-4900
Ottendorfer, 135 Second Ave.; (212) 674-0947
Roosevelt Island, 524 Main St.; (212) 308-6243
Terence Cardinal Cooke-Cathedral, 560 Lexington Ave.; (212) 752-3824
Webster, 1465 York Ave.; (212) 288-5049
Yorkville, 222 E. 79th St.; (212) 744-5824

West Side
115th Street, 203 W. 115th St.; (212) 666-9393
Andrew Heiskell Braille & Talking Book Library, 40 W. 20th St.; (212) 206-5400; voice mail (212) 206-5425; TDD (212) 206-5458
Bloomingdale, 150 W. 100th St.; (212) 222-8030
Columbus, 742 Tenth Ave.; (212) 586-5098
Countee Cullen, 104 W. 136th St.; (212) 491-2070
Donnell Library Center, 20 W. 53rd St.; (212) 621-0619
Fort Washington, 535 W. 179th St.; (212) 927-3533
George Bruce, 518 W. 125th St.; (212) 662-9727
Hamilton Grange, 503 W. 145th St.; (212) 926-2147

Harlem, 9 W. 124th St.; (212) 348-5620

Inwood, 4790 Broadway; (212) 942-2445

Jefferson Market, 425 Avenue of the Americas; (212) 243-4334

Kips Bay, 446 Third Ave.; (212) 683-2520

Morningside Heights, 2900 Broadway; (212) 864-2530

Muhlenberg, 209 W. 23rd St.; (212) 924-1585

Riverside, 127 Amsterdam Ave.; (212) 870-1810

St. Agnes, 444 Amsterdam Ave.; (212) 877-4380

Seward Park, 192 E. Broadway; (212) 477-6770

Washington Heights, 1000 Saint Nicholas Ave.; (212) 923-6054

Downtown

Battery Park City, 175 North End Ave.; (212) 790-6598

Chatham Square, 33 E. Broadway; (212) 964-6598

Hamilton Fish Park, 415 E. Houston St.; (212) 673-2290

Hudson Park, 66 Leroy St.; (212) 243-6876

New Amsterdam, 9 Murray St.; (212) 732-8186

Tompkins Square, 331 E. 10th St.; (212) 228-4747

THE **BRONX**

Bronx Library Center, 2556 Bainbridge Ave. (at Fordham Road); (718) 579-4244

Bronx Reference Center, (718) 579-4257

Allerton, 2740 Barnes Ave.; (718) 881-4240

Baychester, 2049 Asch Loop North; (718) 379-6700

Belmont Library–Enrico Fermi Cultural Center, 610 E. 186th St.; (718) 933-6410

Castle Hill, 947 Castle Hill Ave.; (718) 824-3838

City Island, 320 City Island Ave.; (718) 885-1703

Clason's Point, 1215 Morrison Ave.; (718) 842-1235

Eastchester, 1385 E. Gun Hill Rd.; (718) 653-3292

Edenwald, 1255 E. 233rd St.; (718) 798-3355

Francis Martin, 2150 University Ave.; (718) 295-5287

Grand Concourse, 155 E. 173rd St.; (718) 583-6611

High Bridge, 78 W. 168th St.; (718) 293-7800

Hunt's Point, 877 Southern Blvd.; (718) 617-0338

Jerome Park, 118 Eames Place; (718) 549-5200

Kingsbridge, 280 W. 231st St.; (718) 548-5656

Melrose, 910 Morris Ave.; (718) 588-0110

Morrisania, 610 E. 169th St.; (718) 589-9268

Morris Park, 985 Morris Park Ave.; (718) 931-0636

Mosholu, 285 E. 205th St.; (718) 882-8239

Mott Haven, 321 E. 140th St.; (718) 665-4878

Parkchester, 1985 Westchester Ave.; (718) 829-7830

Pelham Bay, 3060 Middletown Rd.; (718) 792-6744

Riverdale, 5540 Mosholu Ave.; (718) 549-1212

Sedgwick, 1701 Dr. Martin Luther King Jr. Blvd.; (718) 731-2074

Soundview, 660 Soundview Ave.; (718) 589-0880

Spuyten Duyvil, 650 W. 235th St.; (718) 796-1202

Throg's Neck, 3025 Cross Bronx Expressway Extension; (718) 792-2612

Tremont, 1866 Washington Ave.; (718) 299-5177

Van Cortlandt, 3874 Sedgwick Ave.; (718) 543-5150

Van Nest, 2147 Barnes Ave.; (718) 829-5864

Wakefield, 4100 Lowerre Place; (718) 652-4663

Westchester Square, 2521 Glebe Ave.; (718) 863-0436

West Farms, 2085 Honeywell Ave.; (718) 367-5376

Woodlawn Heights, 4355 Katonah Ave.; (718) 519-9627

Woodstock, 761 E. 160th St.; (718) 665-6255

BROOKLYN

Central Library, Grand Army Plaza (Flatbush Avenue and Eastern Parkway); (718) 230-2100; www.brooklynpubliclibrary.org; Telephone Reference, (718) 230-2100, ext. 5

Arlington, Arlington Avenue at Warwick Street; (718) 277-6105

Bay Ridge, Ridge Boulevard at 73rd Street; (718) 748-5709

Bedford, Franklin Avenue at Hancock Street; (718) 623-0012

Bedford Learning Center, (718) 623-2134

Borough Park, 43rd Street near Thirteenth Avenue; (718) 437-4085

Brighton Beach, Brighton First Road (near Brighton Beach Avenue); (718) 946-2917

Brooklyn Heights, 280 Cadman Plaza West (at Tillary Street); (718) 623-7100

Brower Park, St. Marks Avenue near Nostrand Avenue; (718) 773-7208

Brownsville, Glenmore Avenue at Watkins Street; (718) 498-9721

Bushwick, Bushwick Avenue at Seigel Street; (718) 602-1348

Business Library, 280 Cadman Plaza at Tillary Street; (718) 623-7000

Canarsie, Rockaway Parkway near Avenue J; (718) 257-6547

Carroll Gardens, Clinton Street at Union Street; (718) 596-6972

Clarendon, Nostrand Avenue near Farragut Road; (718) 421-1159

Clinton Hill, Washington Avenue near Lafayette Avenue; (718) 398-8713

Coney Island, Mermaid Avenue near West 19th Street; (718) 265-3220

Coney Island Learning Center; (718) 265-3880

Cortelyou, Cortelyou Road at Argyle Road; (718) 693-7763

Crown Heights, New York Avenue at Maple Street; (718) 773-1180

Cypress Hills, Sutter Avenue at Crystal Street; (718) 277-6004

DeKalb, Bushwick Avenue at DeKalb Avenue; (718) 455-3898

Dyker, Thirteenth Avenue at 82nd Street; (718) 748-6261

Eastern Parkway, Eastern Parkway at Schenectady Avenue; (718) 953-4225

Eastern Parkway Adult Learning Center; (718) 778-9330

East Flatbush, 9612 Church Ave. near Rockaway Parkway; (718) 922-0927

Flatbush, Linden Boulevard near Flatbush Avenue; (718) 856-0813

Flatlands, Flatbush Avenue at Avenue P; (718) 253-4409

Fort Hamilton, Fourth Avenue at 95th Street; (718) 748-6919

Gerritsen Beach, Gerritsen Avenue at Channel Avenue; (718) 368-1435

Gravesend, Avenue X near West 2nd Street; (718) 382-5792

Greenpoint, Norman Avenue at Leonard Street; (718) 349-8504

Highlawn, West 13th Street at Kings Highway; (718) 234-7208

Homecrest, Coney Island Avenue near Avenue V; (718) 382-5924

Jamaica Bay, Seaview Avenue at East 98th Street; (718) 241-3571

Kensington, Ditmas Avenue near East 5th Street; (718) 435-9431

Kings Bay, Nostrand Avenue near Avenue W; (718) 368-1709

Kings Highway, Ocean Avenue near Kings Highway; (718) 375-3037

Leonard, Devoe Street at Leonard Street; (718) 486-3365

Macon, Lewis Avenue at Macon Street; (718) 573-5606

Mapleton, 60th Street at Seventeenth Avenue; (718) 256-2117

Marcy, DeKalb Avenue near Nostrand Avenue; (718) 935-0032

McKinley Park, Fort Hamilton Parkway at 68th Street; (718) 748-8001

Midwood, East 16th Street near Avenue J; (718) 252-0967

Mill Basin, Ralph Avenue near Avenue N; (718) 241-3973

New Lots, New Lots Avenue at Barbey Street; (718) 649-0311

New Utrecht, 1783 86th St. (at Bay 17th Street); (718) 236-4086

Pacific, Fourth Avenue at Pacific Street; (718) 638-1531

Paerdegat, East 59th Street near Flatlands Avenue; (718) 241-3994

Park Slope, Sixth Avenue near 9th Street; (718) 832-1853

Red Hook, Wolcott Street at Dwight Street; (718) 935-0203

Rugby, Utica Avenue near Tilden Avenue; (718) 566-0054

Ryder, Twenty-third Avenue at 59th Street; (718) 331-2962

Saratoga, Thomas S. Boyland Street at Macon Street; (718) 573-5224

Sheepshead Bay, East 14th Street near Avenue Z; (718) 368-1815

Spring Creek, Flatlands Avenue near New Jersey Avenue; (718) 257-6571

Stone Avenue, 581 Mother Gaston Blvd. at Dumont Avenue; (718) 485-8347

Sunset Park, Fourth Avenue at 51st Street; (718) 567-2806

Ulmer Park, Bath Avenue at Twenty-sixth Avenue; (718) 265-3443

Walt Whitman, 93 St. Edwards St. (at Auburn Place); (718) 935-0244

Washington Irving, Irving Avenue at Woodbine Street; (718) 628-8378

Williamsburg, 240 Division Ave. (at Marcy Avenue); (718) 302-3485

Windsor Terrace, East 5th Street at Fort Hamilton Parkway; (718) 686-9707

QUEENS

Central Library, 89–11 Merrick Blvd. (between Eighty-ninth and Ninetieth Avenues); (718) 990-0700; www.queenslibrary.org; Telephone Reference, (718) 990-0714 or (718) 990-0728

Arverne, Beach 54th St.; (718) 634-4784

Astoria, 14–01 Astoria Blvd.; (718) 278-2220

Auburndale, 25–55 Francis Lewis Blvd.; (718) 352-2027

Baisley Park, 117–11 Sutphin Blvd.; (718) 529-1590

Bayside, 214–20 Northern Blvd.; (718) 229-1834

Bay Terrace, 18–36 Bell Blvd.; (718) 423-7004

Bellerose, 250–06 Hillside Ave.; (718) 831-8644

Briarwood, 85–12 Main St.; (718) 658-1680

Broad Channel, 16–26 Cross Bay Blvd.; (718) 318-4943

Broadway, 40–20 Broadway; (718) 721-2462

Cambria Heights, 220–20 Linden Blvd.; (718) 528-3535

Corona, 38–23 104th St. (between Thirty-eighth and Thirty-ninth Avenues); (718) 426-2844

Court Square, 25–01 Jackson Ave.; (718) 937-2790

Douglaston/Little Neck, 249–01 Northern Blvd.;(718) 225-8414

East Elmhurst, 95–06 Astoria Blvd.; (718) 424-2619

East Flushing, 196–36 Northern Blvd.; (718) 357-6643

Elmhurst, 86–01 Broadway; (718) 271-1020

Far Rockaway, 1637 Central Ave.; (718) 327-2549

Flushing, 41–17 Main St.; (718) 661-1200

Forest Hills, 108–19 Seventy-first Ave.; (718) 268-7934

Fresh Meadows, 193–20 Horace Harding Expressway; (718) 454-7272

Glendale, 78–60 73rd Place; (718) 821-4980

Glen Oaks, 256–04 Union Tpk.; (718) 831-8636

Hillcrest, 187–05 Union Tpk.; (718) 454-2786

Hollis, 202–05 Hillside Ave.; (718) 465-7355

Howard Beach, 92–06 156th Ave.; (718) 641-7086

Jackson Heights, 35–51 81st St.; (718) 899-2500

Kew Gardens Hills, 72–33 Vleigh Place; (718) 261-6654

Langston Hughes, 100–01 Northern Blvd.; (718) 651-1100

Laurelton, 134–26 225th St.; (718) 528-2822

Lefferts, 103–34 Lefferts Blvd.; (718) 843-5950

Lefrak City, 98–25 Horace Harding Expressway.; (718) 592-7677

Long Island City, 37–44 21st St.; (718) 752-3700

Maspeth, 69–70 Grand Ave.; (718) 639-5228

McGoldrick, 155–06 Roosevelt Ave.; (718) 461-1616

Middle Village, 72–31 Metropolitan Ave.; (718) 326-1390

Mitchell–Linden, 29–42 Union St.; (718) 539-2330

North Forest Park, 98–27 Metropolitan Ave.; (718) 261-5512

North Hills, 57–04 Marathon Parkway; (718) 225-3550

Ozone Park, 92–24 Rockaway Blvd.; (718) 845-3127

Peninsula, 92–25 Rockaway Beach Blvd.; (718) 634-1110

Pomonok, 158–21 Jewel Ave.; (718) 591-4343

Poppenhusen, 121–23 Fourteenth Ave.; (718) 359-1102

Queensboro Hill, 60–05 Main St.; (718) 359-8332
Queensbridge, 10–43 Forty-first Ave.; (718) 937-6266
Queens Village, 94–11 217th St.; (718) 776-6800
Ravenswood, 35–32 21st St.; (718) 784-2112
Rego Park, 91–41 63rd Dr.; (718) 459-5140
Richmond Hill, 118–14 Hillside Ave.; (718) 849-7150
Ridgewood, 20–12 Madison St.; (718) 821-4770
Rochdale Village, 169–09 137th Ave.; (718) 723-4440
Rosedale, 144–20 243rd St.; (718) 528-8490
St. Albans, 191–05 Linden Blvd.; (718) 528-8196
Seaside, 116–15 Rockaway Beach Blvd.; (718) 634-1876
South Hollis, 204–01 Hollis Ave.; (718) 465-6779
South Jamaica, 108–41 Guy R. Brewer Blvd.; (718) 739-4088
South Ozone Park, 128–16 Rockaway Blvd.; (718) 529-1660
Steinway, 21–45 31st St.; (718) 728-1965
Sunnyside, 43–06 Greenpoint Ave.; (718) 784-3033
Whitestone, 151–10 14th Rd.; (718) 767-8010
Windsor Park, 79–50 Bell Blvd.; (718) 468-8300
Woodhaven, 85–41 Forest Parkway.; (718) 849-1010
Woodside, 54–22 Skillman Ave.; (718) 429-4700

STATEN **ISLAND**

Dongan Hills, 1617 Richmond Rd.; (718) 351-1444
Great Kills, 56 Giffords Lane; (718) 984-6670
Huguenot Park, 830 Huguenot Ave.; (718) 984-4636
New Dorp, 309 New Dorp Lane; (718) 351-2977
Port Richmond, 75 Bennett St.; (718) 442-0158
Richmondtown, 200 Clarke Ave.; (718) 668-0413
St. George Library Center, 5 Central Ave.; (718) 442-8560
South Beach, 21–25 Robin Rd.; (718) 816-5834
Stapleton, 132 Canal St.; (718) 727-0427
Todt Hill–Westerleigh, 2550 Victory Blvd.; (718) 494-1642
Tottenville, 7430 Amboy Rd.; (718) 984-0945
West New Brighton, 976 Castleton Ave.; (718) 442-1416

APPENDIX D:

NEW YORK CITY RECREATION CENTERS

Additional information for the following parks can be found at **www.nyc govparks.org.**

MANHATTAN

Alfred East Smith (Lower East Side)
80 Catherine St. (off Cherry Street, between Madison and South Streets); (212) 285-0300

Dance classes, open basketball, badminton, gardening club, basic computer courses, kickboxing and karate classes.

Asser Levy (Midtown East Side)
East 23rd Street and Asser Levy Place (at FDR Drive); (212) 447-2020

Indoor and outdoor pool, group fitness classes, martial arts classes, swim classes, guitar lessons, yoga, senior programs.

Chelsea Recreation Center
430 W. 25th St. (between Ninth and Tenth Avenues); (212) 255-3705

Indoor pool, cardio and fitness strength-training equipment, basketball, volleyball, game room, computer resource center, and a variety of fitness classes.

East 54 (Upper East Side)
348 E. 54th St. (between First and Second Avenues); (212) 754-5411

Extensive schedule of fitness, yoga, and dance classes; indoor pool, track; after-school and senior programs.

Hamilton Fish (Lower East Side)

128 Pitt St. (at East Houston Street); (212) 387-7687

Olympic-size outdoor pool, game room, fitness room, basketball courts, wrestling, computer classes, karate class.

Hansborough (Central Harlem)

35 W. 134th St. (between Lenox and Fifth Avenues); (212) 234-9603

Outdoor rooftop sundeck, indoor pool, outdoor and indoor track, aerobic classes, fitness room, seniors programs.

Highbridge (Washington Heights)

Amsterdam Avenue and West 173rd Street; (212) 927-2012

Basketball courts, game room, computer center, dance and martial arts classes, after-school program.

Jackie Robinson (West Harlem)

85 Bradhurst Ave. (at 146th Street); (212) 324-9607

Olympic-size outdoor pool, fitness room, computer classes, volleyball, teen cooking classes, after-school program.

J. Hood Wright (Washington Heights)

351 Fort Washington Ave. (at 174th Street); (212) 927-1563

Fitness room, computer center, softball and basketball tournaments, game room, two athletic fields, tennis court, handball courts, teen and senior programs.

Morningside Park (West Harlem)

410 West 123rd St. (at Morningside Avenue); (212) 280-0209

Operates primarily as an after-school and senior center.

North Meadow (Upper East and West Side)

Central Park (mid-park at 97th Street); (212) 348-4867

Tai chi and yoga classes, youth adventure programs, climbing wall (open-climbing hours are free for eight- to twelve-year-olds; adults $5), basketball clinics, and Field Day Kits. (Borrow a sack of equipment from them for a fun day in the park. The kit includes a basketball, ten cones, three bats, a horseshoe set, playground ball, Nerf ball, football, Frisbee, two handballs, a soccer ball, jump rope, two Wiffle balls, and hula hoops.)

Pelham Fritz (West Harlem)
18 Mount Morris Park West (at 122nd Street); (212) 860-1380

Outdoor pool, computer room, aerobics classes, dance classes, drumming, extensive senior programs, game room, basketball courts.

Recreation Center 59 (Midtown West)
533 W. 59th St. (between Tenth and Eleventh Avenues); (212) 397-3159

Indoor pool, small fitness room.

Thomas Jefferson (East Harlem)
2180 First Ave. (at East 112th Street); (212) 860-1383

Olympic-size outdoor pool, fitness room, basketball courts, athletic fields, martial arts classes, aerobic classes, boxing, handball courts, game room.

Tony Dapolito Recreation Center (West Village/SoHo)
1 Clarkson St. (near Seventh Avenue South and Houston Street); (212) 242-5228

Very popular center. Indoor and outdoor pools, handball courts, two fitness rooms, indoor track, boccie court, fitness classes, basketball and flag football leagues.

BROOKLYN

Brooklyn Senior Center (Fort Hamilton)
9941 Fort Hamilton Parkway. (at 100th Street); (718) 439-4296

Line dancing, tap dancing, social dancing, arts and crafts, day trips, bingo, computer access.

Brownsville

1555 Linden Blvd. (between Mother Gaston and Christopher Streets); (718) 345-2706

Indoor pool, computer center, aerobics classes, martial arts classes, game room, basketball clinics, handball courts, track and field, music studio.

Metropolitan Pool and Fitness Center (Williamsburg)

261 Bedford Ave. (at Metropolitan Avenue); (718) 599-5707

Indoor pool, fitness room, computer center, computer and digital video classes, play schoolroom, and "arguably the best indoor pool in New York City," says the *Village Voice*.

Red Hook

155 Bay St. (between Henry and Clinton Streets); (718) 722-3211

Outdoor pool, computer center and classes, aerobics, martial arts, yoga.

St. John's Recreation Center

1251 Prospect Place (at Schenectady Avenue); (718) 771-2787

Indoor pool, computer center and classes, fitness room, aerobics, tai chi, SAT classes, quilting, senior programs.

Sunset Park

Seventh Avenue and 43rd Street (at 42nd Street); (718) 965-6533

Outdoor pool, computer center, fitness room, boxing room, aerobics classes, *tae bo* classes, game room.

Von King Cultural Arts Center

670 Lafayette Ave. (between Marcy and Tompkins Avenues); (718) 622-2082

Computer center, aerobics classes, game room, dance room, athletic fields, handball courts.

THE BRONX

Haffen Park

Hammersley Avenue at Ely, Gunther, and Burke Avenues; (718) 379-8347

Outdoor pool, tennis courts, senior center, handball courts.

Hunts Point

765 Manida St. (between Lafayette Street and Spofford Avenue);
(718) 860-5544

Fitness room; dance, aerobics, and karate classes; volleyball and basketball courts; movies on the last Fri of every month.

Kingsbridge

3101 Kingsbridge Terrace (between Perot Street and Sedgwick Avenue);
(718) 884-0700

After-school teen and senior programs, computer and back-to-work classes.

Mullaly

East 164th Street (at River Avenue); (718) 590-5743

Outdoor skate park.

Owen Dolan

1400 Westchester Sq.; (718) 822-4282

Small facility with some family-oriented classes.

St. James

2530 Jerome Ave. (at 192nd Street); (718) 367-3658

Computer center, tennis courts, basketball courts, handball courts, teen and senior programs.

St. Mary's

450 St. Ann's Ave. (at 145th Street); (718) 402-5160

Indoor pool, computer center, fitness room, basketball courts, aerobics classes, boxing, cooking, karate, tae kwon do, teen programs, scuba classes, tennis courts, athletic field.

West Bronx
1527 Jessup Ave. (at 172nd Street); (718) 293-5934

After-school programs, basketball courts, weight room, and tae kwon do classes.

Williamsbridge Oval
3225 Reservoir Oval East (between 208th Street and Bainbridge Avenue); (718) 654-1851

Fitness room, tennis courts, basketball courts, handball courts, outdoor track, play schoolroom, karate classes, twenty-two-acre playground, senior programs.

QUEENS

Detective Keith L. Williams (Jamaica)
173rd Place and Liberty Avenue (at 106th Street); (718) 523-6912

Outdoor pool, tennis courts, handball courts, cooking classes, garden, arts and crafts.

Lost Battalion Hall (Rego Park)
93–29 Queens Blvd. (at Sixty-second Avenue); (718) 263-1163

Computer center, boxing room, fitness center, karate, kickboxing, rhythmic gymnastics, Gymboree, senior program.

Louis Armstrong (Corona)
108th Street and Northern Boulevard; (718) 651-0096

Fitness room, karate classes, dance classes, boxing, GED program, community groups, basketball, handball.

Passerelle
Flushing Meadows Corona Park (between National Tennis Center and Shea Stadium); (718) 760-6937

Fitness room, computer center, REACH program for people with disabilities. "We are more like a visitor center. We invite groups to come to us—school groups, organizations, seniors, etc."

Roy Wilkins Family Center (St. Albans)
177th Street at Baisley Boulevard; (718) 276-8686

Indoor pool, fitness room, outdoor track, extensive senior program.

Sorrentino (Far Rockaway)
18–48 Cornaga Ave. (at Beach 19th Street); (718) 471-4818

Fitness room, computer center, double Dutch program, computer classes, play school, senior programs.

STATEN ISLAND

Cromwell Center
Murray Hulbert Avenue at Pier 6; (718) 816-6172

Fitness room, aerobics classes, computer classes, wood carving and ceramics classes, kid and teen programs.

Greenbelt Recreation Center
Brielle Avenue (between Walcott and Rockland Avenues, across from Sea View Hospital); (718) 667-3545

Tennis courts, basketball courts, soccer field, arts and crafts room, performance space, croquet lawn.

INDEX

A Choice Nanny, 119
Acker Merrall & Condit Co., 97
African-American Day Parade, 275
after-school programs, 123
Agata & Valentina, 85
Aguilar Library, 130
AIDS Clinical Trial Information
    Service, 165
airports, 229
Aji Ichiban, 85
Alfred East Smith Recreation
    Center, 284
Alliance Française, 190
Ambassador Wines & Spirits, 94
American Academy of Dramatic
    Arts, 20
American Barber Institute, 111
American Folk Art Museum, 250, 256
American Museum of Natural
    History, 262
Amish Market, 90
AM New York, 193
Angel Street, 206
Animal Care & Control of New York
    City, 210
Animal Cracker, 212
Animal General, 211
Anthology Film Archive, 45
Apple Store, 150
art galleries, 237
art galleries, Chelsea, 238
art galleries, opening receptions,
    240, 245
art galleries, other galleries around
    New York, 245
art galleries, SoHo, 241
art galleries, Williamsburg,
    Brooklyn, 243
Arthur's Tavern, 30

Artists Space, 242
Art Now's Gallery Guide, 239
arts and crafts, children and
    teens, 124
arts, education, 144
Art Shack, The, 124
Ashton's, 77
Asian Classics Institute, The, 157
Asia Society, 257
ASPCA, 210
Asser Levy Pool, 180
Asser Levy Recreation Center, 284
Astoria Pool, 182
Astor Wines & Spirits, 101
Atlantic Theater Company, 6
Atlas Barber School, 112
Audience Extras, 17
Audubon Terrace, 250
Austrian Cultural Forum, 215
Auto Driveaway Company, 226
Aveda Institute, 112
Ayurveda's Beauty Care Spa & Bioticare
    Holistic Center, 163

Back Fence, The, 27
Bakery Soutine, 88
Balthazar Bakery, 85
BAM Rhythm & Blues Festival, 36
Bank Street Bookstore, 139
Barbara Gladstone Gallery, 239
Barbès, 45
Barking Zoo, 212
Barnes & Noble, 140
Bartow-Pell Mansion Museum, 257
Battery Park City Parks, 132, 171
Battery Park City Walking Tours, 215
Baychester Library, 54
Bay Ridge Library, 54, 131
beaches, 183

Beacon Schools, 123
beauty, makeup, 115
beauty schools, 111
beauty services, 103
Beekman Liquors, 94
beer, Brooklyn, 96
Bellevue Hospital Center, 164
Belvedere Castle, 267
Belvedere Castle/Henry Luce Nature
    Observatory, 136
Bergdorf Goodman, 114
Best Cellars, 95, 98
Beth Israel Medical Center, 165
Betsy Head Pool, 181
Bide-A-Wee, 211
Bierkraft, 96
Big Apple Greeters, 215
Big City Fishing, 133
Bike New York, 175
biking, 175
Bikram Yoga NYC, 155
Birthright Israel, 230
Black Hound New York, 86
blogs, 195
Bloomingdale Branch, 130
Bloomingdales, 114
Blue Man Group, 6
boating, 179
Books of Wonder, 140
Boomerang Theatre Company, 20
Brazen Head, The, 84
Brighton Beach, 183
Brighton Beach Library, 54
Broadway Dance Center, 69
Broadway Windows, 245
Bronx Library Center, 130
Bronx Museum of the Arts, 257
Bronx Puerto Rican Day Parade, 274
Bronx Week Parade, 273
Bronx Zoo, The, 265
Brooklyn Botanic Garden, The, 233
Brooklyn Brewery, 96, 216
Brooklyn Children's Museum, 136

Brooklyn GreenBridge & Urban
    Composting Project, 235
Brooklyn Heights Music Society, 33
Brooklyn Irish American Parade, 272
Brooklyn Museum, 258, 262, 268
Brooklyn Pride Parade and Festival, 273
Brooklyn Public Library, 152
Brooklyn Public Library's Business
    Library, 151
Brooklyn Puerto Rican Day Parade, 275
Brooklyn Queens Conservatory
    of Music, 34
Brooklyn Senior Center, 286
Brower Park Library, 131
Brownsville Recreation Center, 287
Bryant Park, 37, 171
Bryant Park Skating Rink, 175
Bryant Park Summer Film Festival, 46
Bumble & Bumble, 106
Burgundy Wine Company, 101
Bushwick Clinic, 169
Bushwick Houses Pool, 181
BWAC Pier Shows, 246

Café Amrita, 91
Café Angelique, 91
Calling All Pets, 211
Candlelight Wines, 98
Capla Kesting Fine Art, 244
Captive Nations Parade, 274
Carnegie Hall, 251
Carnegie Hall Neighborhood Concert
    Series, 34
Carsten Institute, 108
Casa Italiana Zerilli-Marimò, 46
Castle Clinton, 251
Celebrate Brooklyn, 37, 47, 65
Center for Anti-Violence Education,
    The, 133
Center Watch, 165
Central Harlem STD Clinic, 168
Central Library, Brooklyn, 54, 131
Central Library, Queens, 132

Central Park, 172
Central Park Conservancy, 269
Central Park Conservatory Gardens, The, 233
Central Park SummerStage, 37, 65
Central Park tours, 216
Chambers Pottery, 144
Channel 4, 80
Charles A. Dana Discovery Center, The, 39, 133
Charley O's Bar & Grill & Bar, 80
Chatham Square Library, 53
Cheim & Read, 239
Chelsea Market, 86
Chelsea Recreation Center, 284
ChelseArt, 239
Chelsea STD Clinic, 168
Chelsea Wine Vault, 98
Cherry Lane Theatre, The, 6
Child Health Plus, 135
children and teens, 121
children and teens, after-school programs, 123
children and teens, arts and crafts, 124
children and teens, films, 128, 129
children and teens, fun stores, 137
children and teens, health insurance, 135
children and teens, museums, 136
children and teens, sports and games, 132
children and teens, storytelling, 139
Children's Evangelical Parade, 273
Chinatown Independence Day Parade and Festival, 274
Chinese Lunar New Year Celebration and Festival, 271
Choristers, 124
Christine Valmy International School for Esthetics, 112
Circus Amok, 24
City Bakery, The, 91

CityParks Kids, 141
CityParks Theater, 24
City Parks Youth Tennis, Track and Field, and Golf, 134
Clairol Product Evaluation Salon, 104
Claremont Pool, 181
Classic Stage Company, 7
clinical studies, 162
Clinton Veterinary Center, 212
Cloisters, The, 262
Club Getaway, 227
Colbert Report, The, 56
Coler-Goldwater Memorial Hospital, 164
Colombia Day Parade, 274
Columbia-Presbyterian Medical Center, 162
Columbia University, 154
Columbia University tour, 216
Columbus Day Parade, 276
Columbus Library, 130
Columbus Wines & Spirits, 99
comedy, 61
Commodore Barry Pool, 181
community gardens, 236
Coney Island, 183
Coney Island Hospital, 166
Coney Island Library, 131
Cool Music for Warm Summer Days, 38
Cooper-Hewitt, National Design Museum, 125
Cooper Union for the Advancement of Science and Art, The, 151
Cork & Bottle, 95
Corona STD Clinic, 169
Cosi restaurants, 86
Country Vet, The, 211
Crocodile Lounge, 83
Cromwell Center, 290
Crops for Girls, 106
Crotona, 181
Crush Wine Co., 95

Cuban Day Parade, 273
Cucina di Pesce, 83
Culture Project, The, 7
Cumberland Diagnostic & Treatment
     Center, 166
Cutler Salon, 108
Czech Center at Bohemian National
     Hall, 47

Daily Show with Jon Stewart, The, 56
dance, 64
dance, doing it, 68
Dance of Love, 266
Dance Tango, 68
dance, watching it, 65
dance, work-study classes, 69
Dancing in the Streets, 66
dating, 266
Deitch Projects, 242
Dempsey's Pub, 27
depression/mental health clinical
     trials, 167
Detective Keith L. Williams Recreation
     Center, 289
Deutsches Haus, 47
DIA Center for the Arts, 242
Dial-a-Teacher, 122
Dias y Flores, 155
Dieu Donne Papermill, 144
directory assistance, free, 225
D. J. Reynolds, 80
Domestic Placement Network, 119
Dominican Republican Day Parade, 274
Donnell Library Center, 53
Douglas and Degraw Pool, 181
Douglas Kelley Show List, The, 240
Downtown Boathouse, The, 179, 267
Downtown Community Television
     Center, 48, 145
Downtown Express, 194
Downtown NYC River to River
     Festival, 40
Downtown Third Thursday, 145

Dramatics NYC, 107
Drawing Center, The, 243
Dr. Susan Smith McKinney Nursing and
     Rehabilitation Center, 166
Dry Dock Pool, 180
Dumpster dining, 202

East 54 Recreation Center, 284
Easter Parade, 272
East Harlem STD Clinic, 169
East New York Diagnostic & Treatment
     Center, 166
Echo Free Clinic, 161
education, 143
education, arts, 144
education, body, 155
education, food and wine, 148
education, gardening, 235
education, libraries, 152
education, mind, 150
education, spirit, 157
Eglise Français Du St. Esprit, 151
Ehrlich Wines & Spirits, 95
8th Street Walking Tour, 217
80 Washington Square East
     Galleries, 246
86th Street Corner Wine & Liquor
     Company, 99
86th Street Wine & Liquor, 96
11th Street Bar, 83
Eli's, 86
Elmhurst Hospital Center, 166
El Museo del Barrio, 38, 263
Empire Beauty School, 113
Empire Skate Club of New York, 176
Encores, 7
English Classes for Speakers of
     Other Languages, 153

Faber Pool, 182
Face Station, 107
Falun Dafa, 157
Family Extensions, 119

Fantasma Magic, 73
F.A.O. Schwarz, 138
Fashion Institute of Technology
    Museum, 251
Feature Inc., 246
Federal Hall National Memorial, 252
Federal Reserve Bank, The, 217
festivals, 40
Field Day Kit, 266
52nd Street Project, 20
55 Bar, 31
58th Street Library, 53
films, 44
films, at libraries, 53
films, children and teens, 128
films, free, 45
films, free screening passes, 50
Film/Video Arts, 145
First Saturday Night, 268
Fisher Landau Center For Art, The, 252
Fisher Pool, 182
fitness, fun, and games, 170
fitness, fun, and games, beaches, 183
fitness, fun, and games, boating, 179
fitness, fun, and games, parks, 171
fitness, fun, and games, public
    pools, 180
fitness, fun, and games, recreation
    centers, 174
Flatbush Library, 131
Floating the Apple, 179
Flushing Library, 132
food, 76
food, eat late, eat cheap, 90
food, education, 148
food, free samples, 84
food, happy hour, 77
Food Not Bombs NYC, 82
Fools Co. Inc.'s New York School for
    Performing Arts, 125
Forbes Magazine Galleries, 252
Fordham Library Center, 130
Fort Greene STD Clinic, 169

Fort Totten Pool, 182
Foundation Center, The, 189
Free Braking and Safety Clinic in
    Central Park, 178
Free Concerts in Parks, 38
Freecycle, 199
Freegans, 202
French Institute, 190
French Institute/Alliance Française, 47
fruit stands, 207
furniture and household goods, 198
furniture, curbside shopping tips, 200
furniture, favorite finds, 200

Gagosian Gallery, 239
Galerie Lelong, 240
gardening, education, 235
gardens and gardening, 232
gardens, community, 236
gardens, public, 233
Gateway National Recreation Area, 184
Gay Men's Health Crisis (GMHC), 168
General Grant's National Monument, 253
German-American Steuben Day
    Parade, The, 275
Goethe Institute, 190
Go NYC, 194
Good Morning America, 57
Gorilla Rep, 24
Gotham Girls Roller Derby, 177
Gourmet Garage, 87
Gouverneur Nursing Facility and
    Diagnostic & Treatment Center, 164
Governors Island, 172
Gowanus Dredgers Canoe Club, The, 180
Grand Central Station area tour, 218
Grand Central Terminal tour, 217
Grand Concourse Library, 131
Grand Tour, The, 218
Gran Parada Dominicana del Bronx, 274
grants and scholarships, 189
Greek Independence Day Parade, 272
Greenbelt Recreation Center, 290

Green Guerillas, 236
Greenmarket Farmers Market, 87
GreenThumb, 236
Greenwich House Pottery, 146
Groove, 31
Guggenheim Museum, 258

Haffen Park, 288
Haffen Pool, 181
hair and beauty, product testing
   centers, 104
hair, beauty, and massage, 103
hair salons, 105
hair salons, training programs, 108
Haitian Flag Day Parade, 273
Hall of Fame for Great Americans, 253
Halloween Adventure, 138
Hamilton Fish Pool, 180
Hamilton Fish Recreation Center, 285
Hank's Saloon, 28, 84
Hansborough Recreation Center, 285
Hans Christian Andersen statue, 141
happy hour, 77
Hare Krishna Day Parade, 273
Harlem Hospital Center, 164
Harlem Meer Performance Festival, 39
Harlem Week/Harlem Jazz and Music
   Festival, 39
HB Playwrights Foundation, 21
health and medical, 160
health and medical, clinical
   studies, 162
health and medical, depression/mental
   health clinical trials, 167
health and medical, free clinics, 161
health and medical, free condoms, 168
health and medical, Health & Hospitals
   Corporation, 164
health and medical, STD clinics, 167
health and medical, student
   clinics, 163
health and medical, websites for
   clinical studies, 165

Health & Hospitals Corporation, 164
health insurance, children and
   teens, 135
Heimbolt Family Children's Learning
   Center, Scandinavia House, 140
Henry George School of Social
   Science, 153
Here Performance Art Cafe, 8
Heritage of Pride Parade, 274
Highbridge Pool, 181
Highbridge Recreation Center, 285
High Vibe Health & Healing, 156
Hispanic Day Parade, 276
Holland Tunnel, 244
Hostelling International New
   York, 219
household goods, 198
Housing Education Program, 153
Housing Partnership Development
   Corporation, 118
Housing Works Thrift Shops, 206
Howard Pool, 181
Hudson River Festival, 40
Hudson River Park, 173
Hudson Warehouse, 24
Hunts Point Recreation Center, 288
HurryDate, 269

Idiotarod, 271
India Independence Day Parade, 275
in-line skating, instruction, 178
Institute for Fine Arts at NYU, 146
Instituto Cervantes, 48
Instituto Cervantes Library, 191
Integral Yoga Natural Foods, 91
Interchurch Center, The, 34
International Center of
   Photography, 258
International Cultures Parade, 274
International Wines & Spirits, 99
Inwood Shakespeare Festival, 24
Iris & B. Gerald Cantor Film Center
   at NYU, 48

Irish Arts Center, 8
Irish Repertory Theatre, 8

Jackie Robinson Pool, 181
Jackie Robinson Recreation Center, 285
Jack's 99¢ Stores, 205, 206
Jackson Park. *See* Osaka Garden.
Jacobi Medical Center, 164
Jacob Riis Park, 183
Jamaica STD Clinic, 169
Jazzmobile, 39, 125
Jazz Museum in Harlem, The, 146
Jefferson Market, 87
Jefferson Market Library, 53, 130
Jeffrey Stein Salon, 107
Jewish Museum, 259
Jewish Sentinel, 194
J. Hood Wright Recreation Center, 285
jobs, colleges and universities, 154
jobs, live-in service, 119
John Jay Pool, 181
John J. Harvey Fireboat, 218
Joyce Theater, The, 9, 66
Juilliard School, The, 21, 35

Kenkeleba Gallery, 246
Kennedy Airport, 229
Kennedy's, 80
Kings Bay Library, 131
Kingsbridge Recreation Center, 288
Kings County Hospital Center, 166
Kitchen, The, 66
Korean Parade, 275
Kosciusko Pool, 182

Labor Day Parade, 275
La Guardia Airport, 230
Lakeside Lounge, 28
Lamb's Theatre, The, 9
Langan's, 80
Lasker Pool, 181
Lasker Rink, 134
Late Night with Jimmy Fallon, 57

*Late Show with David Letterman,
The,* 57
Learn to Play . . . Soccer, Baseball,
Lacrosse, Basketball, Baseball, 134
Learn to Swim Program, 135
Leffert's Homestead, 137
Lesbian, Gay, Bisexual & Transgender
Community Center, The, 168, 191
Liberty Pool, 182
libraries, 188
libraries, branch locations, 277
libraries, children's DVDs, 129
libraries, children's films, 129
libraries, classes, 152
libraries, films, 53
libraries, free access, 186
libraries, private, 190
libraries, research centers, 187
Lifestyle Resources, 119
Lincoln Center Out of Doors
Festival, 67
Lincoln Medical and Mental Health
Center, 164
Lincoln Square tour, 219
Litter and Leashes, 211
live-in service jobs, 119
Live with Regis and Kelly, 58
Living Room, The, 28
Logos Bookstore, 141
Lord & Taylor, 114
L'Oréal Technical Center, 105
Lost Battalion Hall Recreation
Center, 289
Louis Armstrong Archives, 253
Louis Armstrong Recreation Center, 289
Lucille Lortel Theater, 9
Luhring Augustine Gallery, 240
Lululemon Athletica, 156
Lyons Pool, 182

Macy's, 114
Macy's Fourth of July Fireworks, 274
Macy's Thanksgiving Day Parade, 276

Madison Square Park, 40
magic, 72
Magnet Theater, 62
makeup, 115
makeup, over the counter, 114
Manhattan Beach, 184
Manhattan Jewish Experience, 158
Manhattan Neighborhood Network, 147
Manhattan School of Music, 35
Manhattan Theatre Club, 10
Manhattan Theatre Club at the
    Biltmore Theatre, 4
Mannes College of Music, 35
Mapes Pool, 181
Mapleton Library, 54
Marcus Garvey Pool, 181
Marcy Library, 131
Marijuana March, 273
Martha, 58
Martin Luther King Jr. Concert
    Series, 40
Martin Luther King Jr. Parade, 271
massage, 103, 113
Matrix Global Academy, 107
Matthew Marks Gallery, 241
Maui Tacos, 74
Maury Show, The, 59, 268
McCormack's Public House, 78
MCC Theater, 10
Melrose Library, 131
mental health clinical trials, 167
Mermaid Parade, 274
Met in the Parks, 41
Metro Pictures, 241
Metropolitan Hospital Center, 164
Metropolitan Museum of Art, 263
Metropolitan Pool and Fitness
    Center, 287
Mexican Day Parade, 275
Mexican Fine Arts Center Museum. *See*
    National Museum of Mexican Art
Midland Beach, 185
Mid-Manhattan Library, 53

Midsummer Night Swing at Lincoln
    Center, 68
Minardi Beauty Focus, 108
Mint Theater Company, 10
Mister Wright Liquors, 97
Mitchell-Lama Housing Companies, 120
Miwa Alex Hair Salon, 108
Momenta Art, 244
Monday Movie Series, 49
MoonDance, 68, 266
Morningside Park Recreation
    Center, 285
Morrell & Company Wine & Spirits
    Merchants, 100
Morrisania Diagnostic & Treatment
    Center, 165
Morrisania Library, 131
Morrisania STD Clinic, 169
Mount Sinai Medical Center, 167
Movement Research, 67, 70
Movies Under the Stars, 49
Movies with a View, 49, 266
MTA Arts for Transit Music Under
    New York, 32
MTA New York City Transit, 225
Mullaly Pool, 181
Mullaly Recreation Center, 288
Murray's Cheese Shop, 87
Museum of American Illustrators, 254
Museum of Arts and Design, 259
Museum of Chinese in America,
    259, 263
Museum of Jewish Heritage, 260
Museum of Modern Art, The, 49, 126,
    128, 260
Museum of the City of New York, 263
Museum of the Moving Image, 260
museums, 249
museums, always free, 250
museums, children and teens, 136
museums, sometimes free, 256
museums, with suggested
    donations, 262

music, 26
Music at Castle Clinton, 41
music, classical, 33
music, jazz and blues, 30
music, outdoor summer concerts, 36
music, rock, pop, folk, and
    alternative, 27
music, underground, 32
Muslim Day Parade, 275
MyOpenBar, 99

Nanny Authority, The, 119
National Cancer Institute, 165
National Center for Complementary
    and Alternative Medicine, 165
National Institutes of Health, 165
National Museum of the American
    Indian, 254
Natural Gourmet Institute for Food
    and Health, The, 148
Natural Pet, The, 211
Naumburg Orchestral Concerts, 41
NBA Store, 138
Neuropsych Research Associates, 167
Nevada Smiths, 78
Newark Liberty Airport, 231
New Dorp Branch Library, 54
New Dramatists, 22
New Group Theater, The, 11
New Lots Library, 132
News Cafe, 92
New School Culinary Arts
    Program, 100
New School Food Studies Program, 149
New School for Drama, The, 22
newspapers, 192
New World Stages, 11
New York Academy of Medicine
    Library, The, 191
New York Blade News, 194
New York Botanical Garden Adult
    Education, 235
New York Botanical Garden, The, 234

New York City Department of Parks
    and Recreation, 182
New York City Hall tour, 219
New York City Housing Development
    Corporation, 117
New York City Marathon, 276
New York City Police Museum, 263
New York City Recreation Centers, 123
New York Classical Theatre, 24
New York Doll Hospital, 138
New York Fire Museum, 263
New York Hall of Science, 261
New York Headache Center, 162
New York International Beauty
    School, 113
New York Medical Centers, 165
New York Philharmonic, 42
New York Press, 195
New York Psychiatric Institute, 167
New York Public Library, 142, 152
New York Public Library for the
    Performing Arts, The, 187
New York Public Library Humanities and
    Social Sciences Library, The, 188
New York Public Library tour, 220
New York Shakespeare Festival, 22
New York Tartan Day Parade, 272
New York Theatre Workshop, 11
New York Unearthed, 254
New York University, 67, 154, 266
New York University Graduate Acting
    Program, 23
New York University Program in
    Educational Theatre, 126
Next Magazine, 195
Nicholas Roerich Museum, 255
Nigerian Independence Parade, 275
Niketown Running Club, 176
96th Street Library, 130
Nintendo World, 139
Ninth Avenue Vintner, 100
Noguchi Museum, The, 261
North Central Bronx Hospital, 165

North Meadow Recreation Center, 285
Norwegian-American 17th of May
  Parade, 273
NYBS Creative Arts, 115
NYC Condom, 168
NYC Free Clinic, 162
NY Metro Parents, 196
NY Nanny Center, 119
NYU AIDS Clinical Trials Unit, 165
NYU Department of Music and
  Performing Arts Professions, 36
NYU Langone Medical Center, 165
NYU Program in Educational
  Theatre, 142

Ocularis, 50
O'Flaherty's Ale House, 81
Ohashi Institute, The, 156
Oh My Rockness, 28
One Fish Two Fish, 78
125th Street Branch Library, 130
Onion, The, 196
Open Center, The, 158, 163
Orchard Beach, 184
Orchard Street Walking Tour, 220
O'Reilly's Townhouse, 81
Oscar Bond Salon Spa, 110
Ottendorfer Branch Library, 53
Owen Dolan Recreation Center, 288

Pace Gallery, The, 241
Pacific College of Oriental Medicine &
  Acupuncture, 163
Paddy Reilly's Music Bar, 29
Pakistan Independence Day
  Parade, 275
parades, 271
parks, free fun and games, 171
Parkside Lounge, 29
Parlor, 108
Parlor Jazz at Marjorie Eliot's, 31
Parrots and Pups, 212
Passerelle Recreation Center, 290

Pat Parker/Vito Russo Center
  Library, 191
Paul Labrecque Salon, 108
Pearl Theatre Company, The, 12
Pelham Bay Branch Library, 131
Pelham Fritz Recreation Center, 286
Pennsylvania Station Tours, 220
People's Court, The, 59, 268
People's Improv Theater, The, 62
Performance Space 122, 12
Performance Space 122 gallery, 247
Peridance, 70
Persian-Iranian Parade, 272
Pet Bar, 212
Petco, 211
Peter's Restaurant, 81
pets, 208
pets, adoptions, 210
pets, low-cost care, 210
pets, postings, 211
Pet Stop, 212
pets, websites, 209
Phagwah: Hindu New Year's
  Parade, 272
Philippine Independence Day
  Parade, 273
Pierogi 2000, 245
Pig 'n Whistle, 81
Pig 'n Whistle on 3rd, 78
Play by Play, 17
Playwright Irish Pub, 79
Playwrights Horizons, 12
Pommes Frites, 88
Pool Parties, The, 42
pools, public, 180
Postcrypt Coffeehouse, 29, 267
product testing centers, 104
Professional Nannies Institute, 119
Prospect Park Audubon Center, 127, 221
P.S. 1 Contemporary Art Center, 263
Public Theater's Shakespeare Lab Jr.,
  The, 127
Public Theater, The, 22

Puerto Rican Day Parade, 273
Pulaski Day Parade, 275

Queens Botanical Garden, The, 234
Queens County Farm Museum, 255
Queens Hospital Center, 166
Queens Museum of Art, 263
Queens Pride Parade, 273
Queens Public Library, 152
Queens Village Library, 132
Quintessence Reiki, 113

Rachael Ray Show, 59
Rattlestick Playwrights Theatre, 13
Rattlestick Theatre Company, 23
real estate, 116
real estate, low-rent, no-fee
   apartments, 117
Recreation Center 59, 286
recreation centers, 174, 284
Red Hook Pool, 182
Red Hook Recreation Center, 287
Redken Exchange, The, 109
Redken Testing Center, 105
Red Lion, The, 30
Renaissance Diagnostic & Treatment
   Center, 164
Resident magazine, 196
Riccardo Maggiore Salon, 110
Richmond STD Clinic, 169
ride-share listings, 228
Right Rides, 31
Ringling Brothers, Barnum & Bailey
   Circus's Elephant Walk, 272
River & Blues, 42
River Flicks, 51, 129
Riverside Park, 173
Riverside Park South, 51
Riverside STD Clinic, 169
Rockaway Beach, 185
Rockaway STD Clinic, 169
Rodeo Bar, 79
Rolf's, 79

Roller Derby, 177
romance, 266
Ronald Feldman Fine Arts, 243
Rosenberg + Kaufman Fine Art, 243
Rotunda Gallery, The, 247
Roundabout Theatre Company,
   The, 5, 13
Rowe Camp & Conference Center, 228
Roy Wilkins Family Center, 290
Rudy's Bar and Grill, 81
running, 175

Saks Fifth Avenue, 114
Salon de Quartier, 110
Salon Ishi, 109
Salon Ziba, 110
Salute to Israel Parade, 273
Salvation Army Thrift Store, 201
Sandra Cameron Dance Center, 69
Saturday Night Live, 60
Scandinavia House, 140
scholarships, 189
Scholastic Store, The, 142
Schomburg Center for Research in
   Black Culture, 189
schools, beauty, 111
Science, Industry, and Business
   Library, 189
Scott J. Salons & Spas, 109
Sea Grape Wine & Spirits, 102
Seaport Music Festival, 40
Seaside Summer Concert Series, 43
Sea View Hospital Rehabilitation
   Center and Home, 166
Second Stage Theatre, 14
Segundo Ruiz Belvis Diagnostic
   & Treatment Center, 165
17 @ 17 Thrift Store, 207
Shakespeare in Central Park, 25
Shakespeare in the Park(ing Lot), 24
Shambhala Center of New York, 159
Sheepshead Bay Library, 54
Sheltering Arms Pool, 181

Shige Kosuda Salon, 109
shopping, 204
shopping, 17th Street, 206
shopping, 32nd Street, 205
shopping, children and teens, 137
shopping, curbside tips, 200
shopping, fruit stands, 207
Signature Theater Company, The, 14
Sikh Cultural Society Parade
   & Festival, 272
67 Wines & Spirits, 100
skating, biking, and running, 175
skating, in-line, 178
Sky Rink at Chelsea Piers, 177
Small Business Development Center, 154
Snug Harbor Botanical Gardens, 234
Society of American Magicians, 73
Socrates Sculpture Park, 247
Socrates Sculpture Park's Outdoor
   Cinema, 52
SoHo Playhouse, 14
Sony Wonder Technology Lab, 52, 137
Sorrentino Recreation Center, 290
South Beach, 185
South Street Seaport, 43
Spoiled Brats, 212
sports and games, children
   and teens, 132
Sri Sri Radha Govinda Manir, 82
St. Agnes Library, 53, 130
Stapleton Library, 132
Staten Island Ferry, 226, 269
Staten Island Zoo, 265
STD clinics, 167
Steinway & Sons factory tour, 221
Steps on Broadway, 70
St. James Recreation Center, 288
St. John's Recreation Center, 287
St. Luke's/Roosevelt Hospital, 167
St. Mary's Recreation Center, 288
St. Nick's Jazz Pub, 33
St. Patrick's Day Parade, 272
Studio 54, 5

Studio Museum in Harlem, The, 261
Summer in the Square, 43
Sun Room, The, 82
Sunset Park Pool, 182
Sunset Park Recreation Center, 287
Swedish Institute for Massage
   Therapy, The, 114
Swedish Institute, The, 163
swimming, public pools, 180

Take a Walk, New York!, 222, 268
Tannen's, 74
Tannen's Magic Studio, 74
television tapings, 55
theater, Broadway, 4
theater, cheap seats, 17
Theater Extras, 17
Theater for the New City, 24
theater, free, 20
theater, free in the parks, 25
TheaterMania Gold Club, 18
theater, Off Broadway, 6
theater, standing room, 18
theater, volunteer ushering, 3, 4
theater, with suggested donations, 24
Theatre Row, 15
Theatreworks USA, 23
Thirsty Scholar, The, 83
Thirteen/WNET tour, 222
Thomas Jefferson Pool, 181
Thomas Jefferson Recreation
   Center, 286
303 Gallery, 241
Three Jewels Community Center, 157
Three Kings Day Parade, 271
Tibet House New York, 255
Time Out New York, 63
Times Square New Year's Eve,, 276
Times Square Walking Tour, 222
Time's Up, 177
TKTS Booth, 19
Todaro Bros., 88, 92
Tonnie's Minis, 88

Tony Dapolito Pool, 181
Tony Dapolito Recreation Center, 286
Tony & Guy Hairdressing Academy, 111
Tottenville Pool, 182
travel, 224
travel, getting around New York, 225
travel, getting out of New York, 226
travel, getting to the airports, 229
Travis Fourth of July Parade, 274
Tremont Branch Library, 131
Trinity Church, 36, 222
Tri-State College of Acupuncture, 163
Turkish American Day Parade, 273
Two Little Red Hens, 89
Ty's Bar, 83

Union Market, 89
Union Square Walking Tour, 223
Union Square Wine & Spirits, 97
Upright Citizens Brigade, 63, 267
Urban Center, 256
Urban Glass, 148
Urban Park Rangers, 223, 269

Van Cortlandt Pool, 181
Veterans Day Parade, 276
Vidal Sassoon, 109
View, The, 60
Village Halloween Parade, The, 276
Village Voice, The, 197
Vineyard Theatre, The, 15
Vipassana Meditation Center, 228
Von King Cultural Arts Center, 287
Vosages Haute Chocolat, 89

Wagner Pool, 181
Wakefield Branch Library, 54
walking tours, 214
Wall Street Walking Tour, 223

Watering Hole, The, 79
Wave Hill Public Garden and Cultural
    Center, 235
Wednesday Evening Skate club, 178
West Brighton Pool, 182
West Bronx Recreation Center, 289
Westchester Square Library, 131
West Indian American Day Carnival Day
    Parade, 275
Westside Animal Hospital, 212
West Side Arts Coalition, 248
West Side Dance Project, The, 71
West Side Spirit, 197
Whiskers, 212
White Columns, 248
Whitney Museum at Altria, 256
Whitney Museum of American Art, 262
Whole Foods Market, 89
Who Wants to Be a Millionaire, 60
Williamsbridge Oval Recreation
    Center, 289
Williams-Sonoma, 90, 149
Windsor Court Wine Shop, 97
wine classes, 100
wine, education, 148
wine tastings, 93
Wine Workshop, The, 98, 100, 150
Women's Project at the Julia Miles
    Theater, 15
Woodhull Medical and Mental Health
    Center, 166
Wooster Group, The, 16, 128

York Theatre Company, 16, 25
Yorkville Library, 54, 130
Younghee Salon, 109

Zabar's, 92
zoos, 264

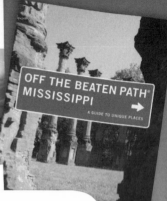